P9-DVD-005

Reading

Henry James

in French Cultural Contexts

PIERRE A. WALKER

Reading

Henry James

in French Cultural Contexts

NORTHERN ILLINOIS UNIVERSITY PRESS

DeKalb 1995

© 1995 by Northern Illinois University Press

Published by the Northern Illinois University Press,

DeKalb, Illinois 60115

Manufactured in the United States using acid-free paper ∞

Design by Julia Fauci

Endleaf art, "PARIS—Le boulevard des Italiens," courtesy of the

Bibliothéque nationale, Paris, France.

Library of Congress Cataloging-in-Publication Data

Walker, Pierre A.

Reading Henry James in French cultural contexts/Pierre A. Walker

p. cm.

Includes bibliographical references (p.   ) and index.

ISBN 0-87580-192-7 (acid-free paper)

1. James, Henry, 1843–1916—Knowledge—France. 2. James,

Henry, 1843–1916—Knowledge—Language and

languages. 3. French philology in literature. 4. France in

literature. 5. National characteristics, French, in

literature. 6. Stereotype (Psychology) in literature. I. Title.

PS2127.F7W35 1994

813'.4—dc20   94-21528

CIP

Dedicated to the memory of my grandfather

André F. Cournand

ॐ

Cet exemple d'une vie consacrée

à l'étude et au développement

scientifique et

humanistique

Contents

Acknowledgments

*I*t is a convention of scholarly books on literature to acknowledge the contributions of all those who helped the author make the book possible. Several people gave considerable help and advice at various stages of the composition of this book, and they all deserve my deepest gratitude. Jonathan Arac, Pierre Force, Ann Douglas, William Stowe, and Adeline Tintner all read various versions of this book while it was in progress and offered intelligent and useful advice that is by no means a small factor in whatever success my work merits. Michael Riffaterre was the first person to encourage me to pursue the approach to Henry James worked out in this book; his support, inspiration, constructive criticism, and encouragement as a teacher, dissertation sponsor, and reader of at least two stages of my manuscript were invaluable. A version of part of chapter 2 was first published as "The Princess Casamassima's 'Sudden Incarnation' and Octave Feuillet," in *Texas Studies in Literature and Language,* and a version of a portion of chapter 4 first appeared as "Reading the Berne Bears in the End of James's *The Ambassadors,*" in *Modern Language Studies.* I am grateful to the University of Texas Press, in the case of the first article, and to the Northeast Modern Language Association, in the case of the second, for their permission to reproduce the full and revised versions in this book. Versions of chapter 6 were worked out at the Henry James session of the 1991 Northeast Modern Language Association annual convention and the James's Literary Criticism session of the Henry James Sesquicentennial conference at New York University in 1993. I am grateful to Phillip Barrish and to Sarah Daugherty, who respectively chaired those two sessions, for the opportunity they gave me to test my ideas about *Washington Square.*

Dan Coran and the staff of the Northern Illinois University Press deserve thanks for their support. In spite of efforts to the contrary, Janus-like, Thomas L. Ashton has been a continuing inspiration for all my scholarly endeavors. Finally, I want to thank Meg Anderson for all her patience and help.

Introduction

Many critics have, with good reason, investigated the subject of Henry James and France. James visited France as a tourist and as a guest of French friends, lived in France both as a child and as an adult, had close French friends, spoke French, read and wrote criticism about French literature, admired and wrote about the French theater, wrote a travel book about the French provinces, and frequently interspersed his conversations, letters, and prose with French. James attended school in France and in the French-speaking part of Switzerland (but in no other European country);[1] he published a translaton from the French of Alphonse Daudet's *Port Tartarin*;[2] he wrote more of his letters (at least his published ones) in French than in any language other than English; and he wrote more criticism about French literature than about any other national literature.[3] Indeed, James served, to an extent rarely fully acknowledged, as a spokesperson to the American and English reading public for contemporary French literary movements. Finally, he slipped France and the French language, as Edwin Sill Fussell has shown,[4] into his fiction to a greater extent than he did any other language and foreign country (with the possible exception, as a setting, of Italy). Surely James was immersed in French culture.

Not only do many of James's novels partly or fully take place in France, represent French characters, and contain French phrases, but from *Watch and Ward*, which imitates the plot of Molière's *L'École des femmes*, to *The Golden Bowl*, with its central premise of a rich bourgeois father who buys an impoverished, aristocratic husband for his daughter, derived from Emile Augier's *Le Gendre de Monsieur Poirier* (which is itself derived from Molière's *Le Bourgeois Gentilhomme*), James's novels copy, refer to, and generally situate themselves in a context of French culture. Thus, James's readers logically should want to be aware of how this context can be understood to work in James's fiction. Even if one cries "intentional fallacy" at this and says that the fact that James was immersed in French culture means nothing for how we read his fiction, the fiction itself shows how much it is immersed in French culture, not only through the French settings, the use of the French language, or the derivative plots (from Balzac and others) but also through its evocation of clichés, stereotypes, and conventions of French culture. That the texts are immersed in French culture implies that their reading should be, too (since how can one separate a text from the reading of it?). The thesis of this book is that it makes sense to read James from a perspective immersed in French culture (along with American and English culture) and that reading James from such a perspective leads to insightful interpretations of his fiction.

My contribution to the subject of James and France grows out of the convergence of several trends in the study of James and France and of James scholarship in general. In the past, the majority of comparative studies of James's fiction and French literature have been influence or source studies, ranging from Adeline Tintner's many articles,[5] which attempt to pinpoint particular characters or situations from literary antecedents that perhaps serve as models for a character or situation in one of James's fictions, to works such as Philip Grover's *Henry James and the French Novel*[6] and Lyall Powers's *Henry James and the Naturalist Movement*,[7] which try to describe the ways in which intellectual and literary movements in France, in the mid-to-late nineteenth century, may have influenced James's fiction.

Peter Brooks and his students have been the principal purveyors of another, more purely comparative type of study of James and French literature. Brooks's *The Melodramatic Imagination*[8] and William Stowe's *Balzac, James, and the Realistic Novel*[9] avoid the notions of "influence" and "source," and use James's fiction primarily for examples—which could be provided by other authors' texts—to illustrate the elaboration of the scholar's overriding concern: in Brooks's case, how the melodrama of the popular French theater translates into nineteenth-century novels, and in Stowe's, a theory of realism. These books hold considerable interest for the reader and critic of James, but James's texts are not their foremost concern. As Brooks writes at the beginning of his conclusion, "We have talked at some length of Victor Hugo, of Balzac and James. We could as well have discussed Dickens, Dostoevsky, Conrad, Lawrence, Faulkner. . . ."[10] Thus the comparative work on James and French literature that is primarily concerned with how to read James's fiction has tended to rely on an older methodology and theory of literary meaning, while Brooks's and Stowe's fresher approaches make James's texts a secondary concern.

The claims of the influence and source studies are often founded on coincidental similarities between the influence and the later writer; Stowe's and Brooks's approaches to James and French literature also rely on the coincidence that both James's and Balzac's works happen to illustrate the respective theories of these two critics. The result is that neither the source studies nor work such as Brooks's and Stowe's is entirely satisfactory in describing the way French culture functions in James's fiction.

To speak of James and France is to enter one of the oldest debates about James's fiction, that of its "nationality." F. R. Leavis saw James's novels as part of the English or "great tradition" of Austen, George Eliot, Conrad, and Lawrence, whereas to Robert Emmet Long (and to Richard Brodhead, to some extent), they are the "legacy" of the American author Hawthorne.[11] One of the implicit arguments of my book is to highlight the "Frenchness" of James's fiction. This is not to say that James is a French novelist rather than an American or an English writer but to emphasize the degree to which James is read in an English, American, *and* French context. One of the most recent contributions to the study of James and France, and the only important work on James that thoroughly argues the same point (that James's fiction is written in a French context) is Edwin Sill Fussell's *The French Side of Henry James*,[12] which, in a fresh twist to the argument over James's "nationality," speaks of the result of James's immersion in English, American, and French literature as "the attachment of literatures,"[13] a phrase Fussell explains by describing James's literary apprenticeship with the following "fable":

> Once upon a time there was born in New York a small squid who at maturity found himself all out and alone in the great worldwide ocean called Literature and who liked his independence well enough but also felt the need of some socialization and as he swam around and pondered these things he encountered various enormous fishes named Greek Literature and Spanish Literature and Latin Literature and German Literature and Chinese Literature but none of them seemed quite right not even English Literature to whom he said in passing "I'll be back" and finally met up with a fish named French Literature, approached, and, with a limber tentacle and powerful suction cup, he attached himself, for ever and a day, to that smoothest of all glistening flanks.[14]

This fable presupposes a particular anxiety of influence relationship on James's part to his literary contemporaries and immediate forebears. The view of James in American literature, so familiar to students of the novelist, is that out of the need to validate his own approach to fictional composition, James "rewrote" the (to him) major monument in American narrative fiction (Hawthorne) into a failed practitioner of the art of fiction.[15] Because he had thus redefined the terms of what constituted a great American novelist, James made it possible to aspire himself to the position of the great American novelist. However persuasive this view may be, it tends to see James in the isolation of one national literary context, while Fussell's fable demonstrates that James's relationship to his literary models and cultural frame of reference is best understood in a pan-Western context. Each of the national literatures, except for French literature, was an inadequate model to James. And French literature ultimately proved inadequate too, since James (unlike, say, Samuel Beckett, three-quarters of a century later) never considered becoming a French author, and because differing moral standards meant he could not literally write French novels in English.[16] Thus, the fable implies, James had to undervalue and value at the same time all possible literary models in order to craft his own unique version of realistic fiction. Previous discussion on the topic of James's literary models generally takes a more limited either/or form—James is understood in either an English or an American context—with Leavis, for example, implying that Austen and George Eliot were the important forebears and the American side (Long and Brodhead) saying that it was Hawthorne. Fussell's fable takes the discussion away from this binary opposition and points to an appreciation of the transnational context in which James ideally should be read (and, I add, this context affects how one reads and interprets James). One of the arguments of Fussell's book is that James was really a frustrated French novelist and that this frustration manifested itself in the creation of Franco-Anglo-American novels (or, another way to conceive it, of French novels written in English with English or American protagonists and with, variously, English, American, or French settings). The French sprinkled throughout the dialogue, the Gallicisms, and the French settings are the ostensible results—indeed the dramatization—of this frustration.

Fussell's argument is compelling, and inasmuch as one of the principal arguments of my book is that the reader and interpreter of James's fiction benefits from sharing James's trinational context, I consider my argument an extension of his. My argument also goes a step beyond Fussell's to argue that James did not stop at the use of the French language and settings in his fiction but incorporated conventions and stereotypes of French culture along with explicit and implicit references to French literary texts in the process of "attaching" French literature. Furthermore, I argue that these conventions, stereotypes, and references have a function both in James's texts and for interpretations of several James novels. My claim is that readers who see James's fictions as invoking a French cultural context and who then read those fictions from a French cultural perspective will be rewarded by new understandings of some of those texts and by the possibility of resolving the interpretive cruxes that have arisen around other texts.

One drawback, from today's perspective, to virtually all the comparative studies on James and France is that they limit their discussion exclusively to canonical French texts.[17] As a result, if the relationship of James's fiction to French culture is described at all, it is only in relationship to a particular part of French culture. There is no question that James had his favorite and less favorite French writers or that many of his preferences—Balzac especially, Zola begrudgingly, Flaubert finally—correspond more or less to late-twentieth-century canonical taste. My investigation is indiscriminate in its attention to both canonical and forgotten French texts in relation to James, and in this respect my study intersects with a growing and important tendency in the last decade to view James's literary work in a wider cultural context.

The literary context for James was always a canonical one until the appearance of William Veeder's *Henry James—the Lessons of the Master*, which traces the evolution of the style of the early James and its relation to contemporary fictional stylistic conventions,[18] and of Marcia Jacobson's *Henry James and the Mass Market*, which describes the popular context for James's novels.[19] In each of her book's chapters, including those on *The Princess Casamassima*, *The Tragic Muse*, and *The Awkward Age*, Jacobson catalogues the points of comparison between several James novels and other, now-forgotten, popular novels of the same years that treated the same sorts of subjects as James's. For example, the chapter on *The Tragic Muse* cites a number of recent English novels (such as Mrs. Humphrey Ward's) that, like James's, treat the actress, and the chapter on *The Awkward Age* reminds us of English novels of the period that also used the *roman dialogué* form. Jacobson's claim is that these treatments of related subjects are the "context within which James was working," and that "[o]ur awareness [of this context], in turn, enhances our understanding of both the writer and his fiction."[20] In other words, an awareness of related, popular contemporary fiction is both an important presupposition to James's reader and an important element in generating how we understand James's fiction, points with which I agree entirely and which I argue throughout the following chapters.

One of the values of Jacobson's approach is that it teaches readers of James to see beyond the "assumed persona" of "James the Master" that James contrived in "the New York Edition prefaces,"[21] an image of the author and his works that has, as Jacobson suggests, overly influenced the way James's fictions are read and understood.[22] It is partly because of this contrived "persona" that twentieth-century critics have so generally situated James's texts in a literary context consisting only of the works of monumental figures like Dickens, Hawthorne, Trollope, and Balzac, while the reading of James's fictions in relation to contemporary, popular literature has only recently begun to transcend this traditional context.

In recent years, other critics have also argued against the image Henry James constructed of himself in the prefaces (and that James's younger acquaintances like Ford Madox Ford and Percy Lubbock, and later Leon Edel, also contributed so much to creating): John Carlos Rowe, in *The Theoretical Dimensions of Henry James*, describes James's efforts to fashion an image of himself as a "Master" that has—as Jacobson argues in relation to the prefaces—overdetermined subsequent readers' responses to James.[23] Anne T. Margolis's *Henry James and the Problem of Audience* and Michael Anesko's *"Friction with the Market"*[24] demonstrate the importance of the relationship between James's novels and popular English and American fiction and, in so doing, further contribute to the deconstruction of the standard view of James as an artist devoted only to "high" art and renouncing material matters by presenting a James far more concerned with the literary marketplace and popular success.

While Rowe's, Margolis's, and Anesko's books serve the same valuable purpose as Jacobson's of expanding the literary context beyond the canonical one in which James is read, they—like *Henry James and the Mass Market*—speak little, if at all, of James and his French literary context. My book follows the example of these critics insofar as it attempts to expand the French literary context in which James has customarily been read. While comparative critics of James have concentrated primarily on his relationship to major French authors, and while James may have devoted more of his critical writings on French literature to the writers we would today label as mainstream, he nonetheless read, wrote about, and was interested in, for example, the works of such now largely forgotten writers as the post-Hugo and post-Musset playwrights, the *Revue des Deux Mondes* novelists,[25] and the fin-de-siècle practitioners of the *roman dialogué*. Reading James suggests that the works of writers such as these merit consideration in the comparative study of James and French culture as much as those of, for example, Balzac.

My study of James and French popular literature differs from Jacobson's study of James and English and American popular literature in two important respects. First, by showing the relevance to James of popular, contemporary French texts as a context for his own works, I take the logical next step beyond Jacobson's attention to the English-language popular context for James's work. Second, in arguing that French texts have functions within James's works, I seek to delineate specific contexts and to describe how those contexts affect our reading of James. If Jacobson's book is open to any criticism, it is to the same one that is leveled at much New Historicist study, which, like Jacobson's book, often juxtaposes non-"literary" or non-canonical texts with canonical literary texts without providing strong evidence that the juxtapositions are obligatory or even valid.

In the following chapters, I argue that James's novels ask their readers to perceive connections with particular French texts; this happens often with explicit references, such as the one in *Daisy Miller* to Victor Cherbuliez's *Paule Méré* (which in turn invokes a French cliché of the Swiss personality). These connections often invoke connections to other texts, not all of which are necessarily French, as in *The Princess Casamassima* with its oblique allusion to Octave Feuillet's *La Veuve* and *Histoire d'une parisienne* and its connection to James's own *Roderick Hudson*, or with *The Ambassadors* and its interweaving of explicit references to Balzac's *Louis Lambert,* Hugo's *Notre-Dame de Paris,* Goldsmith's *The Vicar of Wakefield,* and Thackeray's *Pendennis* and *The Newcomes.*

James's texts also ask their readers to see connections to conventions or traditions in French literary culture, as in *The Princess Casamassima,* which invokes, in order to deconstruct, a tradition of French novels about ambitious outsiders, or in *The Awkward Age,* which through the name of its protagonist associates itself with a series of French novels and plays about innocent "fallen" women and through its *roman dialogué* form rewrites Gyp's treatment of adolescent girls and their marriages. Finally, James can use a character as an emblem of an entire school of French literature, as in *Washington Square,* where Dr. Sloper represents French naturalism in James's fictional dramatization of his own ambivalence about the contemporary novel.

In all of these instances, I argue not only that there are points of comparison between James's novels and texts by French writers but furthermore that James's fictions call their readers' attention to particular French texts that are more than just coincidentally comparable with James's and that serve specific functions in the interpretation of James's works. Thus I argue both that James's novels and stories are best read in a context at least partly French and that it is James's texts themselves that best help us sketch this context.

The French structural and semiotic traditions of literary criticism use the term "intertextual" to describe both meaningful relations and connections between texts and at the same time very narrowly defined intertextual relations.[26] In recent years, critics of all types have adopted the term "intertextuality," and as a result, depending on whom one reads, the term can mean anything and everything. While critics and theorists today disagree about much, the one thing they are likely to agree about is that some kind of context or intertext is, if not *the*, then at least *a* source of literary meaning. There is precious little debate over whether this is right or wrong—from the moment we agree that readers and their preconceptions make up at least part of the context to reading a text and that there cannot be literary meaning without a reader, how could there be? Debates over literary meaning are over the definition or description of the contexts, or intertexts, and how they function as a determinant of literary meaning. One of the things I complain about in this book is how all too easily critics from Tintner to Jacobson have claimed particular popular and literary intertexts for James. Where I see these critics as sometimes erring is in making connections of questionable validity. My own approach errs, when it does, in the opposite sense, in perhaps passing over plausible connections; however, this is a necessary result of a deliberate choice to concentrate on connections between texts that I am convinced can be defended under a variety of prevailing theoretical assumptions.

I have chosen to adhere to a narrow version of intertextuality and discuss other texts that I am confident James's texts mean their readers to perceive as contexts. My purpose is not just to catalogue all the mid-to-late-nineteenth-century French cultural treatments of, say, terrorists and anarchists or mixed-blood illegitimate children (in relation to *The Princess Casamassima*) but, rather, to show how French cultural contexts invoked in a James novel like *The Princess Casamassima* lead readers to understand that novel. I am arguing, then, for particular interpretations and for a particular perspective—that of a tricultural (Anglo-Franco-American) reader—from which to read James. Despite the various trends in literary criticism that have come and gone in an attempt to replace interpretation as a model for literary study,[27] I emphasize interpretation as an integral part of reading, particularly in respect to James, who again and again dramatized the act and problems of interpretation in the worlds he represented in his fictions. James's novels and stories dramatize interpretation in two senses: they confront a character with a social situation that challenges the character's understanding and engages that character in a series of attempted interpretations, and through the limitations of narrative point of view, they offer the reader a correlate to the opacity the character encounters.[28] Just as the situation told about in the James text mystifies the character, so too the telling of that situation mystifies James's reader. And just as James's texts tell the story of his characters' attempts to find some basis on which to build their more or less successful understanding of—to demystify—their situation, so too literary criticism of James is the story of James's readers' search for a basis on which to build an understanding of the texts. My claim is that there is such a basis and that it can be found in the texts' specific invocation of a French cultural context.

On the most general level, my book argues that meaning is constituted through context: it is a reader's perception of a text's differences and similarities to other texts that generates its meaning. Today this is already an old theory of literary meaning, although it is old because it accommodates most of the theories of literary meaning of the twentieth century. My argument for the generation of meaning in novels by James through attention to French cultural contexts is open to the charge of the Stanley Fish anti-stylistics crusade during the 1970s that most literary theories are self-fulfilling prophecies and circular reasoning:[29] I begin by claiming that meaning is generated through attention to French contexts for James's texts; I proceed to show meanings and interpretations that result from attention to French contexts; and I conclude that meaning is the result of attention to French contexts—my point of departure. If this appears to be circular reasoning, it is primarily because it is a convention of writing literary interpretation to begin with the end, to start by sketching what one's work demonstrates and proves, even though this apparent beginning point is really the result of considerable reading, reflection, research, and writing.

My own reading process follows only in an ideal sense the path these subsequent chapters tread; when I actually read James, it is natural for me to pay attention to the way his fictions refer to and then establish similarities within differences or differences within similarities to French popular and literary texts and cultural conventions. My reading practices are a natural result of my background, genetic makeup, life experience, and formal and informal training (my *formation*, as the French say) as a literary critic. I usually find a coherent pattern to the references, both in and among themselves and to other features in James's texts, and that is when I arrive at the point the following chapters seek to fix, when the references to things French and their relations—similarities and/or differences—among themselves and to other elements of James's fictional text coalesce into an appreciation of what kind of representation of reality James's text creates and what it shows happening in that represented reality.

The success of this approach to interpreting James's fiction now lies outside my control, for the ultimate proof is in the pudding; either my readings of James will convince, or they will not. In *Is There a Text in This Class?* Stanley Fish argues what remains true today: "interpretive strategies are always being deployed," and "interpretaton is the only game in town."[30] As Tobin Siebers says, "theories in general tend toward stupidity when they call a halt to interpretation."[31] Interpretation is what all literary critics do, and the success of an interpretation lies not in its verifiability against some fixed authority but in its ability to persuade. "Some interpretations are more adequate to particular stories. We experience a fit, and if this fit survives, it will influence other forms of adequation. Validity in interpretation will never be more than this."[32]

Note on Texts Cited

Scholars and critics of Henry James's fiction invariably have to choose which version of James's revised texts to cite and to defend that choice. Since my primary concern is to argue for a French context for reading James, and since I argue that this context is contemporary to the time James composed his fictions, it seemed to me more appropriate to use James's original book versions of his novels and stories rather than the revised editions of 1907–1909, the New York Edition. Furthermore, in an effort to reconcile the respective advantages of a reliable critical text with widespread availability, I have quoted from modern, commonly found editions of James's fictions. When available, the Library of America text has been my choice of text, the Norton Critical Edition has been my second choice, and the widely distributed but sometimes inaccurate latest Penguin edition has been my final choice. In the case of *The Ambassadors,* this means that I have had to use the text from the New York Edition, but since the lapse of time between James's initial composition and his revised New York Edition of that novel is relatively short, the effect of the revisions has little bearing on my thesis. For my sources for James's nonfiction, I have relied on the same principles, quoting from the Library of America edition, if one exists, otherwise from recent, widely distributed modern reprints.

For the ease and convenience of the reader, I give all the page numbers to my citations from the work of Henry James parenthetically in the text, using the following abbreviations as a reference to the corresponding editions:

AA—The Awkward Age. 1899; Harmondsworth: Penguin, 1987.
Amb.—The Ambassadors. 1903; rev. ed. 1908. Reprint, ed. S. P. Rosenbaum. New York: Norton, 1964.

CN—*The Complete Notebooks of Henry James.* Ed. Leon Edel and Lyall H. Powers. New York: Oxford University Press, 1987.

DM—*Daisy Miller[: A Study].* Ed. Geoffrey Moore. 1878; Harmondsworth: Penguin, 1986.

Eur.—*The Europeans. Novels 1871–1880: Watch and Ward, Roderick Hudson, The American, The Europeans, Confidence.* Ed. William T. Stafford. New York: Library of America, 1983.

HJL—*Letters.* Ed. Leon Edel. 4 vols. Cambridge: Harvard University Press-Belknap, 1974–1984.

LC1—*Literary Criticism: Essays on Literature, American Writers, English Writers.* Ed. Leon Edel and Mark Wilson. New York: Library of America, 1984.

LC2—*Literary Criticism: French Writers, Other European Writers, The Prefaces to the New York Edition.* Ed. Leon Edel and Mark Wilson. New York: Library of America, 1984.

LHJ—*Letters of Henry James.* Ed. Percy Lubbock. 2 vols. London: Macmillan, 1920.

LTF—*A Little Tour of France. Collected Travel Writings: The Continent: A Little Tour of France, Italian Hours, Other Travels.* Ed. Richard Howard. New York: Library of America, 1993.

PC—*The Princess Casamassima. Novels 1886–1890: The Princess Casamassima, The Reverberator, The Tragic Muse.* Ed. Daniel Mark Fogel. New York: Library of America, 1989.

RH—*Roderick Hudson. Novels 1871–1880: Watch and Ward, Roderick Hudson, The American, The Europeans, Confidence.* Ed. William T. Stafford. New York: Library of America, 1983.

SA—*The Scenic Art: Notes on Acting and the Drama, 1872–1901.* Ed. and intro. Allan Wade. New York: Hill and Wang–Dramabook, 1957.

TM—*The Tragic Muse. Novels 1886–1890: The Princess Casamassima, The Reverberator, The Tragic Muse.* Ed. Daniel Mark Fogel. New York: Library of America, 1989.

TS—*"Swiss Notes." Transatlantic Sketches. Collected Travel Writings: The Continent: A Little Tour of France, Italian Hours, Other Travels.* Ed. Richard Howard. New York: Library of America, 1993.

WS—*Washington Square. Novels 1881–1886: Washington Square, The Portrait of a Lady, The Bostonians.* Ed. William T. Stafford. New York: Library of America, 1985.

Also for the reader's convenience, I give parenthetical references for all quotes from Balzac's *La Comédie humaine* and Zola's *Les Rougon-Macquart* using the following abbreviations for the chosen editions:

Comédie—Balzac, Honoré de. *La Comédie humaine.* Ed. Pierre-Georges Castex. 12 vols. Paris: Gallimard, Pléiade, 1976–1981.

R-M—Zola, Emile. *Les Rougon-Macquart: Histoire naturelle et sociale d'une famille sous le second Empire.* Ed. Armand Lanoux and Henri Mitterand. 5 vols. Paris: Gallimard, Pléiade, 1960–1967.

All translations, unless otherwise noted, are my own.

Reading

Henry James

in French Cultural Contexts

1

Cherbuliez's Geneva in
Daisy Miller

James's fiction abounds with literary references, often to French literature.[1] When the references are made by characters, they serve the obvious purpose of demonstrating those characters' cosmopolitan culture, but they are more than that. The works mentioned in the direct literary allusions invariably convey a situation analogous to the one being represented in the James text. However, the analogous situation is generally less ambiguous than the situation represented in the James text. Because of the parallels such references raise, attentive readers and interpreters of James should not ignore them; because of the frequency of these allusions in James's fiction, and because they convey a parallel situation, readers should not discount their significance.

These allusions—be they, for example, to Cherbuliez in *Daisy Miller,* to Octave Feuillet in *The Princess Casamassima,* to Balzac's *Louis Lambert* in *The Ambassadors,* or to *Notre-Dame de Paris* in *The Ambassadors* and *The Awkward Age*—present unambiguous signs or indications that help James's reader resolve interpretive cruxes or apparent ambiguities of Jamesian texts. The clarity of the indication in the works alluded to relies on the reader's ability to perceive a cliché, such as the French stereotype of the Swiss personality, or the emblematic characteristics of a major character in a French text, such as the innocence of Hugo's Esmeralda; therefore the James text situates itself in a context that is at least to some degree French. The function of direct allusions to French literature is a natural place to begin a discussion of James's incorporation of French culture into his fiction; two of the most obvious examples of such allusions appear in *Daisy Miller* and *The Princess Casamassima.*

Daisy Miller, the novella that made its author's reputation in 1879, represents one person's efforts to interpret another person's or people's motives and behavior, as do so many of James's novels, tales, and novellas. The crucial issue of *Daisy Miller* is the ever-changing opinion that Winterbourne, its central character, has of the title character; parallel to the story of the young girl's adventures in Vevey and Rome runs the story that occurs inside Winterbourne's mind as he tries to decide what to make of the pretty American girl.[2] Is her natural, spontaneous behavior the result of American standards for the conduct of unmarried young women and of an upbringing that was obviously anything but strict? Is she an innocent flirt? Is she a naïve but stubborn young woman unwilling to make allowances for the unavoidable values of the world in which she lives? Is she "a young lady whom a gentleman need no longer be at pains to respect" (*DM* 111, chap. 4)? Or is she an innocent and tragically misunderstood figure whose poignant calls for affection are misconstrued?

During the course of the text, Winterbourne decides that Daisy Miller is each of these (it should be noted that critical commentary on *Daisy Miller* raises the same questions Winterbourne faces and offers a similarly wide range of answers), and the text is a record of Winterbourne's succeeding understandings of the girl's character. As he is exposed to her, he interprets her behavior and arrives at a conclusion about her that is soon confounded by her subsequent behavior. This leads to a new interpretation, a new conclusion, and a new indictment; the whole process then repeats itself, and its repetition ceases only after Daisy's death at the novel's close. As Millicent Bell has written, Winterbourne's "uneasy journey from one concept to another is the story's profoundest plot and at the same time a dramatization of our reading experience."[3]

A very similar process of interpretation and reinterpretation is central to other James novels. In *The Princess Casamassima,* Hyacinth Robinson tries to understand the other characters he comes into contact with, most especially the intriguing Princess herself, who is in many respects comparable with Daisy—though she is perhaps even more unfathomable. Just as *Daisy Miller* represents Winterbourne's efforts to understand Daisy's sexuality, so *The Ambassadors* represents Lambert Strether's interpretations and understandings of the relationship between Chad Newsome and Mme. de Vionnet. In *The Awkward Age,* the matter of a young, unmarried girl's sexual innocence—the "question of 'does she or doesn't she?' "[4]—is once again central, although with the difference this time that the reader is not granted access to the inner observations of any watcher of the lady in question as in the other texts.

There is a difference between the way this basic situation appears in

Daisy Miller and in the later texts, as Paul Lukacs has implied in his article on ambiguity in James's novella.[5] The reader of *The Ambassadors*, for example, knows what Strether thinks of the situation he finds himself in, but does not know any better than Strether does whether he is thinking, observing, and interpreting rightly. Because Strether is plagued by doubt in a way that Winterbourne is not (both Strether and Winterbourne can be wrong, but Winterbourne always believes he is right, even though he may later realize that he is not), there is a different distance in *The Ambassadors* between the reader and the protagonist's consciousness than in *Daisy Miller*. It is clear to the reader of *Daisy Miller* what at first inspires Winterbourne's interest in the title character, what makes him defend her fundamental innocence to his scandalized aunt, Mrs. Costello, and equally shocked friend, Mrs. Walker, and what makes him at last decide to drop Daisy.

It is not clear in the same way to the reader of *The Ambassadors* what makes Strether change his mind from insisting Chad return to America immediately, to insisting he stay in Paris, and then to insisting he still stay in Paris even though he has stumbled upon undeniable evidence of Chad's adulterous relationship with Mme. de Vionnet.[6] This is not to say that the reader cannot know what makes Strether change his mind; rather, because other characters withhold the truth, or mislead him about it (whether intentionally or not), or even lie outright, what prompts each of Strether's new interpretations is as problematic to the reader as the interpretation itself. Thus the reader is aware that Strether's interpretations involve his deceiving himself, which is not the case with Winterbourne. Winterbourne is often just as wrong as Strether about things, but his incorrect views seem perfectly correct on the basis of the evidence available at the moment, whereas in *The Ambassadors*, the reader perceives that Strether has missed or misinterpreted crucial evidence.[7]

Since *Daisy Miller* is a simplified version, as it were, of the standard James narrative, I take it as the introductory example of the function of French literature in James's fiction. Because *Daisy Miller* is a representation of the limitations of subjectivity and the problems of interpreting a situation, the reader encounters the same sorts of limitations in interpreting the novel that Winterbourne encounters in trying to know what to think of Daisy. However, *Daisy Miller* offers its readers a solution by means of an allusion to *Paule Méré*, an epistolary novel by Victor Cherbuliez, a French novelist of Genevan origin. This novel tells, in many respects, the same story as James's but with the difference that *Paule Méré* leaves its readers in no doubt as to what they are supposed to conclude from that story.

Since part of the purpose of *Daisy Miller* is to provide a mimesis of the very real problems people face in real life about knowing what to think of a situation, James's text cannot leave its readers with the kind of certitude Cherbuliez gives his readers. However, via the allusion, *Daisy Miller* nevertheless provides an indication—albeit obliquely—of what readers are to conclude. The large body of criticism of *Daisy Miller* and the range of interpretive disagreement recorded in that criticism are evidence of the uncertainty this novella causes (as is the case with so much of James's fiction). However, an understanding of the function of the allusion to *Paule Méré* suggests a way of resolving the differing critical interpretations of *Daisy Miller*. Briefly, these interpretations can be grouped into two camps:

> According to one reading, Daisy's innocence means that she is a child of nature as opposed to history. . . . This interpretation sees Daisy's innocence as a virtue that separates her from the unnecessarily "stiff" conventions of an excessively traditional society. If it means that she is inexperienced, it also means that she has nothing to hide. Thus she plays no roles and carries no affectations; and she is innocent also in the sense of being guiltless, innocent, that is, of the charges of vulgarity and indelicacy that repeatedly are brought against her. Indeed, according to this view, those charges actually indict Mrs. Walker and all the other self-appointed arbiters of social *mores* who so cruelly shun Daisy.[8]

According to this reading, Daisy is "like Billy Budd, Huck Finn, or Natty Bumpo, a mythic or archetypal figure"[9] not unrelated to Montaigne's cannibals or Rousseau's noble savage, whose fundamental goodness is gravely misunderstood, and whose tragic end is an indictment of the society that does not understand her.

> Yet a second interpretation has proved equally popular ever since the novel first appeared; and according to it, Daisy is anything but mythic. This second reading takes her innocence to be an experience that manifests itself as willful ignorance, and it finds her guilty of the very charges that the expatriate colony brings against her.[10]

In this second reading, Daisy's innocence is a negative characteristic; the girl's innocence becomes "willful ignorance" because she stubbornly refuses to recognize what people think of her or to care about the consequences of their disapproval, because that would oblige her to modify her behavior.[11]

In the first, "noble savage" reading, the villains are the American expatriates represented by Mrs. Walker and Mrs. Costello. They are the stubborn ones, for their rigid values do not permit them to overlook Daisy's gaucheries. They are even responsible for Daisy's death, since by ostracizing her, they push her all the more into the company of the Italian fortune hunter Giovanelli, who takes her to the Colosseum, where she catches "Roman fever." In the second reading, the villain is Daisy herself, and the text is an indictment of her tragic unwillingness to "do as the Romans do."[12]

Each of these readings involves a judgment of both the title character and the expatriates who ostracize her, because the innocence of the one necessarily implies the guilt of the other. Either Daisy is responsible and the Europeanized Americans are not, or else the girl is not responsible and the expatriates are, for her tragic end. To resolve the differences between the two readings, then, one could focus either on Daisy or on the expatriates. The tendency has been to focus on the former; my intention is to consider the latter.[13]

Daisy Miller requires that the reader carefully examine at least one of the expatriates in the novel, Winterbourne, because he is the character whom the end emphasizes:

> Nevertheless, he [Winterbourne] went back to live at Geneva, whence there continue to come the most contradictory accounts of his motives of sojourn: a report that he is "studying" hard—an intimation that he is much interested in a very clever foreign lady. (116, chap. 4)

This is the last sentence of *Daisy Miller*, and like so many of the endings of James's fictions, it has a considerable effect on the reader's interpretation of the entire text. It repeats practically word for word a passage in the second paragraph of the text describing Winterbourne's life in Geneva before the events of the novella:

> when his friends spoke of him, they usually said that he was at Geneva, "studying." . . . [W]hen certain persons spoke of him they affirmed that the reason of his spending so much time at Geneva was that he was extremely devoted to a lady who lived there—a foreign lady—a person older than himself. (48, chap. 1)

The juxtaposition of these two passages suggests that Winterbourne's life goes on unchanged, in spite of the events of the novella. This raises the question, What effect have Daisy's life and death had on Winterbourne? If they have had some effect, why does the end suggest that his life continues the same, and if they have had no effect, what is the point of telling the story of Winterbourne's acquaintance with Daisy? Because of these questions that the end raises, it is difficult to understand how a reader can have a response to Daisy entirely independent of Winterbourne's response to her.

Whereas the text has carefully represented Winterbourne's various responses to his contact with Daisy up to her death, after her funeral it withholds his thoughts. Until that point, it is always quite clear what prompts Winterbourne each time he changes his mind about the title character. Therefore his final conclusion about Daisy, which Winterbourne expresses in the closing conversation with his aunt, challenges the reader to figure out from the evidence offered in the events of the plot what makes the young American change his mind this final time.[14] It is this aspect of the end that "has led to considerable variety in critical interpretations of Winterbourne's character and of *Daisy Miller* as a whole."[15] Indeed, many of James's fictional endings raise similar interpretive problems and for similar reasons. While, as Frank Kermode has often shown,[16] readers should expect conventional endings to resolve matters neatly and clearly, the kinds of endings James usually writes oblige readers to turn back into the text for the unequivocality upon which to base the interpretations they normally expect from the ending. The voluminous record of interpretations of James's work suggests that this unequivocality is not readily found; however, I argue that such a basis for interpretation lies in the system of reference to other literature and culture that abounds throughout James's fictions.

Several critics have examined allusions in *Daisy Miller* in an effort to resolve the questions raised by the novel and by various critics. The reference to Byron's *Manfred* in the scene in the Colosseum has been treated by John Randall and Susan Koprince.[17] Carl Wood has argued that "several prominent though indirect allusions to . . . 'The Prisoner of Chillon' . . . clarify and underscore the poignancy of Winterbourne's tragic failure to come into full, permanent contact with the genuine human warmth that Daisy offers him."[18] Adeline Tintner and Jeffrey Meyers have considered the implications of the allusion to Velázquez's portrait of Pope Innocent X in a scene that Winterbourne learns of indirectly.[19] Finally, Edward Stone has written on the allusion at the beginning of the third chapter of *Daisy Miller* to Cherbuliez's *Paule Méré*.[20] It is the most significant of these allusions, since it provides James's readers with an unequivocal condemnation of Geneva, the European residence of two of the three permanent American expatriates in *Daisy Miller*.[21] And this in turn provides the readers of *Daisy Miller* with a clear indication of how to perceive these expatriates.

The action of *Daisy Miller* is situated in two places: Vevey and its environs for the first two chapters and the last half-page, and Rome for the remainder of the last two chapters. However, a third place, Geneva, is never far from the reader's and characters' thoughts. As the historical capital of

Calvinism, it is an obvious counterweight to Rome, the seat of the papacy. This leaves Vevey in between, as a neutral ground too cosmopolitan for any one thing to be associated with it (in contrast with Rome and Geneva): it "assumes . . . some of the characteristics of an American watering-place" like Newport or Saratoga; the waiters are "neat German[s]"; and among the hotel guests are "Russian princesses" and "Polish boys" (47–48, chap. 1).

The association between Geneva and Calvinism is made explicitly in the novella's second paragraph, where Winterbourne is introduced: "[h]e had come from Geneva . . . Geneva having been for a long time his place of residence. . . . Winterbourne had an old attachment for the little metropolis of Calvinism" (48, chap. 1). Despite Winterbourne's obvious attachment to Geneva, the few direct mentions of the Swiss city do not represent it in the best light. When Winterbourne meets Daisy's mother, for example, he contrasts her in his mind to "the vigilant matrons who massed themselves in the forefront of social intercourse in the *dark old* city at the other end of the lake" (71, chap. 2; emphasis added).

Geneva, it is suggested, has an effect on the judgments its inhabitants make of others. When Winterbourne first meets Daisy, he wonders at her easy, outgoing manner and then if Geneva is not as much the cause of his bewilderment as Daisy herself.

> Poor Winterbourne was amused, perplexed, and decidedly charmed. He had never yet heard a young girl express herself in just this fashion; . . . He felt that he had lived at Geneva so long that he had lost a good deal; he had become dishabituated to the American tone. (57, chap. 1)

This is the first of three times in the text that the young American wonders if the length of his residence abroad has affected his values and judgments.

Winterbourne expresses the same concern about the effect of his residence in Geneva later, in Rome, to his friend Mrs. Walker, who is shocked at Daisy's walking unchaperoned in the Pincio with Giovanelli and himself. When her effort to convince Daisy not to make such a display of herself fails, she orders Winterbourne into her carriage and scolds him for associating with someone so badly behaved. Winterbourne's response to this scolding is surprisingly self-revealing: " 'I suspect, Mrs. Walker, that you and I have lived too long at Geneva!' " (*DM* 94, chap. 3).

Winterbourne repeats the suspicion that extended residence in Geneva has prevented him from judging Daisy fairly at the end of the novella, when he is reunited with his aunt at Vevey several months after the girl's death. Their conversation is the last occasion for the reader to learn what the young man thinks of Daisy; it is the last stage represented in his series of interpretations of the girl and immediately precedes the closing sentence about his subsequent life in Geneva quoted above. His late-night accidental meeting with Daisy and Giovanelli in the Colosseum had convinced Winterbourne that what the other Americans were suggesting about her was true; she was not a decent girl: "He felt angry with himself that he had bothered so much about the right way of regarding Miss Daisy Miller" (111, chap. 4). But Daisy's illness and death, Mrs. Miller's report of Daisy's delirious message to Winterbourne, and finally Giovanelli's admission at Daisy's funeral that the girl "was the most beautiful young lady I ever saw, and the most amiable . . . [a]nd she was the most innocent" and that "[s]he would never have married me, I am sure" (115, chap. 4) led Winterbourne to modify his opinion of James's title character one last time.

> Winterbourne had often thought of Daisy Miller and her mystifying manners. One day he spoke of her to his aunt—said it was on his conscience that he had done her injustice. . . . "You were right in that remark that you made last summer. I was booked to make a mistake. I have lived too long in foreign parts." (115–16, chap. 4)

Thus Winterbourne has come full circle in his interpretations of Daisy. Once again she is the "pretty American flirt" he had concluded she was at their first meeting (58, chap. 1). Her running about with Giovanelli and alternately pretending and then denying to be engaged to him (109, chap. 4), like her teasing Winterbourne for being "stiff" (93, chap. 3; 98, 99, 108, chap. 4), her scolding him for not visiting her sooner in Rome (81, 83, 87, chap. 3), her making a scene about his returning to Geneva after such a short stay in Vevey (77–78, chap. 2), and her provoking him into insisting on taking her out at night in a rowboat on the Lac Léman (71–74, chap. 2) are only harmless manifestations of her flirtatious nature. All she wants is to provoke Winterbourne into making a "fuss" (73, chap. 2) about her, to show he has some interest in her. This last conclusion about Daisy, like the first, ends with the reflection of having lived too long abroad, especially in Geneva. Thus the question of Geneva is inextricably related to the reader's full response to Winterbourne, for deciding whether the young man (and by extension, the other expatriates) has done Daisy justice in his opinion of her becomes a question of deciding whether living in Geneva indeed has altered his view of people, whether he really has "lived too long at Geneva."

The reader aware of the French stereotype of the Swiss in general and of Genevans in particular would know the sort of effect Geneva would have on Winterbourne. Pierre Larousse, that invaluable source of nineteenth-century French cultural conventions, expresses this stereotype in his description of Geneva's old and new sections in terms that James's "*the dark old city* at the other end of the lake" seem to echo:

> . . . la ville nouvelle . . . manque d'originalité; mais *la vieille Genève, la grave et sombre* Genève de Calvin, dont les maisons sont entassées sur une colline, intéressera vivement les touristes. . . .

> [. . . the new city . . . lacks originality; but *old Geneva, the stern and dark Geneva* of Calvin, with its houses piled up on a hill, will greatly interest tourists. . . .][22]

According to this stereotype, the Swiss are dull and repressed, conform blandly to conventional values, and are concerned primarily with business and money. They are everything that Daisy Miller is not; she is anything but repressed, she certainly is not dull, and she is clearly a nonconformist. She is in every way the exact opposite of the typical Genevan or Swiss. Having lived so long in Geneva, Winterbourne and Mrs. Walker have become like its citizens, and Daisy's nonconformity cannot possibly please them.

James's readers sufficiently versed in French culture and its stereotypes would need no more than the reference to Calvin and "the dark old city" to make the necessary association with the cliché of the Genevan and Swiss character as dull, repressed, and conformist, and to perceive that it is operative in *Daisy Miller;* but a less cosmopolitan reader might not.[23] In order that readers not miss this view of the Swiss and consider how it functions in *Daisy Miller,* James's novella provides the explicit allusion to *Paule Méré* at the beginning of its third chapter. In the letter Mrs. Costello sends Winterbourne inviting him to join her in Rome, she writes a few lines on the escapades of the Millers and follows them with an apparently unrelated instruction:

> Those people you were so devoted to last summer at Vevey have turned up here, courier and all. . . . They seem to have made several acquaintances, but the courier continues to be the most *intime*. The young lady, however, is also very intimate with some third-rate Italians, with whom she rackets about in a way that makes much talk. Bring me that pretty novel of Cherbuliez's— *Paule Méré*. (*DM* 79, chap. 3)

The juxtaposition of the gossip about the Millers and the instruction to bring the book are, on the surface, unrelated, but the very fact of their

juxtaposition, plus the similarities between Cherbuliez's and James's novels, suggest that what is said about the Millers and *Paule Méré* have a great
deal to do with each other. Viola Dunbar has briefly discussed similarities
of theme between Cherbuliez's and James's novels,[24] and Stone has discussed the similarities of their plots, concentrating on this passage in particular. He argues that James was "capable on occasion of providing the initiated reader of a fiction with a more strategic clue . . . that would turn out
to be nothing less than a key to the understanding of an entire fiction of
his own."[25] Daisy's innocence, as Stone reminds us, is "the central question
of James's story," and the first three sentences of Mrs. Costello's letter
remind the reader of that question; the fourth sentence—the allusion to
Paule Méré—is "the key to its answer."[26]

While Winterbourne and Mrs. Costello may not see any connection between the Millers' unconventional behavior and *Paule Méré*, James's juxtaposition of the two in the letter shows that there is a relation. The passage
comes at "the exact center" of *Daisy Miller*[27] (it appears in the first paragraph of the third of the four chapters of the American edition of 1878 and
the first paragraph of the second of the two installments of the serial version). The purpose of placing the allusion in this central position, continues
Stone, is "a dead giveaway . . . imply[ing] disapproval of [Mrs. Costello's]
snobbery by furnishing the initiated among [James's] readers a parallel situation."[28] Thus not only does the juxtaposition imply a relation but its chronological centrality suggests how central it is to the novel's interpretation.

The "parallel situation" lies in the similarities between the two texts of
plot and characterization of the hero and heroine. Cherbuliez's "Paule is
. . . essentially as headstrong as Daisy. Like Daisy, she has been slan-
dered";[29] innocent sketching excursions have been "falsely interpreted,"[30]
just like Daisy's unchaperoned escapades in Rome.

> Marcel Roger, Cherbuliez' hero . . . [l]ike Winterbourne . . . is about thirty,
> wealthy, a self-styled "*spectateur désoeuvré*," and cosmopolitan in upbringing
> and point of view. The ambivalence of his attitude toward the maligned hero-
> ine corresponds to Winterbourne's. . . .[31]

Like *Daisy Miller, Paule Méré* tells the story of a man interested in a very
attractive young woman who is the subject of scandalous gossip. At first
Cherbuliez's Marcel, like Winterbourne, pays no heed to the rumors, but
he becomes increasingly suspicious; and when he catches a glimpse of Paule
furtively introducing a strange man into her home, Marcel takes this as
definite evidence of Paule's shame and breaks off their engagement. He
discovers too late that the stranger was his intended father-in-law. Hurt
that Marcel even suspected her of wrongdoing, Paule becomes gravely ill,

and the novel ends with her near death and Marcel on the verge of insanity. The final lines of the text, spoken by a friend of both, reinforce the critique of Genevan values as the novel's central theme: "Mais, monsieur, dites-moi, quelle est donc cette faiblesse d'écouter un monde qu'on méprise?" [But tell me, sir, why this weakness of listening to a world one scorns?].[32]

The most obvious similarity between the two novels is that both heroines are unjustly criticized by people from Geneva and that the man who initially defends her against these criticisms ends up agreeing with them. As Stone emphasizes, both novels "relate, with varying sympathy, the sad fate of an admirable girl whose actions run afoul of rigid Genevan standards of deportment."[33] Stone and Dunbar do not make clear that the significant difference between the two texts is that *Paule Méré* expresses its attitude about Geneva and its society clearly and unequivocally. That is what is really important about the allusion to *Paule Méré* in *Daisy Miller*, for since James's text does not overtly emphasize the negative characterization of Geneva, other than to call it "the little metropolis of Calvinism" and "the dark old city at the other end of the lake," it needs a means of indicating to the reader what to make of the Swiss city and of the characters who represent its conventions. This means is provided by the allusion to Cherbuliez's novel. From the very first paragraph of *Paule Méré*, where Marcel explains why his stay in Geneva had been far shorter than planned, the Swiss city and its society are presented in the poorest of lights.

> Le premier jour, elle [ma mère] a été presque tendre; le lendemain, elle m'a questionné; le surlendemain, elle s'est inquiétée et m'a fait sonder par ses amis. L'un d'eux me demanda "ce que je comptais faire"; un autre calcula sur ses doigts ce qu'avaient dû coûter mes longs voyages dans le Levant; le troisième m'examina sur les matières de doctrine; le quatrième. . . . J'ai pris ma fuite et je cours encore.

> [The first day my mother was practically tender; the next day, she started questioning me; the following day, she got worried and had her friends sound me out. One of them asked me "what I was planning to do"; another calculated on his fingers what my long trips to the Levant must have cost; the third one examined me on matters of doctrine; the fourth. . . . I took flight, and I am still running.] (*PM* 3, part 1)

The image of Geneva portrayed here could not be clearer. The city's inhabitants are concerned only with practical matters—business plans and money—or with "doctrine"—matters of conscience. This attitude toward Geneva and its society—the French stereotype of the repressed and conformist Genevan, in short—prevails throughout *Paule Méré*. Marcel says:

Les Genevois sont un peuple très-estimable, ils ont du coeur et de l'esprit; mais ils accompagnent leurs qualités d'un travers qui gâte tout . . . ils aiment percher. Oui; ils sont toujours perchés sur quelque chose, l'un sur ses aïeux, l'autre sur ses écus, celui-ci sur ses vertus, celui-là sur ses écrits.

[The Genevans are a highly estimable people, they are clever and honorable; but their qualities are accompanied by a defect that ruins everything . . . they like to harp. Yes; they are always harping on something, some on their ancestors, others on their money, these on their virtues, those on their writings.] (41–42, part 1)

The same sentiment is repeated by Paule in her long account of her childhood when she describes the society that met in her grandparents' home.

Le commérage et la médisance défrayaient le plus souvent la conversation; on parlait aussi de Dieu et des affaires, et ces deux sujets étaient traités sur le même ton, ou, pour mieux dire, ces gens-là parlaient de Dieu en hommes d'affaires et des affaires avec une sorte de religieuse onction.

[Gossip and rumor were the principal subject of conversation; God and business were also spoken of, and these two subjects were treated with the same tone, or rather, these people spoke of God as if they were businessmen and of business with a sort of religious unctuousness.] (*PM* 159, part 2)

All these passages describe what Dunbar calls "the highly artificial character of life in Geneva,"[34] although the artificiality she speaks of is cast in the French stereotype of the repressed Swiss as the Genevans' nature. Nevertheless, because of the pervasiveness of this characterization of Geneva throughout Cherbuliez's novel, it makes sense for *Daisy Miller* to allude to it. The key point is that the allusion to *Paule Méré* has a function within James's text, which is to indicate to the reader that Geneva is to be understood in the way it is portrayed in Cherbuliez's text. Again, the juxtaposition in Mrs. Costello's remarks of the gossip about the Millers and her request for *Paule Méré* confirms this significance: *Paule Méré* expresses the contempt of Genevan "commérage" and "médisance," and Mrs. Costello's letter is a perfect example of just such gossip and rumor-spreading. While both Dunbar and Stone have demonstrated how the two novels are alike, they have placed less emphasis on the significance of the allusion in James's text to *Paule Méré* and how it affects the reader than on arguing that the allusion is evidence of an authorial intention.[35]

Stone and Bell both point out that Cherbuliez was a well-known author in America in the 1870s.[36] If they are right that readers of *Daisy Miller* could be expected to know *Paule Méré*, the function of the allusion to it at the beginning of the third chapter is to make available to American readers, who may not have otherwise been aware of it, the significance of the French stereotype of the repressed Genevan to James's novella. Cherbuliez's book serves as a bridge between a French cultural convention—the cliché repressed Swiss—and American readers who otherwise might not have access to it. It is a crucial sign for such readers, for it shows them what to make of the Americans in the novella who live in Geneva and therefore of what to make of their attitude toward Daisy.

Because of this allusion, it is clear that Winterbourne and Mrs. Walker have indeed lived too long in Geneva. They have come to see things the Genevan way, and that is why they do not accept Daisy for the innocent young girl the text otherwise shows her to be.[37] The young girl's first name ought to be indication enough of her innocence, and the text provides several other signs: she first appears to Winterbourne and the reader in a "garden" (*DM* 51, chap. 1), she lives "as they did in the Golden Age" (103, chap. 4), and in the scene in the Colosseum, she compares herself to the "Christian martyrs" whom the Romans fed to "the old lions or tigers" (110, chap. 4). The Europeanized Americans, however, are far too swayed by their Genevan mentality to recognize her innocence. Thus the first of the two readings of *Daisy Miller* that I summarized at the beginning—the "noble savage" reading—is the more convincing one. Daisy is misunderstood and innocent—although her innocence is not a naïve one, as her final message to Winterbourne demonstrates—and the expatriate colony is to blame for not being able to understand her because it has been overly influenced by the stuffy "little metropolis of Calvinism."

Paule Méré is also an exposé of the damage to human life and happiness caused by restrictive morality, and the allusion to it in James's novel allows his readers to see that *Daisy Miller* is a critique of a society characterized by gossip and narrow-mindedness too. We know this because of the word "pretty," which Mrs. Costello uses to describe Cherbuliez's novel when she asks Winterbourne to bring it to her. The reader who knows Cherbuliez's novel recognizes the irony in Mrs. Costello thinking Paule Méré's story "pretty" at the same time she holds a far less pretty view of the similar story of Daisy Miller. The irony is that Mrs. Costello is a hypocrite, and if the novel casts her as a hypocrite, it is because the novel is a critique of the hypocrisy of the society to which she belongs.

Righteous-minded undergraduate students of *Daisy Miller* never tire of pointing out Winterbourne's hypocrisy in having a mistress in Geneva at the same time that he permits himself to judge the apparent "looseness" of Daisy's behavior and relations. Such students realize just how right they are if they see what this hypocrisy implies about the extent to which *Daisy Miller* is a critique of social manners. The double standard that applies to Winterbourne applies to privileged American and European society in the nineteenth century as a whole, and *Daisy Miller* is one of the many literary protests lodged against it.

To see *Daisy Miller* as a protest against the hypocritical double standard for men and women is to see an entirely different meaning to the message the dying Daisy tries to send Winterbourne. As Mrs. Miller tells Winterbourne, Daisy wanted to tell him that "she never was engaged to . . . Giovanelli. . . . And [she wanted] to ask you if you remembered the time you went to that castle, in Switzerland" (114, chap. 4). Winterbourne appears, at the end of the novel, to have taken this message as a sign of affectionate interest: " 'She sent me a message before her death which I didn't understand at the time. But I have understood it since. She would have appreciated one's esteem.' " It is not clear how far Winterbourne believes this esteem is meant to go, but it is clear what his aunt thinks: " 'Is that a modest way . . . of saying that she would have reciprocated one's affection?' " (116, chap. 4).

Because Winterbourne neither contradicts nor agrees with his aunt, we do not know if he assents to the implication of her question, and as a result, we never know Winterbourne's interpretation of the message. We could accept Mrs. Costello's interpretation, which would perceive Daisy as saying "Remember the good times we shared," and conclude that Daisy's message is an appeal for affection or esteem, but there is less ground for us to do so than there is for us to conclude that Daisy's message is an attempt at self-vindication.

The logic behind Mrs. Costello's question is that if Daisy sent a death-bed message (note that Winterbourne does not tell Mrs. Costello the content of the message) then she cares for the person she sent it to. A reader who adopts this logic runs the danger of thinking that in reminding Winterbourne of the visit they made to Chillon Castle, Daisy is appealing to his memory of a happy moment they shared. However, this cannot be why Daisy recalls the trip. It is true that the castle visit is the one extended time Winterbourne and Daisy spend alone in each other's company, but as it is described, it does not merit fond remembrance. Daisy is completely unimpressed by the castle and what Winterbourne tells her of it (*DM* 76, chap. 2), and the return to Vevey is anything but cheerful (78, chap. 2). Two things stand out in the episode: the maneuvers Winterbourne attempts for the sake of his and Daisy's intimacy—he prefers they travel in a carriage (74, chap. 2), apparently so he can be alone with her, and he tips the custodian "generously" to ensure the couple's privacy (76, chap. 2)—and the jealous scene Daisy makes when Winterbourne announces his impending return to Geneva (77–78, chap. 2).

There is no reason to view the visit to Chillon as a fond memory, but there is a reason for Daisy to remind Winterbourne of it after he has discovered Giovanelli and her in the Colosseum, for what Winterbourne suspected both Daisy and Giovanelli of was not too different from the spirit of "adventure" (*DM* 75, chap. 2) that prompted Winterbourne to arrange the visit to Chillon. Daisy's message does not say "Remember the good times"; what it says is "Don't blame Giovanelli and me for doing in the Colosseum exactly what you were doing at Chillon." If Daisy was a flirt, than Winterbourne was certainly a womanizer; regardless of one's view of the moral propriety of his involvement with the "very clever foreign lady" (116, chap. 4) in Geneva, Winterbourne was certainly guilty of carrying on a romantic, or sexual, pursuit of Daisy at the same time; Daisy's message attempts to remind Winterbourne, and does remind the reader, of this and appeals for equal standards for judging flirts and womanizers.

From a comment Daisy makes at Mrs. Walker's party—"[Flirting] seems to me much more proper in young unmarried women than in old married ones" (*DM* 99, chap. 4)—the reader knows Daisy is aware of the double standard applied to men and women at the time, and therefore there is nothing unreasonable in seeing her final message as expressing an awareness of the hypocrisy of this double standard and as a reminder to Winterbourne that in a fairer society he would be in no position to condemn her. We cannot be certain that Winterbourne appreciates Daisy's message as a protest against his and society's hypocrisy, but it does not matter; what matters is that the reader understand that Daisy's message and the end of *Daisy Miller* condemn the society the novella represents, just as *Paule Méré* does.

In James's novella, this condemnation is made obliquely; that it is made is confirmed if we once again see *Paule Méré* as the unambiguous parallel for James's story. Cherbuliez's novel ends with the question already quoted, "Mais, monsieur, dites-moi, quelle est donc cette faiblesse d'écouter un monde qu'on méprise?" [But tell me, sir, what is this weakness of listening to a world one scorns?] (352, part 4), which is the final expression of the novel's criticism of Genevan values. *Daisy Miller* ends with Mrs. Costello's question of whether Daisy's message meant that she desired Winterbourne's affection, but because we recognize Mrs. Costello's interpretation of the message as wrong, we see that *Daisy Miller* lodges a criticism of the same kind of society as Cherbuliez's novel. *Paule Méré* ends on a note of scorn for Genevan morality—"un monde qu'on méprise"— and so, though less obviously, does *Daisy Miller*.

2

Princess Casamassima and
Octave Feuillet

lthough it is not likely to be among the texts mentioned
by people who read Henry James for entertainment, *The
Princess Casamassima* has become one of the novels that
scholarly critics of James write about most often. There are a number of
obvious reasons for this, not least of which is that as the James novel (along
with *The Bostonians* and *The Tragic Muse*) that most overtly treats politics
as a topic and the only one about poor people, it has a particular appeal to
neo-Marxist and New Historicist critics. Also, because of the mixed French
and English ancestry of Hyacinth Robinson, the novel's protagonist, and
because of the significance of the episodes situated in Paris, *The Princess
Casamassima* invariably receives detailed attention from critics of James
interested in James and France. Indeed, all the book-length studies of
James and French literature, with the exception of Brooks's, offer significant chapters on *The Princess Casamassima*. Lyall Powers claims that
James's long novels of the mid- and late 1880s are markedly different from
his fiction up to and through *The Portrait of a Lady* (1880–1881) because
of the influence of the realist and naturalist "grandsons of Balzac": Turgenev, Flaubert, Daudet, Zola, Edmond de Goncourt, and Maupassant,
whom James came to know personally after 1875.[1] *Henry James and the
Naturalist Movement,* Powers's book on the novels of this "Naturalist Period" of James's career,[2] interpolates the "principles" of Zola's naturalism
into James's "experimental novels":[3] *The Bostonians, The Princess Casamassima,* and *The Tragic Muse.* Philip Grover's *Henry James and the French
Novel* is similar to Powers's, emphasizing the influence of French realism
and the "art for art's sake" movement on James's fiction.

It is not surprising that chapters on *The Princess Casamassima* are high points of both Powers's and Grover's books, because James himself is partly responsible for comparisons between the works of the French naturalists and the novels—especially *The Princess Casamassima*—of the later 1880s. James spent the month of February 1884 in Paris, during which time he renewed his contacts with the members of Flaubert's "*cénacle*," whom he had frequented during his Paris residence in 1875–1876, and none of whom he had seen since before his "final glimpse of Turgenev" in November 1882.[4] Letters written during James's stay in Paris to his brother William and to William Dean Howells testify to his interest in Goncourt, Daudet, and Zola and their fiction.[5] In December 1884, James visited Millbank Prison, which was to become the scene of Hyacinth's visit to his dying mother, in chapter 3 of *The Princess Casamassima*. He was given an extensive tour of the prison, and upon his return home, he told Thomas Sergeant Perry: "I have been all the morning at Millbank Prison (horrible place) collecting notes for a fiction scene. You see I am quite the Naturalist" (*HJL* 3:61). Because of this reference to and adoption of Zola's and the Goncourts' well-known research habits, and because of the uncharacteristic portrayal of working-class characters throughout the novel, critics like Powers and Grover have been eager to argue the numerous points of comparison between *The Princess Casamassima* and French naturalism.

I do not mean to discount the "naturalist" tendencies in *The Princess Casamassima* (slum settings, working-class characters, the note gathering at Millbank Prison) or to suggest that there are no similarities between *The Princess Casamassima* and the novels of Zola and others. That James was especially interested in French naturalist fiction during the period of his career that he was conceiving and writing *The Princess Casamassima* is indicated by the fact that the majority of the criticism he published during the first half of the 1880s was either devoted specifically to contemporary French realist or naturalist writers or else, as in "The Art of Fiction" (1884), contained important considerations of French naturalism.

This criticism, and in fact virtually all his critical essays and letters to friends and acquaintances in the world of English and American letters, shows James to be a persuasive and important spokesman for the French realist novel, and the role James (along with Howells) played in paving the way for the full-blown American naturalists of the turn of the century (Crane, Garland, Norris, Wharton, London) cannot be underestimated. However, the tendency to emphasize James's interest in French realism has obscured the fact that the French novelists whom we, a century later, consider the major authors of the time were not the only ones James read and took seriously.[6]

That literary tastes change over time is a commonplace every student of James's literary criticism knows applies to the evolution of James's critical career. Not only did his taste change over the course of his career but late-twentieth-century standards are no guideline for his preferences. Balzac is the only French writer, and Turgenev the only contemporary of James, who received unqualified praise and admiration throughout James's critical career. James criticized Flaubert harshly early in his career, classed him among the "minor French novelists" in 1876,[7] and came late in his career to only a begrudging appreciation of the author of *Madame Bovary.* James's earlier writing on Zola could be extremely critical,[8] and any praise was always heavily qualified.[9] If James's last essay on Zola[10] is an unqualified appreciation of Zola's career, reservations about his achievement nevertheless continued to appear in James's critical essays of the same period.[11] While James was expressing reservations about Zola during his "Naturalist Period," the only French naturalist who received unreserved appreciation was Alphonse Daudet, whose importance is certainly perceived today as of a lesser magnitude than Zola's. During at least the first decades of James's career, however, writers such as Cherbuliez, Octave Feuillet, Gustave Droz, and Jules Sandeau received as much attention and at least as much praise as the now canonical writers of the time.

What I am suggesting is a parallel to the central argument of Marcia Jacobson's *Henry James and the Mass Market.* Jacobson first argues that the tendency in James scholarship has been to consider James's work only in relation to canonical literature, and then shows the many striking points of comparison between James's fiction—including *The Princess Casamassima* (and *The Awkward Age,* the subject of a later chapter)—and contemporary, popular but now forgotten, novels. Jacobson limits herself, however, to discussing English-language parallels, and I am arguing that the attention paid to James's literary relations to French writers of the stature of Balzac and Zola, however justified that attention may be, has eclipsed the importance of the relations of other contemporary French writers, who were well known in their day but are obscure today.

This raises the question of the grounds on which one compares the work of Henry James with that of his French contemporaries. Following Edwin Fussell's lead, I have been arguing that throughout James's fictional writings we see a variety of strategies for incorporating French literature into the James text. In the previous chapter, I discussed one manifestation of this incorporation, a specific literary allusion, and the role that allusion plays in providing the reader of *Daisy Miller* with a basis for an interpretation of the novella. *The Princess Casamassima* contains a number of allusions, several of which have received attention from Adeline Tintner, that indefatigable chronicler of James's literary and artistic allusions.[12] One of these allusions, which Tintner has incorrectly identified,[13] is to the work of Octave Feuillet. It plays a far more complex role in *The Princess Casamassima* than the *Paule Méré* allusion does in *Daisy Miller:* first, it is an obscure allusion, giving only the author's name and leaving out the title, and second, while the *Paule Méré* allusion served to confirm a particular resolution of the interpretive cruxes in *Daisy Miller,* the Feuillet allusion in *The Princess Casamassima* is really to a network of references, consisting of three novels: Feuillet's *Histoire d'une parisienne* and *La Veuve* and James's *Roderick Hudson.* Furthermore, while the *Paule Méré* reference only served as a basis for supporting a particular interpretation of *Daisy Miller,* the Feuillet reference breaks the interpretation of *The Princess Casamassima* wide open by pointing to a view of the title character that is radically different from the one generally held by commentators on this novel.

On the first day of his visit to Medley, the Princess Casamassima's country house, Hyacinth and his hostess decide to take a walk together in the park. Before this walk begins, the text refers to Octave Feuillet, a now forgotten, though once fashionable and famous, French novelist and playwright:

> [the Princess] left [Hyacinth] for a short time, giving him the last number of the *Revue des Deux Mondes* to entertain himself withal, and calling his attention, in particular, to a story of M. Octave Feuillet (she should be so curious to know what he thought of it); and reappeared . . . presenting herself to our young man, at that moment, as a sudden incarnation of the heroine of M. Feuillet's novel, in which he had instantly become immersed. (*PC* 265)

Perhaps because Feuillet is obscure today, the allusion to him in *The Princess Casamassima* has received very little attention from the commentators on James's novel.[14] Nevertheless, this reference to Feuillet is a very significant clue to understanding the major cruxes of *The Princess Casamassima:* Hyacinth's and the Princess's friendship, the Princess's supposedly capricious personality, and the end of the novel.

This reference is deliberately secretive; the passage does not say what the Feuillet story is, why the Princess "should be so curious to know what [Hyacinth] thought of it," or how the Princess could appear to incarnate Feuillet's heroine. At the same time, the reader acquires some information—there is an interesting Octave Feuillet story, and the heroine of that story bears a marked similarity to the Princess Casamassima—that ought to appear irrelevant to the novel. This combination of secretiveness and the divulgence of apparently irrelevant information engages the reader's curiosity about the allusion, the identity of the story and the nature of its heroine's similarity to the Princess, and the full significance of the allusion. This combination is also typical of one of this novel's most fundamental patterns, one too often repeated to be discounted. This pattern, which we see from the very beginning of the novel, consists of introducing information only in partial form, thereby raising as many questions in the reader's mind as it answers. When the Princess calls Hyacinth's attention to Feuillet's story, she also calls the reader's, and her curiosity ("she would be so curious to know what he thought of it") excites the reader's own. But once the curiosity is created, the text refuses (at least overtly) to satisfy it. The reader learns neither what the story is nor what is so interesting about it. The reader is all the more frustrated when the Princess appears as "a sudden incarnation of the heroine of M. Feuillet's novel," for the text does not divulge how the Princess resembles a Feuillet heroine.

Tintner has suggested that Hyacinth sees Christina as an "incarnation" of the heroine of Feuillet's 1859 novel, *La Petite Comtesse,* but the grounds for this comparison are not very convincing: James's Princess must be an "incarnation" of Feuillet's countess, says Tintner, because James vividly recalled the French author's protagonist in the 1914 autobiographical *Notes of a Son and Brother;* because there are various points of comparison between *La Petite Comtesse* and other works by James, such as *Confidence,* "The Diary of a Man of Fifty," "The Beast in the Jungle," and *The Ambassadors;* because *The Tragic Muse* and *The Wings of the Dove* have plots similar to Feuillet's *Les Amours de Philippe;* and because of "the resemblance between [Feuillet's] frivolous noblewoman and 'la capricciosa,' Christina Light."[15]

It is true that the Princess has left her husband and moved to a foreign land, that she goes through three different *cavalieri serventi* during the two years that she figures in the novel, and that she takes an interest (that would seem curious for someone of her rank) in the life of the lower classes and abruptly leaves her luxurious Mayfair mansion for a dingy lower-middle-class lifestyle. Of all the characters in the novel, Madame Grandoni is certainly the person who has known Christina the longest and the most intimately. This would appear to add special credibility to her description of the Princess as "a *capricciosa*" (*PC* 261), but it does not prove that Madame Grandoni's is the last word on Christina's character or even that it is correct. Madame Grandoni is as well situated as anybody to pass judgment on her companion's character, but that does not mean that we should not read her remarks with skepticism.

Madame Grandoni's motivations in general—and thus her general reliability—are never satisfactorily explained; for example, although she denies being a spy (466), she certainly serves the Prince as his informer. This is not in itself conclusive, but it does permit us—indeed obliges us—to weigh the evidence against her remark on Christina's capriciousness. Furthermore, even if the Princess were "a *capricciosa*," it does not automatically follow that capriciousness is the prime motivator of the Princess's actions in respect to Hyacinth, as critics like Tintner and John Roland Dove believe:[16]

> She is essentially a bored and capricious woman, like Mathilde [de la Mole in Stendhal's *Le Rouge et le noir*]; and, as Hyacinth sadly realizes, her interest in him, like her interest in the problems of the proletariat, was prompted mainly by ennui and the desire for novelty.[17]

Certainly the Princess frequently expresses boredom, which suggests there is something to Captain Sholto's belief that her interest in proletarians is superficial (*PC* 305–6). However, her interest in "the social question" (*PC* 304) is not simply capricious. In truth, nothing in *The Princess Casamassima* supports Madame Grandoni's and Sholto's belief (shared also by the Prince) that Christina's acts are motivated by pure caprice. The only time the text passes what appears to be an authoritative judgment on Madame Grandoni's characterization of the Princess comes when Hyacinth, having returned from Europe, discovers the Princess's Mayfair house in South Street boarded up and recalls "Madame Grandoni's account" of the Princess as a "*capricciosa*" (*PC* 357). But this recollection means neither that Hyacinth decides Madame Grandoni is right nor that her remark is confirmed in an objective sense.

Actually, everything the Princess does in the novel is inspired by the deepest motives; they are not often immediately apparent—the Prince, Madame Grandoni, and Sholto are proof of many people's limited ability to comprehend her psychology—but they are there. The Princess's cultivation of Hyacinth and later of Paul Muniment, her correspondence with the anarchist leader Hoffendahl,[18] and her move from opulent South Street to dreary Paddington appear capricious to those who only see them as isolated incidents and refuse to accept that these actions can result from carefully thought-out plans. Even in *Roderick Hudson*, James's early novel in which Christina also appears, there is no firm evidence that the Princess is capricious. She is certainly flirtatious, but flirting is not always whimsical. Her behavior appears contradictory at times in *Roderick Hudson*, but when it does, it is because she is caught between other people's conflicting desires and projects for her. A caprice is a sudden and impulsive change of mind or action, and never in *The Princess Casamassima* does the Princess do or say anything that does not result from her hatred of the rich, aristocratic, stuffy Casamassimas and their like.

There is evidence from other texts that James made assumptions about what a typical Feuillet character was like. During his trip through Provence described in *A Little Tour in France,* James mentions meeting a man at the Pont du Gard who looked like he "might have stepped out of a novel of Octave Feuillet" (*LTF* 188). The "gentleman" was "followed by his groom and mounted on a strikingly handsome horse," and he had "good looks and [a] charming manner" (*LTF* 188). Only after the comparison with a Feuillet character does James mention the young man's château, and it is several pages before he gives a description of that edifice (*LTF* 191). Since he says nothing further to describe the man, James clearly has a particular type in mind when he evokes Feuillet here. In each of his three reviews of a Feuillet novel, James almost immediately mentions the one point about the French author's fiction that immediately strikes a reader: Feuillet's novels are invariably situated among the highest aristocracy, and his heroes and heroines are always young, elegant, dashing, charming, handsome, and rich. In the earliest of the three reviews, of *Monsieur de Camors,* James writes that Feuillet's "works treat almost wholly of fine ladies, and seem as if they were meant to be read by fine ladies" (*LC2* 281). In the second review, of *Un Mariage dans le monde,* James calls Feuillet

> . . . the fashionable novelist—a gentleman or lady without a *de* to their name is, to the best of our recollection, not to be found in all his tales. He is perhaps a trifle too elegant and superfine; his imagination turns out its toes, as it were, a trifle too much; but grant him his field—the drawing-room carpet—and he is a real master. (*LC1* 42)

Finally, in the opening paragraph of his review of *Les Amours de Philippe,* James complains of Feuillet:

> His defect is a too obvious desire to be what we call in English a "fashionable" novelist. He relates exclusively the joys and sorrows of the aristocracy; the loves of marquises and countesses alone appear worthy of his attention, and heroes and heroines can hope to make no figure in his pages unless they have an extraordinary number of quarterings. (*LC2* 286–87)

These passages demonstrate that James recognized a stereotypical Feuillet character and that that character is a paragon of aristocratic, haut monde elegance.[19] The minimal explanation in the reference to the man at the Pont du Gard demonstrates that by 1883, at least, when *A Little Tour in France* was serialized, James presumed his reader would recognize the stereotypicality of a Feuillet character.[20]

The irony in the Feuillet reviews, especially in the last one—"the loves of marquises and countesses alone appear worthy of his attention, and heroes and heroines can hope to make no figure in his pages unless they have an extraordinary number of quarterings"—indicates that James considers that Feuillet situates his stories in an "unreal" or fantastic world. When Hyacinth's imagination incarnates the Princess as a Feuillet heroine, it is transposing her from his everyday real world into an ideal one. This is not surprising on Hyacinth's part, since the Medley visit, as a whole, is a gratification of the young man's fantasies, "his dream come true, down to the detail of the *Revue*."[21] Considerably before his first meeting with the Princess, in the middle of a passage of reflection on Millicent Henning, Hyacinth lets "his imagination wander among the haunts of the aristocracy, and fanc[ies] himself stretched in the shadow of an ancestral beech, reading the last number of the *Revue des Deux Mondes*" (*PC* 114). At Medley, he does not stretch under "an ancestral beech," but he does read "the last number of the *Revue des Deux Mondes*" (*PC* 265), thus fulfilling his earlier fantasy. The *Revue des Deux Mondes* is significant, because it is a recurring sign of highbrow intellectual chic all through French fiction; in Flaubert's *L'Education sentimentale,* for example, it adorns Mme. Dambreuse's salon.[22] In his earlier fantasy, the *Revue des Deux Mondes* is one of the elements of the good life; when Hyacinth reads it at Medley, it is a synecdoche standing for the apparent realization of that good life.[23]

What Hyacinth sees when the Princess reappears is not so much Feuillet's character as his own idealization—the fairy-tale princess he continuously wants the Princess Casamassima to be. Most of all, he wants her to be *his* fairy-tale princess, who will take him out of his dreary existence, who will recognize that he is not a frog (we recall his French ancestry) but a true prince (we recall his other, his aristocratic, ascendants). When Hyacinth idealizes his Princess, he also idealizes himself. If he makes Christina incarnate an ideal heroine, he must also want to be an idealized "Feuillet hero" himself.

This confirms a central point in John Roland Dove's reading of *The Princess Casamassima.* Hyacinth idealizes Paul, Millicent, and Christina, says Dove, but is rejected by each of them when they opt for erotic love over the ideal love that Hyacinth offers.[24]

> The Jamesian protagonist appeals to the beloved to rescue him from a personal life that has become too complex and problematic, and he expects to escape from his own individuality by dedicating himself to the other and identifying himself with him completely. This presupposes an idealistic and

exalted attitude towards the other who is, indeed, regarded in a redemptive light. In the Jamesian dialectic of the personal, this attitude invariably turns out to be unfounded, the protagonist is betrayed, and his appeal is denied.[25]

Dove is not concerned, as I am, with the ways that James's text leads its reader to see the centrality of idealization in Hyacinth's story, yet the Feuillet allusion is one important example of how *The Princess Casamassima* dramatizes Hyacinth's desire for the kind of ideal of which Dove speaks.

Seeing the Feuillet allusion as a sign of Hyacinth's desire to become a typical Feuillet hero would be enough to explain both the presence and the secretiveness of the allusion, thus satisfying the curiosity it arouses in the reader. However, the allusion to Feuillet in *The Princess Casamassima* is to actual texts by Feuillet. The Princess mentions "the last number of the *Revue des Deux Mondes*," and James's text explicitly states, only a few pages before, that Hyacinth's stay at Medley occurs in late April (*PC* 258). The Medley chapters take place in the spring following the "Sun and Moon" episode in chapter 21, which Leon Edel maintains occurs "during the hard winter of 1880–81."[26] The "Sun and Moon" chapter says that "the season was terribly hard" (*PC* 241), and readers in 1886 would catch the reference to the recent "hard winter." In addition, "the amnesty to the Communards," which went into effect in July 1880,[27] is mentioned in the "Sun and Moon" episode (*PC* 243).

The Princess Casamassima is consistently exact about time. Hyacinth is fifteen—therefore in 1871 at the earliest—when Mr. Vetch meets the Communard refugee Poupin (*PC* 65), and twenty-four when he meets the Princess (197); the visit at Medley, then, would have occurred no earlier than 1881. The *Revue des Deux Mondes* serialized two Feuillet novels between 1880 and the end of 1885, when James was writing book 3 of *The Princess Casamassima*:[28] *La Veuve* (1883) and *Histoire d'une parisienne* (1881). Of these two, *Histoire d'une parisienne* is the only one—indeed the only Feuillet serial between 1871 and 1886—to appear in April issues of the *Revue des Deux Mondes*.[29]

Since Feuillet was a well-known and fashionable writer (in France, at least) and the *Revue des Deux Mondes* could easily appear, in the late nineteenth century, in any elegant drawing room, it is not at all unlikely in March 1886, when chapter 22 of *The Princess Casamassima* appeared in *Atlantic Monthly,* that a reference to a particular Feuillet piece in the *Revue des Deux Mondes* would evoke actual titles in the mind of a cultivated, cosmopolitan reader (one much like James himself). The Princess's mention of Feuillet, then, not only refers to a stereotype character but also is like the allusions we find in the works of Joyce and T. S. Eliot, which make demands on the extent of the reader's specific literary and general cultural knowledge. Examination of Feuillet's novels *Histoire d'une parisienne* and *La Veuve* can only confirm—because of their various similarities—their relevance to *The Princess Casamassima*.

The title *Histoire d'une parisienne* resonates to the reader who, without having read Feuillet's novel, understands the innuendo in the word "*parisienne*." In French literature, a *parisienne* is very different from a *lilloise*, a *bordelaise*, a *marseillaise*, or a *genevoise*;[30] the supposedly unparalleled charms of the female inhabitants of Paris are equaled only by their experience in sentimental matters and their sexual unscrupulousness.

If Christina, Princess Casamassima, appears as "a sudden incarnation" of Feuillet's heroine, does this mean that she is a *parisienne*? While the reader is not permitted to learn unequivocally about the nature of Christina's romantic life or the full extent of her relations with Sholto, Hyacinth, or Paul Muniment (despite the Prince's certainty of grounds for his jealousy), there are two incidents in *The Princess Casamassima* that link her to the typical Parisian courtesan. After the Princess moves to Madeira Crescent and Hyacinth's visits become regular, "it was understood between them that, except by special appointment, he was to come to see her only in the evening" (*PC* 407). The first thing that any clever and skillful Parisian courtesan imposes on her lovers is a set time to visit, which permits her to have several lovers, each with his own "hour." Second, the Princess and Mr. Vetch, in their only meeting (416–29), act out a scene that is very similar to the obligatory father-figure-confronts-mistress scene in every courtesan story (the second act of Verdi's *La Traviata*, for example). One of the first things the Princess says to Mr. Vetch is "Ah, I hope you haven't come to ask me to give him up!" (*PC* 417), which is exactly what the mistress says to the father in such a scene and clearly establishes the roles of the players: the Princess as the courtesan who has tempted the young man, and Mr. Vetch as the father who pleads with her to give up the son. One remembers that the Princess's maiden name is Light and that the French, whom Christina has "never liked" (426), understand the word *légère*, or light, when applied to a woman to refer to easy virtue.

The "incarnation" of the Princess as Feuillet's heroine is therefore an evocation of all the various attributes of the Parisian woman or courtesan. Again, it is Hyacinth who sees her as such, and this is simply another way of dramatizing the tension between the hero he would like to be and the one he actually is. In other words, he would rather be Alfredo Germont or the Chevalier Des Grieux than a "little bookbinder."

The first pages of *Histoire d'une parisienne* are not about a woman of easy or light virtue. Jeanne, the heroine of Feuillet's novel, is a genteel, attractive young lady whose mother arranges her marriage to the first eligible suitor, M. de Maurescamp. Practically strangers at the time of their wedding, the newlyweds soon realize that they have little in common and quickly cease to get along at all. Mme. de Maurescamp then finds a soul mate in Jacques de Lerne, the son of an older friend. While Mme. de Maurescamp and M. de Lerne realize and even express their love for each other, their relationship remains entirely spiritual. Despite this, and despite his indifference to his wife, M. de Maurescamp becomes jealous, provokes a duel with his wife's friend, and kills him.

Mme. de Maurescamp learns of the duel the night before it takes place, and pleading the innocence of her relationship with de Lerne, she urges her husband to call off the fight. When he refuses, she tells him that if the duel takes place, she will subsequently take every opportunity to give him real reasons to complain about her virtue and his honor. After M. de Lerne's death, Mme. de Maurescamp leaves her husband and goes to live with her mother; after some time she appears to agree to a reconciliation with her husband and ends the separation. After she returns to her husband, Mme. de Maurescamp shows a peculiar interest in his fencing. She regularly visits the gym where he practices, and she learns to judge fencers. Mme. de Maurescamp soon becomes very intimate with Captain de Sontis, an unattractive little man who far exceeds her husband in his ability with the sword. Although this intimacy arouses her husband's jealousy, it takes Maurescamp far longer to provoke a duel with this apparent lover than with de Lerne. Mme. de Maurescamp exults in her husband's cowardice, and just before the inevitable duel finally takes place, she urges de Sontis not to spare her husband. De Sontis obliges and gravely, but not mortally, wounds his opponent. The novel ends with the remark that if Mme. de Maurescamp is no longer the angel she was before her marriage but, rather, "[f]roide, railleuse, mondaine furieuse, coquette à outrance, indifférente à tout" [cold, mocking, furiously hedonistic, outrageously coquettish, indifferent to everything], it is because men, not God, make monsters.[31]

Misguided mothers, who are not careful to whom they marry off their daughters, and obtuse husbands are to blame when innocent young women become true *parisiennes:* ruthless, calculating, vindictive, and flirtatious. Ultimately, Feuillet's novel is a loss-of-innocence story.

Because Hyacinth's changing perceptions and judgment of the world around him are the subject of *The Princess Casamassima* and because of the novel's narrative technique,[32] much that would be obvious in a novel with omniscient narrative is left apparently to conjecture. The paramount enigma is the title character and her motivations. Although it may not always be simple to understand the behavior of characters like Paul, Millicent, and Sholto toward the protagonist, every character is ultimately far more easily fathomable than the Princess. No character's behavior is as complex, and no other character's behavior poses such problems for interpretation as the Princess's. "The Princess is a complex and highly intricate character, delineated with all the keenness and intellectual refinement that typifies James at his best";[33] she is "mysterious" and "unfathomable."[34] None of the many explanations, or psychologies, of her behavior offered in the novel—Madame Grandoni's, the Prince's, Sholto's, Millicent's, Paul's—satisfactorily defines her. In fact, the wide variety of interpretations of the Princess makes it all the harder for the reader to understand her satisfactorily. Hyacinth himself appears to offer no explanation, nor does he seem to understand her any better than the others. Since she lends her name to the title of the book, although she is not the protagonist and is not even mentioned until the twelfth chapter (*PC* 141), understanding her becomes the reader's primary interpretive task.[35]

Besides the general question of her personality, the reader has questions about specific mysteries in the Princess's life. Why does the Casamassima marriage prove such a failure, and why does Christina come to support a social upheaval so actively? Although her husband is constantly jealous (a characteristic that he shares with Feuillet's M. de Maurescamp) and obviously believes Christina has had many lovers, the reader never learns exactly why "she had been turned out of the house by her husband" (*PC* 186). The reasons given for her happiness with her separation from her husband—her general dislike and resentment of Casamassima's relatives (194, 207) and bitterness at her own family for having made a mercenary marriage for her (205) and at herself for having complied (216)—are not precise and are presented either by a third person or in the voice of the narrator's indirect discourse. The allusion to *Histoire d'une parisienne* in chapter 22 makes it possible to answer the questions to which James's text otherwise only provides the vaguest responses and helps to explain the Princess's considerable interest in Hyacinth.

Only a reader of *Roderick Hudson* can know the particulars of Christina's marriage and that, like Feuillet's Mme. de Maurescamp, James's Princess had been married off by her mother. In *The Princess Casamassima*, the information about Christina's marriage is limited to the fact that "[s]he had been married by her people, in a mercenary way, for the sake of a fortune and a title" (*PC* 205) and to Madame Grandoni's belief that "the Princess considers that in the darkest hour of her life she sold herself for a title and a fortune" (216).[36] Hyacinth perceives the Princess's anarchist fervor to be motivated by her hatred of the Casamassimas: "Hyacinth gathered that the force of reaction and revenge might carry her far, make her modern and democratic and heretical *à outrance*" (207). The Princess makes several jargony speeches in favor of anarchist revolution (391, 411) and often criticizes the tediousness of upper-class society. Her "exquisite gratification" in bringing Hyacinth to visit her genteel neighbors at Broome (295) is an indication of the pleasure she receives from successfully organizing and executing a minor revolution against the stuffy aristocracy. None of this, however, elucidates precisely what motivates the Princess's hatred or even confirms Hyacinth's perception of her desiring revenge against her husband, his relatives, and the entire upper classes.

There are critics who believe that Hyacinth's perception is right. According to John Kimmey, "the Princess is ashamed of having been forced into a mercenary marriage. She wants revenge on her class";[37] and Frederick J. Hoffman—in a rare instance of a critic not trying to argue the Princess's fundamental capriciousness—writes "that most of the Princess's motives for her acts come from her hatred and scorn of the Prince and his world, and especially from her resentment over having been 'caught' in a form of *mariage de convenance*."[38] Marcia Jacobson suggests that Christina's "interest in revolution dates from a quarrel with her husband and is colored by resentment of him for trying to control her and of the titled and moneyed class he represents";[39] and John Carlos Rowe has stated: "the Princess understands the roles of wife, woman, princess as her particular bondage, and it is this understanding that turns her submission into a *desire* for rebellion and the *fact* of self-hatred."[40]

My point is that the Feuillet allusion provides the reader with the means to confirm not just these critics' minority view that Christina is not so capricious as she is generally held to be but also Hyacinth's hypothesis that the Casamassima in-laws have driven the Princess to vengeance and socialism and, ultimately, her behavior in general. Christina's interest in the Feuillet novel—"she should be so curious to know what [Hyacinth] thought of it"—and her "incarnation" as its heroine (*PC* 265) suggest that we can comprehend the mysteries of the Princess's motives through her similarity to Mme. de Maurescamp.

The Princess and Mme. de Maurescamp have in common the failure of their marriages and deep hatred of their husbands. Mme. de Maurescamp seeks revenge for her husband's cowardly slaying of her friend, de Lerne (Maurescamp knew, on the eve of the duel, that de Lerne's weakened right arm made it virtually impossible for him to use a sword properly), and Christina at least appears to have both reasons and a desire for revenge. Why else would Christina be made to allude to Feuillet's novel about revenge and Hyacinth be made to compare her to its heroine if not to emphasize the similarity between the two women? And what similarity is more obvious than a common motive of revenge against their jealous husbands?

The similarity between the two heroines is complete: both blame their husbands, or the world the husband represents, as the cause of their own unhappiness (though the Princess's is more general and less obvious than Mme. de Maurescamp's); both seek revenge; and both make use of other men as the instrument of their revenge.

The Princess Casamassima includes several details that appear to confirm this comparison between Feuillet's and James's heroines. We recall the exact words of Hyacinth's hypothesis about the Princess's revenge: "the force of reaction and revenge might carry her far, make her modern and democratic and heretical *à outrance*" (*PC* 207), and we notice that this is a virtual quotation of the end of *Histoire d'une parisienne;* the narrator of *The Princess Casamassima* uses a series of adjectives and the phrase "*à outrance*," just as Feuillet's narrator does to describe his by now completely disillusioned, vengeful, Parisian heroine: "Froide, railleuse, mondaine furieuse, coquette *à outrance*."[41]

Another detail that serves to confirm the similarities of the heroines' plans of revenge involves Tennyson. Hyacinth, after visiting the Princess in Mayfair, "in the immediate heat of his emotion" (*PC* 211) resolves to bind and offer her a volume of the works of the poet (210). The presentation of this book is not portrayed in the novel, but it is associated with Hyacinth's binding of some of the books the Princess stores away instead of selling after her move to Madeira Crescent. During the visit to Medley, Hyacinth and Christina agree on his binding books for her, at which point he mentions that he has brought the Tennyson to give to her (280). This is the last time the volume of Tennyson is mentioned, but it and the binding he agrees at Medley to do for her are metonymically linked. Later, when Hyacinth brings the Princess the work agreed upon at Medley, she hardly shows the slightest appreciation (432–33); in effect, her indifference to the quality of the work Hyacinth has done for her is a rejection of the romantic spirit in which he decided to offer her the Tennyson.

In *Histoire d'une parisienne,* Mme. de Maurescamp, in her early married days, reads Tennyson, and even tries to interest her husband in his verse.[42] At the end of Feuillet's novel, the narrator, to prove that "Jeanne n'est plus romanesque" [Jeanne is no longer romantic], cites the fact that "Elle ne lit plus Tennyson" [She no longer reads Tennyson].[43] James's Princess, after her move to Paddington, becomes as unromantic in her reading tastes as Feuillet's deromanticized avenger; she pays "no attention" when Hyacinth reads to her from Browning's *Men and Women* (*PC* 444), and on her own, she reads "a heavy work on Labour and Capital" (406).[44]

That Christina's desire for revenge against her husband explains her socialism is further indicated by the effect her political activity has on the

Prince. When he learns from Madame Grandoni of the Princess's "plotting
. . . to break up society" (*PC* 468–69), the Prince becomes more upset
than at any other time in the novel (469–71), and rightly so, for being
cuckolded (at least believing he has been) hurts him only in his role as
husband, while Christina's conspiring to overthrow the aristocracy threatens his values, his situation in society, and therefore, his entire identity
(472).

Finally, while the Princess is comparable to Feuillet's Jeanne, and the
Prince and Monsieur de Maurescamp are similar by virtue of their jealousy,
Hyacinth and Captain de Sontis serve as instruments of revenge for the
heroines of the two novels. Jeanne uses the Captain (whose physical stature,
like Hyacinth's, is emphasized as short—indeed he is the only short character in *Histoire d'une parisienne*) to show up her husband's cowardice and
to inflict a near-fatal wound upon him; and the Princess uses Hyacinth as
the source of perverse and private pleasure when he accompanies her to a
neighboring estate to visit the Marchants (*PC* 295), a stuffy aristocratic
family who "produced a very peculiar, and at moments almost maddening,
effect upon her nerves" (275).

The Princess's passion for revenge shows that her interest in working-
class people and her cultivation of Hyacinth as an introduction to the lower
classes are not merely capricious but, rather, premeditated. Her revenge
goes a long way toward explaining why she has such a particular interest in
Hyacinth (although there is also another reason). The parallel between
Mme. de Maurescamp and de Sontis and the Princess and Hyacinth makes
it impossible to avoid the fact that Hyacinth is an instrument of revenge,
even though de Sontis's utility in Feuillet's novel is far more consequential.
This is problematic, because the role of instrument, since it negates Hyacinth's humanity, is particularly unflattering. If Hyacinth is an instrument,
perhaps he is nothing more than one to the Princess. This tension between
instrument and human individual is supported by the meaning of Hyacinth's name: Hyacinth as a flower or precious stone (which is what he is
to Pinnie and Mr. Vetch), suggesting the value of the individual, and Hyacinth the martyred Roman saint, suggesting sacrifice (as Sholto remarks,
"Certainly, he will have to be sacrificed" [*PC* 309]) and suppression of
individual value to a greater cause or force.[45]

For Lyall Powers, in his "naturalist" or Darwinian interpretation of *The
Princess Casamassima*, Hyacinth is a sacrifice not so much to a political
cause as to the conflicting forces of biological nature and social environment: "Nowhere else in James's work does the determining effect of the
heredity and the environment of the hero play so large a role."[46] These
tensions between the conflicting heredities of his proletarian French mater-
nal grandfather and his noble English father, between the environment he

was brought up in and the one the Princess introduces him to, his pledge to Hoffendahl and his new appreciation of civilization's greatest cultural achievements, are perfectly compatible with the tension between Hyacinth as instrument and as individual.

Such tensions, according to Powers, lead naturally to Hyacinth's suicide:

> Hyacinth . . . cannot bring himself . . . to contribute to the downfall of a class and a way of life he believes are responsible for much of the beauty that civilization has produced. He sees that he can never fulfill his oath and, on the other hand, that he cannot betray that oath: in either case he would have to be false to himself. The whole complication, then, is so arranged as to fix Hyacinth in immobility . . . he has no choice left. Or rather he is faced . . . with a single undeniable option . . . suicide.[47]

Oscar Cargill differs from this view by saying that Hyacinth's death proves the supremacy of freedom of the will over predestination; however, he explains the suicide in much the same way as Powers:

> Yet on his death-dealing mission a double specter must have arisen in his consciousness: that of his murdered father and his father's murderess. To escape the dreadful destiny of following precisely in his poor mother's footsteps, thereby demonstrating the utter rule of tainted blood, Hyacinth elects the only other choice left open to him, self-destruction.[48]

These long quotes demonstrate that, regardless of how the commentators tie it into their way of reading *The Princess Casamassima,* a reason must be given for Hyacinth's death. Suicide invariably raises the question Why? and Hyacinth's is no exception. What is more, since the novel ends with the unexplained suicide, interpreting the end and interpreting the death come to the same thing. To the question "Why did Hyacinth kill himself? [t]here is no simple answer," and this is no doubt why "[t]he ending of *The Princess Casamassima* has been interpreted in a variety of ways."[49]

The Feuillet allusion in chapter 22 of *The Princess Casamassima,* in addition to its role in determining the reader's understanding of the Princess, helps to clarify the questions that the end raises: Why does Hyacinth take his life, and why does the Princess seek him out at the moment of his death? So far I have assumed that the Feuillet story in "the last number of the *Revue des Deux Mondes*" that piques the Princess's interest is *Histoire d'une parisienne.* There are two reasons for thinking this assumption correct: first, the similarities I have described between James's and Feuillet's heroines, which are so very relevant to James's text, and second, the historical fact that "the last number of the *Revue des Deux Mondes*" that Christina gives Hyacinth is apparently an issue from April 1881, which is when *Histoire d'une parisienne* was serialized. This fact makes it seem certain, then, that the allusion is to *Histoire d'une parisienne*. We must ask ourselves, however, how a reader in 1886 could be expected to catch the allusion. It would not be too difficult for an alert reader to be aware of the time of year of Hyacinth's visit to Medley—the month of April is mentioned six pages before Feuillet's story—and the memory of the winter of 1880–1881 would still be in English readers' minds. I have already indicated that the *Revue des Deux Mondes* was a status symbol, and Octave Feuillet would be familiar, in name at least, to many readers. Nonetheless, it is difficult to believe that a reader in 1886 could reasonably be expected to recall exactly which Octave Feuillet story was serialized in April 1881. On the other hand, it is not unreasonable to assume that a reader would recall the only two Feuillet novels that were serialized during the first half of the decade: *Histoire d'une parisienne* and *La Veuve*.[50] Since *La Veuve* also has much in common with *The Princess Casamassima*, it, too, could be understood as part of the object of the allusion to Feuillet. And while comparing *Histoire d'une parisienne* with *The Princess Casamassima* helps the reader to interpret the Princess's personality better, considering *La Veuve* in this comparison helps the reader to understand the next greatest interpretive mystery of James's text, Hyacinth's suicide.

Many critics, such as Powers,[51] Daniel Lerner,[52] W. H. Tilley,[53] Eunice Hamilton,[54] and Jeanne Delbaere-Garant,[55] have described the similarities between the protagonists of Turgenev's *Virgin Soil* and of *The Princess Casamassima*. Both Hyacinth and Turgenev's Nezhdanov are the unrecognized, illegitimate sons of noblemen, each gets involved with radical anarchists and then changes his mind about destroying the world of the aristocracy. Both men have important friendships with "steadying older brother" figures,[56] to whom they ultimately concede the objects of their romantic yearnings. And each man commits suicide by shooting himself in the heart. While these similar endings have been documented, the commentators have never noted that the hero of Feuillet's *La Veuve* dies in exactly the same manner. There is no denying that the plots of *The Princess Casamassima* and *Virgin Soil* are remarkably alike, and it is impossible to prove that Turgenev's novel is not a "source" or inspiration for James's.[57] Any basis upon which *Virgin Soil* is argued to be pertinent to reading *The Princess Casamassima* is, however, at least equally applicable to the relevance of *La Veuve* (the author of which—unlike Turgenev—is mentioned in James's text).

Feuillet's *La Veuve* is about two close friends, one of whom, Maurice de

Frémeuse, is short and the other of whom, Robert de la Pave, is tall.[58] Since Feuillet's characters—unless they are especially odious—are invariably idealized, both in their physical appearances and in their personalities, male protagonists are always tall, handsome, and charming. That Maurice de Frémeuse, the hero of *La Veuve*, is short, then, cannot escape notice (especially as the heights of the two friends are mentioned in the novel's first paragraph); and because of the singular emphasis on height in *The Princess Casamassima*,[59] the parallel between Hyacinth's and Paul Muniment's friendship and Maurice's and Robert's in *La Veuve* is striking.

Robert de la Pave is mortally wounded during the Franco-Prussian War,[60] but before dying, he makes his friend Maurice promise that he will tell the young Mme. de la Pave (whom Maurice has never met) that it is his last wish that she never remarry.[61] Although Maurice does not approve of this request, he cannot refuse his dying friend's last wish. Chagrined though he be by the message he must deliver, Maurice feels it a point of honor that he carry out his promise to his dead companion.[62] What Maurice does not bargain for, although the reader expects it from the moment the promise is made, is that he and the young widow, Marianne de la Pave, fall in love.[63] While Maurice has reservations because of Robert's dying wish, Marianne has no scruples at all. Had her late husband not been so imposing, she might have been naturally inclined to remain faithful to his memory, but she feels he had no right to expect and order her to do so.[64] Nonetheless, after the marriage ceremony, Maurice disappears from the wedding reception and is found a little later with a revolver in his hand and a bullet through his heart.[65]

Not only is Maurice's suicide similar in detail to Hyacinth's—both men shoot themselves in the heart—but it is also narrated from the point of view of the woman most directly involved. In this respect, the suicides in *The Princess Casamassima* and *La Veuve* are very different from the one in *Virgin Soil*, which is told entirely from Nezhdanov's point of view. In *La Veuve*, a newspaper account of Maurice's death, telling of Marianne's anxiety at the absence of the bridegroom, a shot she thinks she hears outdoors, and finally the discovery of Maurice's body by a farmer, is reproduced, thus distancing the death from the reader all the more.[66] In *The Princess Casamassima*, the Princess tries to visit Hyacinth at his lodging; discovers Schinkel, the anarchist cabinetmaker, waiting on his doorstep; begins to feel uneasy; and finally persuades Schinkel to break down the door. (In *Virgin Soil*, on the other hand, while Nezhdanov shoots himself, *his* Marianne is blissfully ignorant of any reason for apprehension.) The reasons that Hyacinth and Maurice shoot themselves are also comparable: both men are torn between their sense of honor and their inclination. Maurice and

Hyacinth have made promises that they cannot keep but, at the same time, are unable to break. Most important, the two suicides are not unequivocally explained. The newspaper report at the end of *La Veuve* finds little reason for Maurice to take his life, except that perhaps an old war wound "a déterminé subitement chez lui un désordre cérébral" [had suddenly set off a cerebral disorder].[67]

Powers's explication of Hyacinth's suicide, quoted above, is equally applicable to *La Veuve,* for Maurice, on the one hand, must betray his oath to Robert, "and, on the other hand, . . . cannot betray that oath."[68] Just as with Hyacinth, the situation fixes Maurice "in immobility." In both cases, the heroine's apparent change of affection from one of the two friends to the other has something to do with the suicide. It is true that Maurice is gaining Marianne's affection while Hyacinth thinks he has lost Christina's, but this should not obscure the fact that the Princess Casamassima in the final chapter of James's text plays exactly the same role as Marianne in Feuillet's: her inexplicable anxiety about Hyacinth and her insisting on breaking down the door to his room correspond exactly to Marianne's anxiety over Maurice. While Hyacinth completes his role as Feuillet's hero, the Princess acts out hers as Feuillet's heroine: roles that the text predetermined for them in the Feuillet "incarnation" of chapter 22.

The end of *La Veuve* is strikingly Jamesian; as in *The Ambassadors, The Portrait of a Lady,* and *The Wings of the Dove,* to cite a few instances, a conflict between scruple and self-interest is resolved by the sacrifice of the latter. In *La Veuve* and *The Princess Casamassima,* the ultimate sacrifice is made. No fault can be found with saying, like Powers, that the sacrifice in *The Princess Casamassima* is the result of the protagonist's being trapped between contradictory urges; what this sort of interpretation leaves out, though, is the connection of Hyacinth's death to the theme of idealization signaled by the Feuillet allusion in chapter 22.

If Hyacinth has the Princess incarnate a Feuillet heroine as a function of his yearning for an idealized existence, then the text has Hyacinth incarnate a Feuillet hero. Indeed, he plays the role of more than one Feuillet character; inasmuch as he embodies de Sontis of *Histoire d'une parisienne,* Hyacinth is an instrument of revenge. But de Sontis is a flat character and Hyacinth is not. He is the central consciousness of James's text, which means he has feelings, scruples, a sense of honor, and a heart. There is only one resolution possible to the conflict in Hyacinth as instrument of revenge on the one hand and as the text's central consciousness on the other, and that resolution—that the heart must be eliminated—is dictated by the Feuillet hero that Hyacinth also embodies: Maurice de Frémeuse.

If Hyacinth's "incarnation" of the Princess is a variation on his own fantasy of living the idealized life of a Feuillet hero, the end of *The Princess Casamassima* shows that he has gotten what he wished for; he has not lived the idealized life in the material sense, but he has played the part of two Feuillet characters. This is one of the great ironies of *The Princess Casamassima*: Hyacinth wants to be a Feuillet hero, and he gets to be a Feuillet hero, but not necessarily the one he would like to be. Living an idealized role—the cliché Feuillet aristocrat—is impossible, since such a role is an illusion. Furthermore, even if it were possible, it would not be so wonderful, for even those who have ancestral beeches to stretch under are constrained at times by the demands of the society they live in and the obligations they commit themselves to—in short, by all the sorts of things that drive people like Hyacinth and Maurice to see suicide as the best solution to their predicaments.

The end of *The Princess Casamassima* and the significance of the Feuillet allusion are not completely understood until their relation to yet another text is considered. This text is one of James's own novels, one that demands consideration from the very beginning of *The Princess Casamassima* and the only novel James wrote from which he borrowed characters for later works: *Roderick Hudson*. Had James written novels that, like Balzac's or Trollope's, were full of recurring characters, the reappearance of the Princess Casamassima would be of less consequence. However, the Princess's recurrence is not insignificant, and James's subsequent explanation that she simply "couldn't resign herself not to strike again" (*LC2* 1098–99) is a feeble excuse and perhaps a smoke screen that seems to hide, but really points to, the relevance of *Roderick Hudson* to *The Princess Casamassima*.

A suicide occurs near the end of both novels, and like Hyacinth's in *The Princess Casamassima* (and Maurice's in *La Veuve*), Roderick Hudson's death occurs offstage; the reader and the central consciousness (in this case, Rowland Mallet) learn of it only after the fact (*RH* 509–10). Again, the causes of the suicide are not completely clear; there is no suicide note. Nevertheless, the Princess Casamassima is at least as much, though quite probably far more, the cause of Roderick's death as of Hyacinth's. Roderick's fall from an Alpine hillside, in the last chapter of the novel that bears his name, concludes several months of torpor that began after Christina's marriage to Casamassima. Not only has Roderick clearly been heartbroken ever since Christina's rejection of him, but a chance encounter (*RH* 489–90) between the erstwhile lovers the day before appears to be the immediate impetus for Roderick's final, fatal step.

Roderick's death is different from Hyacinth's in one important respect; the reader has no sense whatsoever of the effect of it on Christina. In the last chapter of *The Princess Casamassima*, Christina's anxiety and concern for Hyacinth are perfectly apparent, whereas in *Roderick Hudson* her feelings are not recorded. Cargill says that the end of *The Princess Casamassima* shows that Christina is not entirely hard and cold-blooded:

> Though she had said to Muniment that she would replace their young friend herself as a more effective instrument in a terrorist mission, this is not her reason for going [to Hyacinth's home]. Something that Rowland Mallet had awakened in her long before has stirred again. Is it not credible that she has drawn a parallel between the finer sensibility of Hyacinth and the talent of Roderick Hudson, to both of which she may seem to herself to have been destructive, or if not, is she not to draw it after covering the body of the poor suicide with her own? The act is as symbolical as it is emotional, and James counterpoints it by having Schinkel, picking up the revolver, wish that it might have been used on its designated object. In his brief relation with her, Hyacinth has had all his sensibilities awakened by the Princess, but does he not reciprocate by reminding her of her duty to the forms, if nothing else? . . . She has now been, in James's meaningful phrase, "completely recorded."[69]

James's remark in his preface that "the Princess of the climax of *Roderick Hudson* still . . . made her desire felt, . . . to testify that she had not been—for what she was—completely recorded" (*LC 2* 1098) is to the point in this respect. *Roderick Hudson* does the Princess a disservice; since her feelings are not recorded, she comes off as insensitive to the loss of life that she is to some extent to blame for. Her revival in *The Princess Casamassima* gives her a second chance to bring about a more flattering conclusion to her story—a chance, perhaps, to try to prevent the self-destruction this time, at least to react with concern to it, to show she does have a heart; that is why she "couldn't resign herself not to strike again."

Christina's heart is dramatized in her next-to-last appearance in *Roderick Hudson*. Mrs. Light hopes that Rowland Mallet can persuade her daughter to accept Prince Casamassima, but Christina tells Rowland that she will not:

> "I have chosen, and I shall hold to it. I have something here, here, *here!*" and she patted her heart. "It's my own. I shan't part with it. Is it what you call an ideal? I don't know; I don't care! It is brighter than the Casamassima diamonds!" (*RH* 432)

This thrice-emphasized heart and the ideal it contains are the "something that Rowland Mallet had awakened in her" that Cargill speaks of. When Rowland and Christina next meet, she has become the Princess Casamassima, having given in, despite her assurance, to Mrs. Light's mysterious "sword of Damocles" (436), and thus having apparently put away forever the "something that Rowland Mallet had awakened." In this final meeting, Christina communicates two things to Rowland: the first, repeated three times, like the triple emphasis on her heart, that "I *was* sincere!" at the earlier encounter (488–89), and the second, a Rastignac-like challenge, "a mysterious menace," against "that 'world' " that had forced her to marry Casamassima (488).[70] This sincerity and idealism are what Mallet awakened, and their locus was Christina's heart, but it requires the destruction of Hyacinth's heart to make them stir again.

Mrs. Light's "sword of Damocles" is guessed by Rowland to be the fact that Christina is actually the illegitimate offspring of her mother's affair with her companion, Giacosa (*RH* 440–41). This "hypothesis" is confirmed in *The Princess Casamassima* and explains Christina's interest in Hyacinth. Hyacinth's first extended discussion with the Princess occurs during his visit to her house in Mayfair, and during this visit, "she related her parentage—American on the mother's side, Italian on the father's" (*PC* 205). The family name, Light, is clearly not Italian, and Christina's maiden name, then, cannot come from her biological father. However, the Princess's maiden name is never mentioned in *The Princess Casamassima,* so the nationalities of her parents remain an unimportant detail unless the reader has also read *Roderick Hudson*. In that case, the Princess's mention of her parentage to Hyacinth not only confirms Rowland Mallet's hypothesis but also shows that Christina was told the truth about her birth.

Thus, one of the mysteries of *Roderick Hudson* (what Mrs. Light's "sword of Damocles" is) is solved for the reader in *The Princess Casamassima,* and the solution explains one of the mysteries of the later novel. Because the Princess is an illegitimate child and also, not initially, a member of the aristocratic class, she, like Hyacinth, is always an outsider and never really belongs to any social group; as a result, her interest in Hyacinth and their close relationship are only natural. What is more, their friendship becomes really intimate only after "he told her the things [about his own origins] that had never yet passed his lips" (*PC* 296).

Surprisingly little of the commentary on *The Princess Casamassima*—a novel where illegitimate birth is so central—mentions the facts of the title character's birth. Louise Bogan,[71] M. E. Grenander,[72] Halliburton,[73] Charles Anderson,[74] and Millicent Bell[75] all mention the similarity of Christina's and Hyacinth's origins, and both Bogan[76] and Anderson call the Princess's illegitimacy "one of the mainsprings of her behavior."[77] Otherwise, most of the commentators ignore this very important point. It is no surprise, then, that so many critics of *The Princess Casamassima* also accept Sholto's and Madame Grandoni's characterization of the Princess as a "*capricciosa,*" especially in respect to her relationship with Hyacinth. A reader who does not notice the common circumstances of their parentage might fail to see a compelling reason for an intimate relationship between Christina and Hyacinth and would all the more easily accept Sholto's belief that Hyacinth is only a part of the Princess's collection of democrats (*PC* 306). But if one understands that the Princess has this reason to remain closely tied to Hyacinth and that in fact she shows genuine concern and interest for him right up to the end of the novel, it is difficult to believe she is as capricious as critics have made her out to be.[78]

The question of Christina in the two novels brings us full turn, back to Feuillet's *Histoire d'une parisienne*. During the course of her loss-of-innocence story, Jeanne de Maurescamp develops from a naïve young girl to an unscrupulous, cold, deceiving woman. It is the world that makes her change this way; she becomes a *parisienne* despite herself. Although the young Christina Light is not the obvious Polly Purebred that Feuillet's heroine is at first, the Princess Casamassima's story is really the same. When older and unhappily married, she has reason to say that "there is nothing in life in which I have not been awfully disappointed" (*PC* 205). As with Feuillet's heroine, it is the world that has made the Princess behave in the complicated way she does.

The Princess's attempt to show her sincere concern at the end of her story goes against the grain of her worldly cynicism, but it is futile, for the tragedy of *The Princess Casamassima* is as much hers as Hyacinth's. Christina's showing Hyacinth the Feuillet story is her effort to communicate something of her essence to the young man; it is her veiled attempt to reach out to him in an intimate way; and it is the preface and parallel to his own communication to her of his illegitimate origins two chapters later. Hyacinth, of course, reads the communication entirely wrong; rather than learning of the Princess's loss of innocence from the Feuillet text, and perhaps catching an inkling of her illegitimacy, he reads his hostess into an idealization. Hyacinth may not read correctly, but the Princess is also unable to communicate successfully, and this inability to express herself clearly and establish an intimate two-way rapport is another part of her tragedy.

Unlike Hyacinth as Feuillet's reader, the reader of *The Princess Casamassima* can unravel the secrets in the *mise en abîme* marked by the allusion to Feuillet's story in chapter 22. Christina's story in *Roderick Hudson* is very similar to Jeanne de Maurescamp's in *Histoire d'une parisienne*. She certainly suffers a loss of innocence about her origins and parentage, and she tells Rowland Mallet, in their last meeting, that she has cast away all scruple. Because of the allusion to Feuillet's story in chapter 22 of *The Princess Casamassima*, because of the Princess's "incarnation" as the heroine of Feuillet's story, the reader discovers the intertextual thread that runs through *Histoire d'une parisienne*, *La Veuve*, and *Roderick Hudson*. The title, *The Princess Casamassima*, which suggests Christina's centrality, and the apparently secondary role the title character plays to Hyacinth in the novel's plot constitute a textual ungrammaticality, which is a sign that there is a significant reason why the text is not titled *Hyacinth Robinson*. This should be more than enough to attract the reader's attention to *Roderick Hudson* and to the discovery—which is made possible only by the conjunction of the two texts—of the secret of Christina's conception. If it is not, the reader is still led to the earlier James novel through the Feuillet texts, the one with its suicide and the other with its heroine's classic loss-of-innocence story.[79]

These three novels together form an intertext that (a) dramatizes the Princess's desire for revenge against her husband and all he cares for; (b) transforms Hyacinth's death into the suicide of *La Veuve*, which means that, ironically, the "little bookbinder" at last accedes to the ideal aristocratic life he desires as a Feuillet hero, complete with a strong code of honor; and (c) represents the Princess's personality in a manner that does not confirm the unreliable judgments of the various other characters but expresses her concern for Hyacinth and her tragedy. Finally, Hyacinth as de Sontis is no more than an instrument of revenge, while as Maurice de Frémeuse he is an object of heartfelt concern. This contradiction or ambiguity expresses the duality of the human condition that is expressed in *The Princess Casamassima*: according to one way of looking at things, a human being is of little consequence, but a human being feels his or her own importance, and that self-importance is confirmed by the attention of others. This is exactly Hyacinth's situation in respect to "the most remarkable woman in Europe" (*PC* 139).

Expectations of Rastignac in
The Princess Casamassima

A narrative called *What Maisie Knew* might be expected to tell you what it was that Maisie knew, but it does not, for the clues lead to no unambiguous *dévoilement. . . .* The exploitation of such opacities is familiar in such works as *The Turn of the Screw,* "The Figure in the Carpet," "The Beast in the Jungle," and, in the most exemplary instance, *The Sacred Fount.*

—Frank Kermode

Kermode could easily apply to *The Princess Casamassima* his remarks on the refusal of *What Maisie Knew* to disclose overtly what its title suggests is its subject matter.[1] A reader would expect a novel entitled *The Princess Casamassima* to be about that Princess; however, James's novel frustrates this expectation, for during the first eleven and a half chapters (approximately a quarter of the novel), there is not the slightest mention of the title character's existence. This is but one of many examples of the disruptive strategies James's text employs to toy with and mystify its readers' expectations. *The Princess Casamassima* constantly introduces the reader—sometimes along with the protagonist—into the middle of a scene, leaving both to try to grasp how the situation had developed, and further confounds the reader by making big chronological leaps in the narrative, by withholding important information only to divulge it much later, and by reversals in characters' intentions.[2]

All of these techniques are paradigmatic of the novel's most significant plot expectation: that Hyacinth's story will turn into a rags-to-riches story exemplified in nineteenth-century fiction by Rastignac's in *Le Père Goriot* and characterized by Lionel Trilling as the "Young Man from the Provinces." *The Princess Casamassima* constantly creates and then confounds the reader's expectations on both a large and a small scale. The most thematically significant expectation the text encourages is that Hyacinth deserves a better life and that he will gain entry to the social and intellectual classes to which he should belong through his encounter with the Princess. As such, the novel deliberately places itself in the context of a tradition of progress or rags-to-riches stories; as Millicent Bell has written, when reading *The Princess Casamassima*, "one is led to expect the fulfillment of the story of the foundling or orphan whose relation to high-placed parents will be revealed at last."[3] And yet it ultimately frustrates the expectations aroused by its apparent adherence to the conventions of the tradition and provides instead a critique of this tradition. As such, *The Princess Casamassima* not only incorporates what had become by 1885 a cliché of French culture (and thanks to the efforts of Horatio Alger was fast becoming a cliché of American culture), but it also aligns itself with what inevitably follows in the wake of a cultural cliché: the cultural undermining of the cliché.

The very beginning of the novel is a model for the rest of the text's repeated frustration and confusion of the reader's expectations. The opening lines drop the reader into the middle of the conversation between Miss Pynsent and the prison guard, Mrs. Bowerbank. The scene is reflected through the point of view of the seamstress, and her struggle to come to grips with the imposing visitor closely parallels the reader's own struggle to understand the situation fully. The very first line of the novel, " 'Oh yes, I daresay I can find the child, if you would like to see him,' Miss Pynsent said" (*PC* 3), poses uncertainties for the reader. Miss Pynsent's speech is clearly a reply to something said by someone else, but exactly what she replies to is never explicitly stated, and the other interlocutor is referred to in this first sentence only as "her visitor, whom she regarded as a high and rather terrible personage" (3). Who "the child" is and why the mysterious visitor might—or might not—want to see him are left unclear.

Some of the questions that the first sentence raises are quickly answered; for example, the reader learns in the third sentence that the child's name is Hyacinth and, in the fourth sentence, that the visitor's name is Mrs. Bowerbank (*PC* 3). But as some questions are answered, others arise. The fifth sentence, while repeating the visitor's name, makes the reader wonder about Miss Pynsent's relationship to the child: "Mrs. Bowerbank had intimated so definitely that she thought it remarkable on Miss Pynsent's part to have taken care of him gratuitously for so many years" (3). By raising the question of why it should be so remarkable for Miss Pynsent to take care of the child for nothing, the narration adds to the mystery that has already arisen about the reason for Mrs. Bowerbank's visit and her wanting to see Hyacinth.

This first paragraph is a typical example of the way *The Princess Casamassima* repeatedly thrusts its reader into the middle of a scene. The novel often uses this technique to introduce a new character or situation. One such instance is the introduction of Paul Muniment, which is accomplished, as many of James's introductions are,[4] in a manner that parallels the bit-by-bit disclosure of information in the first chapter. The narrator does not formally present Paul to the reader at the same time that the Poupins do not properly introduce him to Hyacinth (*PC* 77), referring to him only as "the strange young man" (73, 78) or "the stranger" (79). Only when the Poupins actually call Paul by name does the text also adopt the label (80, 82). Thus both the reader and Hyacinth discover the name as an eavesdropper or spectator of the conversation would.

The teasing and frustration of readers' expectations persists in *The Princess Casamassima* even into the closing chapters. Thanks to a protracted argument among the Poupins, maddening delaying tactics by Schinkel, and an unexpected visit by Mr. Vetch, it takes all of the first two chapters of book 6 (chapters 43 and 44) to complete the delivery to Hyacinth of Hoffendahl's letter. At the end of the second of these chapters, when Hyacinth is finally permitted to read his letter, the reader's suspense is not assuaged, for the text does not reveal the letter's contents. The text has again toyed with the reader's expectations of a *dévoilement* and left the reader to deduce whatever he or she can from what has been presented.

In the transition to the second paragraph of the novel, the text treats the reader to another of its fundamental disruptive strategies: the chronological leap. The first paragraph ends with Miss Pynsent standing on her doorstep, surveying the street for the absent Hyacinth; the second paragraph begins with a spoken sentence: " 'Millicent Henning, tell me quickly, have you seen my child?' " The reader cannot know who is speaking to whom until the following sentence, for only then are the speaker— Miss Pynsent—and her auditor—"a little girl who sat on the doorstep of the adjacent house"—identified (*PC* 4). The text makes an abrupt transition from Miss Pynsent's contemplation of a street empty of the desired object of her sight, to a sentence spoken as from out of nowhere and the introduction of an additional person who was unrepresented and, therefore, unperceived but nonetheless present all the time.

The visit to the prison, which takes place in the third chapter, ends with a similarly abrupt transition. Chapter 3 closes with Miss Pynsent accompanying Hyacinth home and hoping that the boy will not "exercise" his "inquisitorial rights" about the visit too vigorously (*PC* 39). But instead of beginning with Hyacinth's expected inquisition of his foster parent about the prison visit, the following chapter—the fourth—opens like the first, with an unattributed remark spoken out of the blue, this time by the grown-up Millicent (40), thus frustrating the expectation of a confrontation between Hyacinth and Pinnie about his parentage and thrusting the reader into the middle of an unexplained situation by making a leap forward of at least ten years. The end of the third chapter leads the reader to expect an important scene between Hyacinth and Miss Pynsent on the subject of the visit and of Hyacinth's parentage, but in the transition to the next chapter, this scene has been skipped over. Instead, the expectation aroused in the reader of the representation of the climactic scene between Hyacinth and Pinnie about the prison visit and the *dévoilement* of Hyacinth's parentage is not fully satisfied until seven chapters later (120–21).

The tantalizing of the reader through a combination of withholding information and an abrupt transition is conspicuous in the Medley chapters. The final chapter of book 2 is the "Sun and Moon" episode, which concludes with Paul, Hyacinth, Poupin, and the German cabinetmaker Schinkel setting off to visit Hoffendahl. The subsequent chapter opens not with the expected introduction to the revolutionary leader but with Hyacinth waking up in a bedroom of a splendid country house.[5] Equally abrupt is the transition from Hyacinth's stay at Medley to his return to London.[6] Chapter 26 ends with Hyacinth and the Princess entering a drawing room (313), and the next chapter starts with Hyacinth confronting Lady Aurora on the threshold of Pinnie's bedroom (314).[7]

The third disruptive strategy revealed in the first chapter of the novel is the reversal. Pinnie tries to pass off some of the responsibility for deciding whether Hyacinth should visit his mother at the prison by suggesting that Mrs. Bowerbank would judge better if she saw the child, but the prison guard replies, " 'I don't want to judge—it's none of our business!' " This is the most decisive statement made so far in the first chapter, but its decisiveness is immediately undermined by Hyacinth's entrance and Mrs. Bowerbank's passing exactly the judgment she had just refused to make with her "inconsequent cry. 'Is that the child? Oh, Lord o' mercy, don't take *him!* " (11).

The first chapter of *The Princess Casamassima* continually tantalizes the reader with mysteries but withholds their explanation. It is but an initial taste of the novel's propensity for continually postponing a clear "*dévoilement*," to use Kermode's word, and leaving the reader to arrive at an eventual understanding by piecing together different bits of information as pieces in a puzzle. Each time in the first chapter when the reader's questions begin to be answered, the text disrupts this sense of security with the proposal of another mystery, or with a leap such as Miss Pynsent's first speech to Millicent, or with a reversal such as Mrs. Bowerbank's exclamation at Hyacinth's entrance. This disruptiveness is the basic pattern of the novel, and its forms appear in individual paragraphs, whole chapters, or groups of chapters. The reversal is the central structure of the entire novel, for Hyacinth's change from revolutionary to aesthete and the Princess's simultaneous opposite development from aristocrat to revolutionary are the basic elements of the novel's plot.

With its many delays, frustrated expectations, and withheld information, *The Princess Casamassima* constantly arouses expectations at the same time that it never permits its reader to fall into a complacent expectation of omniscient, unequivocal disclosures. The most significant expectations that the novel encourages (at the same time that their fulfillment is consistently postponed) are the same expectations Miss Pynsent holds and encourages Hyacinth to share about his aristocratic relations.[8] The novel makes clear from the very first chapter that Pinnie believes Hyacinth will eventually be taken up by his paternal relatives,[9] and Hyacinth is never able completely to suppress the desire to share this belief.[10] Pinnie's faith that fate has a glorious future reserved for Hyacinth is apparent from the decorations on her parlor walls, which include "a portrait of the Empress of the French . . . framed and glazed in the manner of 1853" (*PC* 41). The mention of the French empress and of 1853 is significant, for that was the year Eugénie de Montijo married Napoleon III; and that marriage, as most of the later nineteenth century knew and as readers of *Roderick Hudson* are reminded (*RH* 274, 330), miraculously lifted that young lady to a position of the greatest wealth and power possible from the relative obscurity of "jeunes années passées loin de tout ce faste royal" [years of youth spent far from such royal pomp].[11] Pinnie's display of the picture of the empress is a reminder that such radical rises from rags to riches can indeed occur. Hyacinth's own wish to be acknowledged as a gentleman is apparent in his envious thoughts as he watches the crowd in Hyde Park:

> He wanted to drive in every carriage, to mount on every horse, to feel on his arm the hand of every pretty woman in the place. . . . There were individuals whom he followed with his eyes, with his thoughts, sometimes even with his steps; they seemed to tell him what it was to be the flower of a high civilisation. (*PC* 119–20)

For John Colmer, this passage "expresses the desire of the 'disinherited' for a full initiation into the life of riches and pleasures and the recovery of a cultural heritage that is his by right of a superior sensibility."[12] As the

Princess later says, Hyacinth's is a case of looking " 'at the good things of life only through the glass of the pastry-cook's window' " (*PC* 296). This is a reminder of the mention in the novel's opening paragraph of Hyacinth's doing precisely that as a boy:

> [T]he boy was often planted in front of the little sweet-shop on the other side of the street, an establishment where periodical literature . . . [was] exhibited in the small-paned, dirty window. He used to stand there . . . spelling out the first page of the romances in the *Family Herald* and the *London Journal,* and admiring the obligatory illustration in which the noble characters (they were always of the highest birth) were presented to the carnal eye. (4)

This scene is an example of the proverbial depiction of the deprived standing on the outside looking in and desiring what is on the inside; in this instance, what Hyacinth sees on the inside are "the noble characters" he later wishes to associate with when, as a young man, he follows the splendid individuals in the park.[13] As Philip Page argues, Hyacinth's gazing through the sweet-shop window is a sign of exclusion and an indication of a mystery to be penetrated.[14]

Hyacinth's position on the outside looking in and his cherished "belief that he was a gentleman born" situate him, as critics have remarked, in the company of heroes of what Lionel Trilling calls "The story of the Young Man from the Provinces."[15]

> *The Princess Casamassima* belongs to a great line of novels which runs through the nineteenth century as, one might say, the very backbone of its fiction. These novels, which are defined as a group by the character and circumstance of their heroes, include Stendhal's *The Red and the Black,* Balzac's *Père Goriot* and *Lost Illusions,* Dickens' *Great Expectations,* Flaubert's *Sentimental Education;* only a very slight extension of the definition is needed to allow the inclusion of Tolstoi's *War and Peace* and Dostoevski's *The Idiot.*[16]

As Trilling says, these novels as a group are distinguished by common features in the protagonist and his background:

> He need not come from the provinces in literal fact, his social class may constitute his province. But a provincial birth and rearing suggest the simplicity and the high hopes he begins with. . . . He may be of a good family but he must be poor. He is intelligent. . . .
> Thus equipped with poverty, pride, and intelligence, the Young Man from the Provinces stands outside life and seeks to enter . . . there is some mystery

about his birth; his real parents, if the truth were known, are of great and even royal estate.[17]

Trilling is emphatic that Hyacinth is a "Young Man from the Provinces": "The hero of *The Princess Casamassima* conforms very exactly to type."[18]

The "Young Man from the Provinces" story "has its roots," says Trilling, in both fairy tale and the most contemporary realism.[19] Because the poor, proud, intelligent hero deserves better, because of the underprivileged situation in which he begins, his story is "in the very heart of the modern actuality."[20] The story is also a variation of the Cinderella tale: the reader is aware that this hero does not deserve to be living in squalor and expects at the same time a Prince Charming figure to intercede and set things right. The squalor of the beginning, by definition in these stories, suggests the intervention of

[s]ome great and powerful hand [which] must reach down into the world of seemingly chanceless routine and pick up the hero and set him down in his complex and dangerous fate. Pip meets Magwitch . . . Pierre Bezuhov unexpectedly inherits [a] fortune . . . powerful unseen forces play around the head of Julien Sorel . . . Rastignac, simply by being one of the boarders at the Maison Vauquer which also shelters the great Vautrin, moves to the very center of Parisian intrigue. . . .[21]

Stendhal's Julien Sorel, in *Le Rouge et le noir,* and Rastignac, in Balzac's *Le Père Goriot,* share underprivileged beginnings, unlimited ambition, intelligence, a faculty of observation that they use to learn acceptable social mannerisms, and the conviction that, despite the handicaps in their origins, they can succeed on the strength of their intelligence, charm, and will—the characteristics Trilling sums up as "poverty, pride, and intelligence." Trilling does not point out, however, that there is a distinction between the "great and powerful hand" in the French texts and in *The Princess Casamassima* and the different form the "hand" takes in the Russian or other English examples. "Powerful unseen forces" do "play around" Julien Sorel's head, and Rastignac's acquaintances at the pension Vauquer do link him "to the very center of Parisian intrigue," but both Julien and Rastignac count on another means to succeed, a means Trilling does not acknowledge but that *L'Education sentimentale* shows is an "*idée reçue*" of French nineteenth-century culture.

Trilling's inclusion in his list of Frédéric Moreau and Flaubert's *L'Education sentimentale*[22] obscures the fact that Flaubert's novel is not an example of the type but a deliberate play on it. Although Frédéric is from the country, he is not terribly poor; at times he has pretenses of ambition, but he is really mediocre and lethargic; he does inherit unexpectedly from an uncle, but the route to success the novel emphasizes from the very beginning, when Frédéric's friend Deslauriers urges him to become Mme. Dambreuse's lover, is sex: "Mais je te dis là des choses classiques, il me semble? Rappelle-toi Rastignac dans *La Comédie humaine!* Tu réussiras, j'en suis sûr!" [But I'm telling you something as old as the earth, no? Remember Rastignac in *The Human Comedy!* You will succeed, I'm sure of it!][23] The phrase "Rappelle-toi Rastignac," refers specifically to *Le Père Goriot*, which is *the* success story in French nineteenth-century fiction, and makes it into a cliché (and Balzac's text into the subject of a parody of Romanticism). Both Rastignac and Julien unscrupulously use women to help them to success, but only Rastignac succeeds.

The allusion to him and to his success through women in Flaubert's novel is a sign that he stands for romantic and worldly success and that he is, by the later nineteenth century, a convention of French culture. That Trilling cites *L'Education sentimentale* indicates that readers recognize the type of the "Young Man from the Provinces" even when, as in Flaubert's novel and in *The Princess Casamassima,* it appears in a play on the type. We recognize the type in these two texts because of the expectation aroused of the intervention of a female "great and powerful hand."

Of all the novels Trilling mentions, *The Princess Casamassima* is most like Flaubert's, for it, too, deliberately evokes the Rastignac type and does something unconventional with it.[24] The "Young Man from the Provinces" has to be an outsider, has to have the kind of charm and intelligence that would be appreciated in high society, and an intercession on his behalf has to be available. Hyacinth has all the requisite characteristics: he is poor and intelligent and has the refined manner that belies his origins; he "stands outside life and seeks to enter," as we perceive from the Princess's remark about "the pastry-cook's window" (*PC* 296); and there certainly is a "mystery about his birth."[25] He has natural nobility in two senses: his nobility is innate, and he is the natural son of nobility; he grows up in the requisite deprived setting and becomes educated nevertheless.

In the English and American texts that belong to the "Young Man from the Provinces" type—Trilling mentions *Great Expectations* and *The Great Gatsby,* but *Little Lord Fauntleroy* should be included—the intercession usually comes from a lost relative or parent figure.[26] The obvious quarter from which any real possibility of rising to the rank of gentleman would come would be Hyacinth's father's family. However, Hyacinth, apparently recognizing the unlikelihood of his story turning out like little Lord Fauntleroy's (which appeared the same year as *The Princess Casamassima*),[27] forbids Miss Pynsent, who hopes openly for this kind of intercession, to talk about his paternal family in his presence.[28]

But there is one other available route to admittance into genteel society, one Miss Pynsent also hints at and that the title of the novel cannot keep far from the reader's mind during the eleven chapters when the title character is not mentioned, the one that frequently occurs in the French texts: a romantic liaison or marriage. It is not an impossible occurrence; if the philanthropic Lady Aurora Langrish can be attracted to the proletarian Paul Muniment and can even be thought seriously to desire to marry him (*PC* 445), there is nothing unreasonable in imagining a lady taking a liking to Hyacinth, who, everybody agrees, looks the part of the gentleman.[29] Hyacinth is intelligent and charming, but most of all, he has "the precious faculty, of inspiring women with an interest" (*PC* 157). This is the clue that unquestionably associates Hyacinth to the ambitious French characters Rastignac and Julien, who both take advantage of women and succeed (inasmuch as they do) largely thanks to their mistresses.[30] In fact, Rastignac, according to Larousse, is the very type of ambitious man who succeeds by means of women: "Rastignac est tout simplement 'l'homme qui arrive par les femmes'" [Rastignac is quite simply "the man who succeeds through women"].[31]

Because Hyacinth is in these ways similar to Rastignac and Julien, because Hyacinth is a male Cinderella, the reader of *The Princess Casamassima* does not need a deliberate evocation of Balzac like the one in *L'Education sentimentale* to believe in Pinnie's and Hyacinth's romantic expectations of the Princess Charming. What Princess Charming could be more satisfactory than Princess "Biggest House" *(casa massima),* and what better way to heighten the expectation of the intercession of such a character than by naming the novel after her and then holding back her entrance for twelve chapters? That these devices are successful in raising expectations is apparent in the tension created in the episode in which Hyacinth at last does meet the Princess.

The encounter between Hyacinth and the Princess takes place at the theater. Two chapters are required to portray the meeting; the first consists mostly of the sort of creation of suspense and excitement of expectations that is typical of *The Princess Casamassima.* Hyacinth and Millicent sit caught up in the third act of the sensational *Pearl of Paraguay:*

> It was at this crisis, none the less, that she asked Hyacinth who his friends were in the principal box on the left of the stage, and let him know that a gentleman seated there had been watching him, at intervals, for the past half hour. . . . "[D]on't hang back. He may make your fortune." (*PC* 132)[32]

Millicent's prediction is perhaps flippant (and ironic, in view of the possibility—apparent at the novel's end—that the gentleman in question will make *her* fortune), but it expresses what the reader expects. The "principal box" in the theater is always occupied by people of distinction, and this distinction is a sign of an important influence taking notice of Hyacinth. Millicent continues to voice the reader's expectation that the hoped-for encounter with the "great and powerful hand" is at last coming about when she says, " 'I say, I say—is it one of your grand relations? . . . Is he your uncle, or your grandfather, or your first or second cousin?' " (133). As always, though, the text frustrates the expectation that it creates, and it does it typically by replacing the expectation with a mystery. The gentleman is not a "grand relation," but Hyacinth does know him. "They had met three times, he and his fellow-spectator; but they had met under circumstances which, to Hyacinth's mind, would have made a furtive wink, a mere tremor of the eyelid, a more judicious reference to the fact than so public a salutation" (133). Before this point, the text has not mentioned the "Sun and Moon" or remarked specifically about Hyacinth's meeting with secret societies, nor has it revealed Hyacinth's acquaintance with the "fellow-spectator." The existence of this person in Hyacinth's life has been entirely concealed up to this point, in yet another example of the novel's tendency to withhold information from the reader.

Not only is the gentleman a mystery, but there are other people in his box about whose identity the text builds some suspense. Hyacinth and Millicent see that one of them is a lady: "her arm, bare save for its bracelets, was visible at moments on the cushioned ledge" of the box (*PC* 132). Instead of satisfying the reader as to who this lady is, however, the text presents yet another unknown person when, a little later, "Hyacinth saw that the chair his mysterious acquaintance had quitted in the stage-box was now occupied by a lady hitherto invisible—not the one who had given them a glimpse of her shoulder and bare arm" (135). Millicent dramatizes the reader's interest in the lady's identity when she asks, " 'Is the old woman his mother? Where did she dig up her clothes? They look as if she hired them for the evening. Does *she* come to your wonderful club, too? I daresay she cuts it fine, don't she?' " (135).

The gentleman disappears from the box, and Hyacinth and Millicent impatiently anticipate his appearance in their balcony. At this moment of high suspense, the text finally satisfies the reader on the subject of the gentleman's identity.

> . . . [Hyacinth] was really excited, dazzled, by an incident of which the reader will have failed as yet to perceive the larger relations. What moved him was not the pleasure of being patronised by a rich man; it was simply the prospect of new experience—a sensation for which he was always ready to exchange

> any present boon; and he was convinced that if the gentleman with whom he
> had conversed in a small occult back-room in Bloomsbury as Captain God-
> frey Sholto—the Captain had given him his card—had more positively than
> in Millicent's imagination come out of the stage-box to see him, he would
> bring with him rare influences. This nervous presentiment, lighting on our
> young man, was so keen that it constituted almost a preparation. . . . (*PC*
> 136)

The revelation of who Sholto is begins with a reminder of how little the
reader knows—"the reader will have failed as yet to perceive the larger
relations"—and, at the same time that the text satisfies the reader on the
Captain's identity, it encourages other expectations by giving a sense of
how much Hyacinth anticipates from his acquaintance.

At last the Captain appears in their section of the theater and tells Hyacinth and his companion the purpose of his errand: " 'One of my ladies has
a great desire to make your acquaintance.' "

> "To make my acquaintance?" Hyacinth felt himself turning pale; the first
> impulse he could have, in connection with such an announcement as that—
> and *it lay far down, in the depths of the unspeakable—was a conjecture that it
> had something to do with his parentage on his father's side.* (*PC* 138–39; em-
> phasis added)[33]

Hyacinth resists the idea of being patronized by a rich man as much as he
earlier resisted sharing Pinnie's hope of his being taken up by his paternal
relatives (124); nevertheless, his reaction to the Captain's announcement
reveals that such a taking up—the occurrence of which the reader has expected from the beginning—is one of Hyacinth's deepest hopes. By this
point, the expectation of the "great and powerful hand" appearing is at its
most feverish pitch. Only now does the text reveal that the lady who wants
to meet Hyacinth—"the most remarkable woman in Europe"—is the Princess Casamassima (140), the title character whose existence has not even
been hinted at in almost twelve chapters.

What makes it unavoidable that the reader perceive the meeting with the
Princess as the hoped-for intervention of the "great and powerful hand" is
where it takes place: a theater. This fact of location is the most significant
link between *The Princess Casamassima* and the figure of Balzac's Rastignac. The evocation of Rastignac in *L'Education sentimentale* makes Balzac's hero a cliché, the stereotype of the successful "Young Man from the
Provinces." Because it is a cliché or stereotype, it is, as Trilling suggested,[34]
linked to legend, to fairy tale; it is part of the society's cultural language.

By placing its protagonist in the stock situation of the theater, *The Princess Casamassima* refers its readers to the cliché that is represented in French culture by Rastignac, and because of this reference, *The Princess Casamassima* is able to offer a critique of the kind of rags-to-riches success story that Balzac's character exemplifies.

Because Balzac has Rastignac first meet Delphine de Nucingen, the future mistress who will be his path to success, at the theater (*Comédie* 3: 152–57), Hyacinth's meeting with the Princess at the theater could be seen as a direct quotation of *Le Père Goriot*. But Rastignac's introduction to Delphine is, in itself, a quotation of the convention that the theater is one of the places for seductive looks and amorous encounters (as in Dumas's *La Dame aux camélias* or in *War and Peace,* for example). What confirms this relation to the convention in Balzac's text is that Rastignac, when seated next to Delphine, plays the conventional lover, literally speaking "sottises stéréotypées" [stereotypical inanities] to her (*Comédie* 3: 156)— the scene is stereotypical and requires stereotypical conversation. Since the theater meeting in *The Princess Casamassima* plays upon this convention, the reader sees in the meeting the beginning of the fulfillment of Hyacinth's Rastignacian destiny. The scene is not so much a direct quote of Balzac's text as an allusion to a conventional story involving a cliché locale, the theater, and the seductive encounter with the cliché lady of destiny.

The Princess Casamassima, which incessantly creates and frustrates expectations on a small scale in its reader, encourages the overriding, large-scale expectation that Hyacinth will find, through a woman, the opportunity to rise into the social circles one is led to consider his proper milieu. This expectation is still encouraged after the theater episode in this passage from Hyacinth's visit to Lady Aurora's house:

> . . . he considered much the extreme oddity of this new phase of his life . . . a phase in which his society should have become indispensable to ladies of high rank and the obscurity of his condition only an attraction the more. They were taking him up then, one after the other, and they were even taking up poor Pinnie, as a means of getting at him; so that he wondered, with humorous bitterness, whether it meant that his destiny was really seeking him out—that the aristocracy, recognising a mysterious affinity (with that fineness of *flair* for which they were remarkable), were coming to him to save him the trouble of coming to them. (*PC* 220)

No expectation that *The Princess Casamassima* creates is satisfied in a straightforward manner, and this proves no less true in the case of Hyacinth's social aspirations. The ultimate irony of the encounter is like the irony of the Princess's announcement under the beech tree. Hyacinth expects to meet his paternal relatives in the theater (and the reader has been led to expect it, too) and to be lifted socially into the world of the nobility. But just as the fantasy of reading a fashionable periodical under the beech tree is realized rather by the Princess's disclosure under a beech tree of her revolutionary connections with Hoffendahl, the person Hyacinth expects to encounter at the theater as the viaticum to social and economic success turns out to be a woman who seeks to make him the guide for her own descent into the worlds of the working classes and of anarchists—though she does inspire the interest he develops (and crystallizes in Paris and Venice) in art and culture.

As with Frédéric Moreau in Flaubert's novel, James's text establishes Hyacinth's similarity to the "Young Man from the Provinces" type in order to do something different with it. In *L'Education sentimentale*, Frédéric tries all the possible routes to a great romantic (in both senses) career and finds them all unfulfilling. The different use of the type in *L'Education sentimentale* turns out to be antithetical—a critique of the type, an elegy of mediocrity and of a world where a Rastignac is no longer possible. The treatment in *The Princess Casamassima* is different from this, because the expectation of the protagonist's Rastignacian destiny is no more than an illusion of the reader, of Pinnie—who is the personification of the expectations—and once in a while, of Hyacinth.

From beginning to end, *The Princess Casamassima* is a struggle between these illusions and a less pleasant reality.[35] Contrasted to Pinnie's and Rosy Muniment's idealized visions of the upper class are Lady Aurora's and the Princess's descriptions of an insipid world (*PC* 172–78, 209–10). The reader may not have noticed it on the first reading, but upon rereading the novel, the way the first chapter puts Pinnie's romantic fantasies about Hyacinth at odds with Mrs. Bowerbank's pragmatism is unmistakable. While Miss Pynsent muses on "her conviction that [Hyacinth] belonged, 'by the left hand,' . . . to an ancient and exalted race" (8) and on the "elements in the boy's life which she was not prepared to sacrifice" (6), Mrs. Bowerbank, "a woman accustomed to looking facts in the face" (6), acknowledges only what was definitely confirmed in the trial of Florentine Vivier and counsels that " '[t]he less said about the poor child's ancestors the better!' " (7).

Similarly, the last chapter contrasts two different outlooks, one practical and pragmatic, the other excited and flustered. As Schinkel and the Princess wait in front of Hyacinth's lodgings, tension and suspense mount between her "intolerably nervous" impatience and his infuriating methodicalness (550). The half-Italian Christina seems to sense that something is wrong (which, indeed, there is) and becomes emotional, while the Teutonic cabinetmaker maintains his "calm and conscientious thoroughness" (517). He agrees to break open the door to Hyacinth's room only after "deliberating" and giving himself a rationale with his recollection that the young man had received a pistol (552).

By juxtaposing the Princess's Mediterranean frenzy with Schinkel's Teutonic deliberation, *The Princess Casamassima* closes with a repetition of the clash at its beginning between the flustered Pinnie and the stolid Mrs. Bowerbank. The purpose of this type of ring composition[36] is to focus attention on the central chapters at Medley; halfway between the opening and closing chapters, which dramatize pragmatism and romanticism at odds, lie the chapters where Hyacinth lives an idealized existence, fulfilling his fantasy of reading the *Revue des Deux Mondes* and "incarnating" his heroine into an ideal—in fact, into precisely the fairy-tale princess she would be were the novel's Rastignacian expectations meant to be fulfilled.[37]

The central Medley episode covers five chapters (*PC* chaps. 22–26), and it is in the middle chapter of that group that the text presents the greatest irony on Hyacinth's fantasy of "stretch[ing] in the shadow of an ancestral beech" (114). If the Medley visit is a fulfillment of that fantasy, it is a fulfillment with an ironic twist. When Hyacinth is at last "standing there under a great beech" (284), the one real beech tree in the novel, it is not to read the *Revue des Deux Mondes* or to be "taken up" by an ideal patroness; rather he is to learn that the Princess is someone quite different, that she is at least as aquainted with Hoffendahl and as involved with revolutionaries as he is. This is the turning point of the novel; at the very moment when Hyacinth appears to have achieved his fantasy, the Princess ceases to be the glamorous figure of the first half of the novel and begins to become the person who, in the second half of the book, gives away her possessions (with a few exceptions) and her money and trots around with Paul Muniment to clandestine meetings.

The Medley chapters are followed by the abrupt transition to Pinnie's deathbed. Hyacinth is irate when he finds out that nobody contacted him at Medley when Pinnie became ill, but when Mr. Vetch tells him that Pinnie herself had not wished his visit to be interrupted because she believed Hyacinth had at last been "taken up" by his rich relatives, Hyacinth promises to "tell her my great relations have adopted me and that I have come back in the character of Lord Robinson" (320). This permits Pinnie to die with her fantasy intact, and her death is really the passing of the living embodiment of those fantasies. The legacy of her meager savings makes Hyacinth's continental trip possible, but the novel after his return to England is largely a record of the crumbling of the young man's earlier illusions. The dreariness of the Princess's new residence is the first shock; it is followed by Hyacinth's disillusionment with the revolutionary ideas they had shared, the evidence (apparent to the reader, at least) of the callousness of Paul's friendship for Hyacinth, and finally the betrayal Hyacinth feels when he views the ambiguous natures of Paul's relationship with the Princess and of Millicent's with Sholto.

The novel divides into two parts. The first represents a fulfilling of illusions that reaches its peak at Medley with the reading of the *Revue des Deux Mondes* and the incarnation of the Princess as a Feuillet heroine. The second begins with the death of the character who personifies the novel's romantic illusions and is a record of disillusionment. The novel ends as it begins. The first and last chapters present a battle of nerves between a hard, practical person and a flustered, emotional one; as such, they sum up the conflict between illusion and reality that is so central to the novel.[38]

Thus the novel represents the growth and subsequent loss of illusions, and through the techniques it uses to encourage and at the same time frustrate their expectations, the novel manages to include readers in this same process. The ultimate illusion in the novel is the expectation of the rise up the socioeconomic ladder, and it is because this expectation is not fulfilled that *The Princess Casamassima* is at the source of a prominent tradition in modern American literature of critiques of the Horatio Alger–like rags-to-riches story, a tradition that includes such texts as Fitzgerald's *The Great Gatsby*, Ralph Ellison's *Invisible Man*, Faulkner's Snopes novels, and Eugene O'Neill's *The Iceman Cometh*. Critics of *The Great Gatsby* and *Invisible Man* usually mention the extent to which those two texts are responses to the myth of work and advancement up the social ladder of the novels of Horatio Alger, whose career as an author was contemporary with much of James's.[39] I do not mean to deny that these texts are responses to the Alger myth (they contain specific references to Alger), but I do want to suggest the existence of an additional line to the tradition in American literature of critiquing the myth of socioeconomic advancement, a line that runs from the novels of Stendhal and Balzac through James and *The Princess Casamassima* to twentieth-century responses such as Fitzgerald's and Ellison's.

By using the theater as the locale for the introduction of the Princess, thus re-creating the stock situation that leads to Rastignac's rise to wealth and power, *The Princess Casamassima* places itself in a French literary tradition of socioeconomic mobility that precedes Alger by a generation. The source of this tradition is historical; as readers of Stendhal's *Le Rouge et le noir* know, it is a result of the social impact of the French Revolution and its aftermath and of the career of Napoleon, Julien Sorel's hero and Stendhal's emblem of the possibility of ambitions achieved and the rise from poverty to power and wealth. Thus *The Princess Casamassima* does not just incorporate French culture, it lies at an important transitional point between a French and an American literary tradition.

Salvation, the Scaffold, and Origen
in *The Ambassadors*

hile one literary allusion in *Daisy Miller* had a single effect on our reading of that novel, in the much longer *The Princess Casamassima,* the reference to Feuillet's heroine alludes to more than one other text at the same time and ultimately relates to another, less specific reference by means of Hyacinth's underprivileged origins and the theater encounter with the Princess: the general type of the "Young Man from the Provinces." In his later *The Ambassadors,* James took the literary allusion a step further and created a network of literary referentiality through allusions to Goldsmith's *The Vicar of Wakefield,* Thackeray's *Pendennis* and *The Newcomes,* Hugo's *Notre-Dame de Paris,* and Balzac's *Louis Lambert.* Each of these works is by a canonical author, and only two of them are French; but as the mention of Feuillet in *The Princess Casamassima* leads to a consideration of the relationships between two Feuillet texts, James's own *Roderick Hudson,* Hyacinth's idealism, and the outsider "from the provinces" as expressed in Balzac's *Le Père Goriot* and subverted in Flaubert's *L'Education sentimentale,* so does the consideration of any one of the literary references in *The Ambassadors* lead to further consideration of its relationship to the various other such references and to other, less obvious and more generally cultural references.

These less obvious references are to the Virgin Mary and Mary, Queen of Scots, to the legend of Origen's self-castration, and to all that they entail. These cultural figures are not exclusively French—though they are at least as much parts of French culture as of English or American—but *The Ambassadors* leads its reader to them (or, to be more precise, to the Virgin Mary and the legend of Origen) and to understanding their effect on how one interprets James's novel through the more specific references to *Louis Lambert* and *Notre-Dame de Paris*.

The first of the literary allusions in *The Ambassadors,* to Thackeray's two novels and to *The Vicar of Wakefield,* relate the situation of James's protagonist, Lambert Strether, as it is established in the beginning of the novel, to a general type of a father figure losing his innocent illusions as he searches for his prodigal child. The reference to Hugo's *Notre-Dame de Paris* ties together a number of motifs that run throughout the text involving scaffolds, salvation, and the name Mary, which is particularly conspicuous, since it is held by the two principal female characters, Marie de Vionnet and Maria Gostrey. Finally, the allusion to Balzac's *Louis Lambert* plays a role in the reader's understanding both of the problematic ending of *The Ambassadors* and of the effect on Strether of his experiences during the course of the novel.

In a novel about a father figure (Lambert Strether) sent to the modern Babylon (Paris)[1] to search for the Newsome family's prodigal son, the allusions to *The Vicar of Wakefield, Pendennis,* and *The Newcomes* are appropriate, as each of these novels—as do Balzac's "Madame Firmiani" and, more recently, Paton's *Cry the Beloved Country*—presents the father figure "rescuing" the prodigal child.[2] There are also two allusions in *The Ambassadors* (37, 304) to the scene in Goldsmith's novel when the London prostitutes masquerade as high society women before the credulous Primroses in their vicarage.

These allusions serve at least two purposes in James's text: *The Vicar of Wakefield* is a perfect example of the innocent father figure searching for the prodigal child, in this case, Dr. Primrose's elder daughter, Olivia. In this story, the rescuing father loses his innocence during his stay in "Babylon," and this is of the greatest relevance to Strether's story. During the course of his search, which takes him to the great, wicked metropolis of London, the doctor learns that virtually everything is the opposite of what he had initially thought. Squire Thornhill, the man Mrs. Primrose hoped, at one time, would be her son-in-law, turns out to be Olivia's abductor, and Mr. Burchell, whom the Primroses have blamed for their misfortunes, proves to be the wealthy and generous Sir William Thornhill, uncle of the villainous Squire. Inevitably, the father figure's eyes are opened, and he learns that he has trusted those he should have feared most, has condemned those who were least to blame, and in short has failed to see that appearances and reality often differ. In Goldsmith's novel, the scene with the disguised prostitutes serves as a metaphorical warning not to trust appearances too closely, and by alluding to it, James's novel—a text in which seeing will have considerable significance—makes much the same point.

The first reference to Thackeray occurs in the third chapter of *The Ambassadors*, when Strether encounters Maria Gostrey, the expatriate American he had met the day before, in the breakfast room of the hotel at which they are both staying in Chester. Eating her breakfast, "she reminded him, as he let her know, of Major Pendennis breakfasting at his club" (34). Two pages later, Maria guides Strether's old friend Waymarsh through the hazards of a European breakfast so successfully that "her subsequent boast to Strether was that she had made their friend fare—and quite without his knowing what was the matter—as Major Pendennis would have fared at the Megatherium" (36).

The Megatherium is mentioned only in Thackeray's *The Newcomes,* but the only scene—and a remarkable one at that—of Major Pendennis breakfasting is the beginning of *Pendennis.* In that novel's opening chapter, Thackeray's retired officer and admirer of all things aristocratic sits down "to breakfast at a certain Club in Pall Mall, of which he was a chief ornament," and peruses "all the fashionable London letters" that "were laid out there in expectation of his arrival."[3] One missive, left for last, is from the Major's widowed sister-in-law and begs him to come immediately to her and do all he can to save his eighteen-year-old nephew, Arthur Pendennis, from marrying an actress "at least twelve years older."[4]

The Ambassadors describes both Maria Gostrey and Waymarsh as breakfasting like Major Pendennis, but neither of James's characters has the meal unpleasantly disrupted by disturbing news, and neither, for the moment at least, appears called upon to save anybody. Strether, the only other character so far introduced, is the only one not compared to Major Pendennis, but this is an irony of the text, for it is Strether whose situation is not unlike Thackeray's Major's: he, too, is called upon by a widow—his patroness, Mrs. Newsome of Woollett—to save her only son, Chad, from as bad a thing—in fact the same thing—as marriage to an actress "at least twelve years older": an immoral relationship with a "bad" (*Amb.* 144) Parisian woman. Maria and Waymarsh breakfast like Major Pendennis only in one sense: they partake of a regal meal. Strether fulfills the other aspect of the Major's breakfast: he is called to the mission of saving the prodigal son.

In addition to the reference to the Major's breakfast and the shared general motif of the surrogate father called upon to rescue the son, there are other similarities of detail between *Pendennis* and *The Ambassadors* that further suggest that the later novel alludes to a conventional situation. In both novels, the mother's hearty disapproval of her son's inclination is counterbalanced by her long-nurtured preference for a younger, innocent eventual partner for her son. In James's novel, Chad is expected, it seems, to marry Mamie Pocock, his brother-in-law's younger sister, while Mrs.

Pendennis's pet project and hope is that her son will one day marry her ward, Laura Bell. In both cases, the mother has already planned the son's romantic career.

More significantly, in both novels the project to rescue the young man from the "bad" woman is specifically referred to as "saving." In *Pendennis*, it is the Major who has "saved Pen,"[5] and in *The Ambassadors*, it is Strether whose task, as Miss Gostrey (*Amb.* 55) and the artist Little Bilham (167) remind him, is to "save" Chad. The theme of salvation becomes a motif that runs throughout *The Ambassadors*; everybody in James's novel at some point seems to be either saving or being saved by someone else. Strether's original mission is expressed almost from the beginning of *The Ambassadors* in terms of saving Chad:

> . . . "Poor Chad!"
> "Ah," said Strether cheerfully, "Mamie will save him!"
> . . . "*You'll* save him. That's who'll save him."
> "Oh but with Mamie's aid. Unless you mean," he added, "that I shall effect so much more with yours!" (55)

When Strether finally sees Chad in Paris, he soon comes to feel that Mme. de Vionnet has already accomplished his mission: "The fact remains nevertheless that she has saved him" (*Amb.* 167). At the same time, Strether's idea of "saving" Chad changes from bringing him back to Woollett to keeping him in Paris, a project that Strether worries in the end has not been successful: "But I'm not sure I've saved him" (344). Mme. de Vionnet in turn looks to Strether to save her by preventing Chad from abandoning her; Strether promises, "I'll save you if I can" (152). Bilham guesses at this new mission: "It strikes you accordingly then . . . as for you all to save *her?*" (168).

While Strether's view of Europe and Chad's situation changes, Waymarsh's does not, and Strether senses that his old friend not only disapproves of his new views but also tries to save him from them: "The sombre glow stared . . . at [Strether] till it fairly sounded out—'to save you, poor old man, to save you; to save you in spite of yourself' " (224). The time Waymarsh spends with Sarah Pocock makes Strether think, "It might . . . be that they had united to save him" (267). Strether hypothesizes that, like himself, Mamie Pocock came to Paris with the aim of saving Chad—"She was to *save* our friend"—only to find that the young man "was, he *is*, saved" already by Mme. de Vionnet (260). As a result, Strether explains to Bilham, it is only natural that Mamie then should make the young artist the new target of her affections: " *You* remain for her to save" (261).[6] Besides

Strether's plea to the American expatriate for her aid quoted above, a parallel between Mme. de Vionnet and Chad, on the one hand, and Maria Gostrey and Strether, on the other, suggests that Miss Gostrey also has saved and in turn needs saving. If Mme. de Vionnet has "saved" Chad by changing the young man into a charming, mature gentleman and in turn deserves to be saved because it would be unfair "to have turned a man out so wonderfully, too, only for somebody else" (169), then Maria's and Strether's situations are analogous, for "She had decked him out for others" (196).

All this emphasis on salvation in *The Ambassadors* ties the allusions to the two father-figure-in-search-of-prodigal-child texts to another significant point, the double use of the name Mary for the novel's two most important women characters, Marie de Vionnet and Maria Gostrey. In turn, both the salvation motif and the Mary motif are linked with the allusion to Hugo's *Notre-Dame de Paris,* as saving and the name Mary constitute a reference to the Virgin Mary, one of Western European culture's most prevalent salvation figures.[7]

One of the central episodes of *The Ambassadors* includes a reference that is difficult to ignore to Hugo's *Notre-Dame de Paris* and establishes the connection of the doubling of the name Mary to the theme of salvation. This episode begins in the novel's middle chapter,[8] when Strether literally looks to Mary for relief. He frequents Notre Dame—Our Lady, the Virgin Mary—for "its beneficent action on his nerves" and as "a refuge from the obsession of his problem" (*Amb.* 170), and during one of these visits, a significant, accidental encounter with Marie de Vionnet occurs (172–82).

Strether's preference could have been for any number of Parisian churches (and had it been for the Madeleine—that is, the Magdalene—which was much more convenient to both his hotel and Chad's apartment, it would signify something quite different), and as Mme. de Vionnet is a frequenter of many of them—"I'm terrible, in general, for churches" (173)—their meeting did not have to take place at Notre Dame. That Notre Dame is Strether's source of relief is no more a coincidence than the subject of his and Marie de Vionnet's subsequent discussion: the "question" of Strether's *saving* her, "what you had meant by saying, the day you came to see me . . . that you'd *save* me" (178; emphasis added). That Lambert and Marie discuss saving after meeting at the cathedral of Our Lady where Strether went in search of relief makes it unequivocally clear that the "metaphor of salvation" in *The Ambassadors* is connected to the figure of the Virgin Mary.

There are two literal Marys—Maria Gostrey and Marie de Vionnet—in *The Ambassadors,* but there are two symbolic Marys as well, for Mary Stuart is as significant to the novel as the Virgin Mary. While the Virgin is related to the text's tendency to present the characters as saving and being saved by each other, Mary Stuart is connected to a metaphor of the scaffold. The first manifestation of this metaphor comes during Strether's and Miss Gostrey's dinner and theater visit together in London, during which Strether mentally contrasts Mrs. Newsome, who "looked, with her ruff and other matters, like Queen Elizabeth" with "Miss Gostrey [who] looked perhaps like Mary Stuart" (43). Strether dwells on the "broad red velvet band with an antique jewel" that Miss Gostrey wears around her throat (42) and that appears to suggest the comparison to Mary Stuart. Strether no doubt "reads" the red velvet as a sign of lasciviousness, but the reader, aware that the Scottish queen was executed at the English queen's order, sees an additional significance in it, for the placement of the band around Maria's throat suggests the Scottish queen's beheading.

The novel explicitly compares Maria Gostrey to Mary Stuart (43); Marie de Vionnet's connection to Mary Stuart is more subtle but no less certain. From the view of Mrs. Newsome (and of Strether before he meets and gets to know her), Mme. de Vionnet is a bad woman, and there is no question that she will have to be abandoned—sacrificed—(which is what happens in the end) for the sake of Chad and the family's career. Mary Stuart shares these two features—being "bad" and being sacrificed (her beheading was supposed to guarantee political stability)—indeed, they are her two predominant features as far as nineteenth-century Western culture is concerned.[9]

In an extension of the Marie de Vionnet as Mary Stuart motif, Strether later compares Marie de Vionnet to another famous victim of the scaffold, Madame Roland, the Girondin:

> His hostess was dressed as for thunderous times, and it fell in with the kind of imagination we have just attributed to him that she should be in simplest coolest white, of a character so old-fashioned, if he were not mistaken, that Madame Roland must on the scaffold have worn something like it. (317)

These remarks occur during Strether's meeting with Mme. de Vionnet the day after his eye-opening encounter with Chad and her at the Cheval Blanc in the Lambinet scene. During this meeting, Marie, who seems to have intuited that both Chad and Strether are about to abandon her and return to America, admits, "Of course I'm afraid for my life" (323), and Strether, before leaving, assures her, "There's something I believe I can still do . . . it may help *you*" (324). Her predicament, metaphorically speaking, has two possible outcomes: salvation—Strether's help will save her—or the scaffold—her fear for her life will be substantiated. She either will or will not turn out to be a Mary Stuart type.

Strether himself is not immune from the threat of the scaffold. As Waymarsh announces to him that Mrs. Pocock is coming to talk to him, Strether reflects, "Yes, he should go to the scaffold yet for he wouldn't know quite whom" (269). As this comes right after Strether's reflection (already quoted) that Waymarsh and Sarah Pocock, in their own way, might have "united to save him" (267), salvation and the scaffold again appear as the two related alternatives.

The doubling of the name Mary in *The Ambassadors* is a reminder that in metaphorical terms there are two types of Marys in this novel, the saving Mary, the Madonna, and the sacrificed Mary, the Queen of Scots. The combined effect of the repeated savings, the scaffolds, and the two Marys would seem to pose the problem of which character, Maria Gostrey or Marie de Vionnet, will play which part. Both women ultimately play both roles; if Strether perceives Miss Gostrey as Mary Stuart early on, he views Mme. de Vionnet as a variant of her near the end when he sees her as Madame Roland (whose first name is Jeanne-Marie). Maria and Marie are also sources of salvation for Chad and Strether, and in need of salvation when abandoned at the end, Maria by Strether and Marie by both Chad and Strether.

The double use of the name Mary, then, is a sign that the two women have the dual nature of being both savior and victim. This dual nature is made all the more apparent by the allusion to Hugo's *Notre-Dame de Paris*,[10] which Strether twice recalls on the visit to Notre Dame Cathedral during which he runs into Mme. de Vionnet. As Strether strolls around the cathedral, his attention is caught by a lady whom he does not yet recognize as his acquaintance, but whom he imagines as "some fine firm concentrated heroine of an old story." Strether takes a seat in the middle of the nave, scans the great building, and tries "to reconstitute a past, to reduce it in fact to the convenient terms of Victor Hugo," on whose complete works he had splurged "a few days before" (*Amb.* 172). At this moment, he and Mme. de Vionnet recognize each other, and Strether refers explicitly to Hugo and *Notre-Dame de Paris:* "He had spoken of the great romancer and the great romance" (*Amb.* 174).

These references to *Notre-Dame de Paris* and Strether's and Mme. de Vionnet's encounter in the cathedral are followed by lunch at an unnamed restaurant (presumably the Tour d'Argent), during which the question of Marie's salvation is discussed (*Amb.* 175–81). That this luncheon is a repetition with a slightly different cast of Strether's dinner before the theater with Maria Gostrey is clear both by virtue of its similar charm as a forbidden pleasure and because of a direct reference to the earlier repast:

[H]adn't one a right to one's snatch of scandal when one was prepared to pay? It was on this pleasant basis of costly disorder, consequently, that they eventually seated themselves. . . . He was to feel . . . that he had travelled far since that evening in London, before the theatre, when his dinner with Maria Gostrey, between the pink-shaded candles, had struck him as requiring so many explanations. (176)

Salvation is the topic of conversation at the later meal; the first comparison to Mary Stuart occurs at the earlier one. Since the two meals are metaphorically the same and since a Mary is Strether's partner at both, salvation, scaffolds, and the question of the two Marys are inextricably bound together.

Strether's reference in the cathedral Notre Dame to the novel *Notre-Dame de Paris* brings together the salvation and scaffold metaphors in *The Ambassadors*. Until the closing chapters, Hugo's novel is a series of near hangings and rescues: first, Pierre Gringoire, the dramatist, is saved by the beautiful gypsy Esmeralda from being summarily hanged by thieves. Then the young girl metaphorically saves Quasimodo, the hunchback, when she brings him water to drink while he is pilloried for his part in Claude Frollo's attempted abduction of the girl. The hunchback returns the favor when he snatches Esmeralda from the hands of her would-be executioners and carries her into the asylum of Notre Dame. The hunchback is able to save Esmeralda from the gallows only temporarily, and the novel ends with a tragic crescendo of corpses: the king dies, Esmeralda is hanged, her mother's skull is cracked on the pavement, Claude Frollo is pushed off one of the cathedral towers, his brother Jehan is killed by Quasimodo during the thieves' attack on Notre Dame, Quasimodo dies in Esmeralda's arms in the mass grave for criminals at Montfaucon, and Pierre Gringoire turns to writing tragedy.

Esmeralda saves Pierre and Quasimodo, is in turn saved, and becomes a victim; she is also explicitly compared to the Virgin Mary several times. Pierre Gringoire tells Claude Frollo that the entire "tribe" of thieves and gypsies "la tient en vénération singulière, comme une notre-Dame" [holds her in a singular veneration, like a Madonna].[11] Claude recites the names of venerable women, but despite himself, the gypsy's name creeps into the list by association: "la Maria, la Sophia, la Esmeral . . ." (*Notre-Dame* 686). In the climactic confrontation between Claude and Esmeralda, at the foot of the permanent scaffold in the place de Grève, the girl is described as "une sainte Vierge au pied de la croix" [a holy Virgin at the foot of the cross] (836).

While Esmeralda is a metaphoric Virgin Mary, she is also a love object, to various degrees of desire and sincerity, for virtually all the men in the text: Pierre Gringoire, Claude Frollo, Phoebus de Châteaupers, and Quasimodo. In the hunchback's heart, the gypsy rivals and replaces a different Mary—the great church bell with which Quasimodo has a psychosexual relationship (602–3) and has fondly named Marie: "Marie avait une rivale dans le coeur du sonneur de Notre-Dame" [Marie had a rival for the heart of the bell ringer of Notre Dame] (680).

The heroine of *Notre-Dame de Paris* is also a Mary, and like the Marys in *The Ambassadors,* she is at different times a savior and in need of a savior, and also a victim of the scaffold, but the similarities of James's Marys to Hugo's Esmeralda are not just coincidental; *The Ambassadors* makes an explicit connection. When Strether notices Marie de Vionnet at Notre Dame, but before he recognizes her, "[s]he reminded our friend . . . of some fine firm concentrated heroine of an old story, something he had heard, read" (*Amb.* 172). The very next paragraph implies which "fine firm concentrated heroine," which "old story" Strether must have been thinking of by mentioning Strether's purchase of Hugo's complete works. Thus Strether has reduced Mme. de Vionnet "to the convenient terms of Victor Hugo," he has transformed her into Esmeralda; he is in the building from which Hugo's novel takes its title, he perceives a lady and imagines her to be the heroine of a romance, of something he had "read," or perhaps just bought, like Hugo's complete works, which he thinks of next. After that, he recognizes that the lady is Mme. de Vionnet, and finally he speaks to her specifically of *Notre-Dame de Paris* ("He had spoken of the great romancer and the great romance" [*Amb.* 174]).

Like *The Ambassadors,* *Notre-Dame de Paris* is a text in which each Mary is both savior and victim: the cathedral—"Notre Dame" or "Our Lady," that is, the Virgin Mary—in Hugo's novel is a refuge but it is also besieged, ironically, in order to save Esmeralda; and the gypsy girl, herself a "notre-dame," both saves and is saved before becoming a victim, too. The allusion to this novel in *The Ambassadors* is a means of confirming this same duality of saviors and victims, of women not as both Mary and Eve, or Madonna and Magdalene, but as both Mary Stuart and the Virgin Mary. If there are two characters named Mary in *The Ambassadors,* it is to serve as a literal reminder that there are two types of Mary and that both Marie and Maria fill either role—indeed both roles.

The length of *The Ambassadors* means that the intertwining of the dual use of the name Mary, of the metaphor of salvation, and of the scaffold motif evolves during the reading. The Mary Stuart–Virgin Mary opposition, for example, is first cast in terms of the two queens: Mary and her cousin Elizabeth, and then in terms of Mary the queen and Mary the Virgin

Mother. Because of this, these three motifs—Mary, saving, scaffold—constitute a complex metaphorical system or subtext whose development parallels the development and changes of Strether's attitudes and views. The text calls attention to the name Mary by giving it to both Miss Gostrey and Mme. de Vionnet, then suggests several possible metaphorical uses of the name and its various relations not only to the saving and scaffold motifs but also to the novel's overall moral oppositions.

The reader's understanding of this subtext as a whole is inextricably related to the evolution of Strether's understanding of his situation throughout the novel. Since the reader's own "reading" of the novel's events is filtered through the protagonist's point of view, both the literal and the metaphorical readings of those events are colored by the way Strether "reads" them. This is complicated by the fact that it is Strether himself who offers the metaphorical readings: *he* sees Maria as Mary Stuart and Marie as Madame Roland, *he* uses the verb "to save," and *he* sees a "heroine" when he notices Mme. de Vionnet at Notre Dame.

When *The Ambassadors* first alludes to Mary Stuart, in the passage from the London dinner quoted earlier, Strether opposes her not to the Virgin Mary but to Queen Elizabeth (43). There are several similarities between the Virgin Mother and the virgin queen (not only is chastity a common trait but Queen Elizabeth, as she is depicted in *The Fairie Queene,* for example, is a national savior, and thus a figure of salvation) in the context of *The Ambassadors,* but this is not apparent until later. For the moment, there is no Virgin Mary–Mary Stuart, savior-victim antithesis, only that of Queen Elizabeth–Mary, Queen of Scots. In history, the two queens were opposed by virtue of their different religions: Elizabeth was the Protestant queen, Mary the Catholic pretender. Their sexual reputations were also diametrically opposed: Raleigh named the colony of Virginia after Elizabeth, while Mary was married several times, had many lovers, and lost her Scottish throne when her marriage to Bothwell (the supposed murderer of her previous husband, Darnley) provoked a revolt in 1567.[12]

By metaphorically representing Mrs. Newsome and Miss Gostrey to himself as Queen Elizabeth and Mary Stuart, Strether pigeonholes these two ladies within the moral opposites of a simplistic American-European dichotomy. Europe and Catholic have already been linked in the passage where Strether imagines Waymarsh must take Miss Gostrey for "a Jesuit in petticoats" as she guides the two American men on their visit to the Rows at Chester (38); their opposites, America and Protestant, are therefore linked, too. Strether's comparison at the pretheater dinner table connects Europe, Mary Stuart, and Miss Gostrey—with her "dress . . . 'cut down' . . . in respect to shoulders and bosom" (42), her red velvet ribbon, and the thrill she provides as sharer in the forbidden pleasure of the tête-à-tête dinner (as the similar scene at the Tour d'Argent will later link Mme. de Vionnet and Paris to Europe and all it represents)—and America, Queen Elizabeth, and Mrs. Newsome—with her prudish "ruff and other matters" (43). In a more general sense, the comparison associates sensual epicureanism with Europe and Paris, and Puritan asceticism with America and Woollett, but that is as far as the reader can take the Mary-Elizabeth contrast for the moment.[13]

The second paragraph of *The Ambassadors* concludes with a warning by the narrator: "He was burdened, poor Strether—it had better be confessed at the outset—with the oddity of a double consciousness. There was detachment in his zeal and curiosity in his indifference" (*Amb.* 18). In the context of the novel as a whole, this means that Strether is susceptible, at least to some extent, to the claims of both the "Woollett" and the "Paris" moral systems and all that is associated with them.[14] As Sallie Sears has put it,[15] Strether's "attitude toward his mission" has three phases and "undergoes two major shifts," each of which involves a readjustment of the relative claims represented by the Americans and the Europeans. In the first phase, Strether "is fully primed with the Woollett concept":[16] he believes that the woman who has supposedly entangled Chad is not, as Sarah Pocock later implies, "even an apology for a decent woman" (278), and that Chad should immediately "return straight home."[17] The first shift comes after Strether finally sees Chad, realizes how much he has changed for the better, and meets Mme. de Vionnet, "who, a little to his disappointment, has nothing about her of the tart he had expected."[18]

In the second phase, Strether reconciles the attractiveness he now sees in the couple to his New England morality by convincing himself of his theory of the "virtuous" attachment, and this serves as his reason for urging Chad to stay with Mme. de Vionnet. The second shift occurs at the Cheval Blanc in the Lambinet scene, when he encounters Chad and Mme. de Vionnet in their boat and realizes "that their attachment is *not* 'virtuous,' that it is sexual, and that he has been deceived."[19] In the final phase, Strether still insists that Chad remain in Paris, but now his reason is duty, the same argument that Puritans use to urge a particular mode of behavior, for example, in James's *The Europeans.* Chad must stay with Mme. de Vionnet because of all she has done for him, because she "has aided him so . . . sacrificed so much for him, and . . . loves him so."[20] "You owe her everything—very much more than she can ever owe you. You've in other words duties to her, of the most positive sort; and I don't see what other duties—as the others are presented to you—can be held to go before them" (*Amb.* 338).[21] These phases and shifts show Strether facing, constructing, and evolving moral oppositions and ethical dilemmas. As these oppositions evolve, so do their textual correlative, the motifs and literary references.

As long as Strether is in the first of the phases Sears describes, when he is "fully primed with the Woollett concept,"[22] the Mary Stuart–Queen Elizabeth dichotomy is easy for him to use. It means that everything fits neatly into one or the other moral extreme and that Strether will have scruples about dining and going to the theater with Maria (*Amb.* 52) and visiting Marie (141–44), for they are Mary Stuarts. But after the first shift in attitude, the opposition ceases to work because Strether realizes that both women are Virgin Marys (saving Marys). This is why Strether must meet first Maria and then Marie: while there is literally only one Mary, metaphorically there is also only one, Mary Stuart, and the only opposition is between her sensuality and Queen Elizabeth's modesty. When there are actually two Marys in the text, the second figurative Mary appears, and the antitheses become more complicated.

After observing Chad's transformation and getting to know Mme. de Vionnet, Strether sees that Marie has "saved" the young man. On the metaphorical level, this corresponds to Marie's no longer being the sensual Mary Stuart and becoming instead the saving Virgin Mary. But in the self-deception of this second phase, of his "virtuous" attachment theory, Strether ignores just as much as before that Marie still is *both* Marys, just as she always has been (and as Maria has). In this manner, Strether sets himself up for his disillusionment in the Cheval Blanc encounter; there he is confronted with the sexuality in Chad's and Marie's attachment, which is to say he is reminded that Marie is also Mary Stuart (which is why she makes him think of the analogous Madame Roland, a sacrificed Mary without the sexual overtones, when he sees her immediately after).

While during the second phase of the development of his attitude Strether forgets that Marie and Maria can be Mary Stuart, the reader does not, for two reasons. I have already mentioned the scene where Waymarsh prepares Strether for his confrontation with Sarah and the proximity in that scene of both Strether's notion that Chad's sister and the lawyer might have "united to save him" (267) and his thought of the scaffold (269). One function of this juxtaposition is to keep the scaffold, and therefore Mary Stuart, in mind within the pervasiveness of all the various projects for salvation. At the same time, because Mary Stuart is associated with both sensuality and capital punishment, the emphasis here on the scaffold is also the text's way of paralleling Strether's obscuring of the issue of sensuality; as he forgets about the sensual side of Mary Stuart, the text reminds the reader of her scaffold side. When Strether encounters the second Marie, Mme. de Vionnet, and realizes she has "saved" Chad and is not "base, venal—out of the streets" (45), the Queen Elizabeth–Mary Stuart opposition is displaced by the motif of salvation and the figurative sense of savior for the name Mary.

Strether jumps from one excessive view to another. Because so many of the characters in the text need salvation even as they try to save someone else, however, the reader still remembers Mary Stuart, but now as the famous victim, as someone in need of salvation. After the conversation between Strether and Little Bilham about just who is to save whom ("she has saved him . . . that was what *you* were to do. . . . It strikes you . . . for you all to save *her*" [*Amb.* 167–68]), potential victims and saviors are inextricably associated. As a result, the antithesis between Mary Stuart and Queen Elizabeth is displaced not just by the new sense of the significance of the name Mary but also by the new opposition of the Virgin Mary and Mary Stuart— but Mary Stuart now as victim.

The second reason Mary Stuart is not forgotten is the reference to *Notre-Dame de Paris,* because Hugo's text unites victim and savior in one, just as *The Ambassadors* does. However, in the person of Esmeralda, *Notre-Dame de Paris* also unites victim and savior to sensuality—Esmeralda becomes a victim, requires saving, and is temporarily saved because she is an object of desire—the attribute that, in contrast to Queen Elizabeth's and Mrs. Newsome's modesty, suggests Strether's comparison of Miss Gostrey to Mary Stuart in the first place. Both the literal presence and the constant menace of the gallows in Hugo's romance are so pervasive that the reference to *Notre-Dame de Paris* at this point in *The Ambassadors* when the Virgin Mary and the motif of salvation are preeminent is an effective reminder to James's reader of the continued presence of the scaffold motif and Mary Stuart. Since Esmeralda is such an attractive object of desire, in addition to being a savior and a victim, the reference to *Notre-Dame de Paris* has the further effect of signaling the continued presence of sexuality in James's text at a moment when Strether has obscured it.

Because Notre Dame in Hugo's text is an asylum, the allusion in James's text supports Strether's sense of the cathedral as a place of relief. The reference, however, is also an indication of Strether's tendency to romanticize and, specifically in this episode, to cast Mme. de Vionnet as the heroine of a romance.[23] On the one hand, it is precisely this that now allows Strether to take "saving" Marie seriously: because she is an innocent heroine and not "base" and "venal," because she has so much the air of a possible victim rather than that of a femme fatale, she can and should be saved. On the other hand, romanticizing is a sign of the limits of "Strether's reading of such matters," an indication that Strether is seeing only one side of the picture. He requires the enlightenment of the book's other "famous recognition scene"—the Cheval Blanc meeting, which the Notre Dame encounter "clearly anticipates"[24]—before he sees both sides of things, both sensuality and virtue. The reader already can do so because of the allusion to Hugo's novel.

In sum, the two Marys and the related network of moral and metaphoric oppositions are important conveyors of significance in *The Ambassadors*. With the references to Major Pendennis eating breakfast, the novel begins by establishing a father-figure-redeeming-prodigal-son situation. And as is the case in this situation, the search of James's father figure for the prodigal child leads the older man to lose his illusions about the world he is represented as living in and to develop a newer and more complete understanding of it. It is true that Thackeray's *Pendennis* is in some respects different from the conventional norm, for it leaves out the father figure's loss of innocence: the text concentrates instead on young Arthur's development, and Major Pendennis, the elder relative called upon to save his nephew, is a relatively flat character who does not undergo a loss of innocence or a gain of knowledge.

This is why *The Ambassadors* includes the references to *The Vicar of Wakefield* and why the references to Major Pendennis breakfasting suggest *The Newcomes* as well as *Pendennis,* since the benevolent father in Thackeray's later novel is a much better example of the innocent older man who comes to the big city. It is also worth pointing out that Madame d'Ivry, the unscrupulous femme fatale in *The Newcomes,* is frequently called "Mary Queen of Scots"[25] and is even contrasted to the old dowager Lady Kew, who tyrannizes her daughters and grandchildren and refers to herself as Queen Elizabeth.[26]

When Strether realizes that Mme. de Vionnet is not "base" and "venal" and reverses his "mission" to bring Chad home, *The Ambassadors* appears to cease to follow the lines of the father-and-prodigal type. Still, the required loss of innocence does occur,[27] for James's text does provide for the father figure's eyes being opened. That is why *The Vicar of Wakefield* is mentioned, for just as Dr. Primrose's perceptions of the two Thornhill men are reversed, so are Strether's perceptions of the world he lives in, though while what Primrose learns is that appearances can be deceiving, the reality that Strether is represented as perceiving is shown to be too complex for simplistic moral worldviews.

In a story like *The Vicar of Wakefield,* the naïve father figure awakens to the fact that apparently good people can harbor evil intentions, an awakening or loss of innocence that involves a lesson in people's often evil nature and the difference between appearance and reality. In many respects, the "awakening" of James's protagonist in *The Ambassadors* follows this pattern. However, Strether's eyes are not so much opened to a truer reality that underlies false appearances—much as that appears to occur at the Cheval Blanc, when Strether is unexpectedly confronted with the inescapable fact that Chad and Mme. de Vionnet's relationship has its carnal side—but rather to a fuller sense of what it means to have a "double consciousness" (*Amb.* 18), that is, to a more complete understanding that reality, as it is represented in this text, is a paradoxical network of polarities, that everything contains both its essence and its opposite.[28]

The knowledge that is gained when the conventional father's innocence is lost can usually be distilled to a simple moral, such as that superficial appearances are deceiving, for the people one thought one could trust were really the most deceitful. *The Ambassadors* is different because its emphasis is so much less on the moral lesson and so much more on the representation of the central character's efforts to understand and on the series of reversals his ability to comprehend takes him through.[29] Furthermore, while James's text focuses more on the process of the gaining of the knowledge rather than on the revelation itself, the knowledge that Strether arrives at cannot be reduced to a simplistic cautionary lesson but is, rather, a complex view of the world and of the people who inhabit it. One more literary reference, to Balzac's *Louis Lambert,* plays a crucial role in indicating to the reader how to understand the complexity of the reality *The Ambassadors* presents and the role of sexuality in that reality.

The problem Strether has during most of *The Ambassadors* is that he consciously grasps only one side of the polarity at one time, and to understand one element of a polarity requires a concentration and emphasis on it (and thus a natural deemphasis of the opposite element). This is the case both before and after Strether's "first shift," as Sears calls it.[30] As long as he subscribes more or less to the morality of Woollett and is therefore prepared to see women like Marie as "base" and "venal," he is more aware of sensuality and less likely to notice other characteristics, although because of his "double consciousness" his view is never as narrow as, for example, Sarah Pocock's. After the "first shift," Strether's tendency is to ignore sensuality and notice other virtues. Neither way of seeing things is "wrong," since both the sensuality and the virtues are there; but each view is incomplete.

With his tendency to see things metaphorically, to romanticize his situation, Strether is represented as choosing simplistic literary models to supplement his incomplete views: according to "the Woollett concept," Strether should find Chad immersed in a morality tale; after his shift, when he watches her at Notre Dame, Strether transforms Mme. de Vionnet into the unjustly suspected heroine of a Gothic romance. Either "reading" is an oversimplification; the only correct way for Strether to "read" the situation is as a complex Henry James novel of manners.

Another example of Strether's transformation of Mme. de Vionnet into a romantic heroine occurs when Strether lets his imagination turn her apartment into a Romantic literary salon: "the world he vaguely thought of as the world of Chateaubriand, of Madame de Staël, even of the young Lamartine, had left its stamp of harps and urns and torches, a stamp impressed on sundry small objects, ornaments and relics" (*Amb*. 145). Similarly, he sees her at Chad's reception as a dramatic heroine: "Above all she suggested to him the reflexion that the *femme du monde*—in these finest developments of the type—was, like Cleopatra in the play" (160). This last passage, with its evocation of "Cleopatra *in the play*," relates to another ongoing and highly significant motif that runs throughout *The Ambassadors*, the play within the play.

Several episodes in the novel are presented as though they were theater. There are two significant scenes set at a theater. The first is in a London theater, where Strether blurs the distinction between the audience and the actors and between the drama unfolding on the stage and the one in which he himself has become involved, mixing up the drama of "a bad woman in a yellow frock who made a pleasant weak good-looking young man in perpetual evening dress do the most dreadful things" (44) with his vision of Chad's situation in Paris. The second scene occurs at the Comédie Française, where at the end of the intermission, the curtain rises not for the entrance of an actor onto the stage but for Chad's unquestionably dramatic entrance into the box shared by Strether, Maria Gostrey, and Waymarsh. If Strether's thoughts at the first theater scene, in London, blurred the distinction between actors and audience, between the action of the play within the play (or within the novel, rather) and that of the novel, the actors and the play within the play give way entirely to the intrigue of *The Ambassadors* itself in the second scene, at the Comédie Française.

In both theater scenes, the role Strether allots himself is largely that of a spectator. His own part in the "romances" and "dramas" he invents, though hinted at all along, becomes clearer later in the novel. In the passage at Sarah Pocock's hotel, following the Pococks' arrival in Paris, Strether takes an active role in playacting for the first time. Mme. de Vionnet is using all the charm she can muster to manipulate Sarah to promise to visit her and to bring Mamie to meet her daughter. The text presents this maneuvering as a comical theatrical performance with Marie as its director and leading lady, and the others in supporting roles. The word "perform" or "performance" appears at least five times in the scene: "they were arranged, gathered for a performance, the performance of 'Europe' . . . the performance could only go on," and Strether wonders "at the odd part he found thus imposed on him" (225–27).

Other passages also remind the reader of Strether's romanticizing and the play within the play: Strether calls Mme. de Vionnet "the heroine" (266), and he compliments Chad: " 'You've been "wonderful, wonderful," as we say—we poor people who watch the play from the pit' " (283). However, the most important episode, one in which the characters of the novel participate in a comic performance turned sour, is the climactic scene in which Strether, prompted by the memory of a landscape painting by "Lambinet that had charmed him, long years before, at a Boston dealer's and that he had quite absurdly never forgotten" (301), spends a "rambling day" (305) in the countryside, stopping for dinner at an inn called the Cheval Blanc, which is situated on a riverbank, and encounters Marie and Chad in a situation that proves to Strether the ludicrousness of his "virtuous attachment" theory. The scene is presented as framed by the painting whose memory had inspired the excursion, but that picture frame is transformed into the frame of a theater stage: "For this had been all day at bottom the spell of the picture—that it was essentially more than anything else a scene and a stage" (306). On this stage, Madame de Vionnet puts on "a performance" (311) but fails to save the situation with "her comedy" (312).

The next day, after he receives a *pneumatique* begging him to come to Mme. de Vionnet's, Strether becomes completely immersed in the play within the play. He goes to the post office to send confirmation of his visit and, as he prepares his reply, observes the other people there. Whether it is the uniqueness of sending a special-delivery *petit bleu* or simply the atmosphere of the post office itself is not clear,[31] but something there intensifies Strether's impression of the romance of the scene: "There was . . . something in the air of these establishments [the post office]; the vibration of the vast strange life of the town, the influence of the types, the performers concocting their messages" (314–15). "Something in the air" is infectious, for Strether's excitement rises as he realizes that he, too, is one of the "performers":

> He was carrying on a correspondence, across the great city, quite in the key of the *Postes et Télégraphes* in general; . . . He was mixed up with the typical tale of Paris, and so were they, poor things—how could [the other postal patrons] all together help being? (315)

The distinction between actor and audience, between the action of the play and the "reality" of the novel, is now completely erased. Since the theater in London, the characters and the world they are represented as inhabiting in *The Ambassadors* have been transformed into a theatrical drama, and at the same time the protagonist has turned the principal female character into the heroine of a romance to such an extent that he has made himself part of the romance, too.

The conclusion to these theatricizing and romanticizing trends has two parts. On the one hand, the drama motif turns into a recognition of futility, a recognition that is emphasized by Strether's mention of the city of Bern. On the other hand, if Strether's tendency to romanticize leads to his becoming a participant in a "typical tale," it turns out that the tale is not a great Parisian romance but a most un-Parisian one, the tale his given names have indicated from the beginning of the novel, Balzac's *Louis Lambert*.

The final chapter of *The Ambassadors* takes place over lunch at Maria Gostrey's apartment. It is only a few pages long, and the two final pages, with Maria's apparent offer of marriage, Strether's refusal, and his declared intention to return to the United States, make up the part that receives most of the attention from critics. Immediately preceding this, Strether admits to Maria that something about Chad "troubles me." Maria responds with the question "What is it then?" (341). Rather than a direct answer to this question, there is instead this passage:

> He came back to his breakfast; he partook presently of the charming melon, which she liberally cut for him. . . . He remembered everything, . . . falling back above all on the great interest of their early time, the curiosity felt by both of them as to where he would "come out." . . . He found on the spot the image of his recent history; he was like one of the figures of the old clock at Berne. *They* came out, on one side, at their hour, jigged along their little course in the public eye, and went in on the other side. He too had jigged his little course—him too a modest retreat awaited. (341–42)

The paragraph concludes with Maria's suggestion that Chad "may after all go back" to America, and then the dialogue between Strether and Miss Gostrey resumes, the subject now the status of his relationship with his erstwhile fiancée, Mrs. Newsome, and the likelihood of "patch[ing] it up" (343):

> His answer came at last in a conclusive headshake. "There's nothing any one can do. It's over. Over for both of us."
>
> Maria wondered, seemed a little to doubt. "Are you so sure for her?"
>
> "Oh yes—sure now. Too much has happened. I'm different for her."
>
> She took it in then, drawing a deeper breath. "I see. So that as she's different for *you*—"
>
> "Ah but," he interrupted, "she's not." And as Miss Gostrey wondered again: "She's the same. She's more than ever the same. But I do what I didn't before—I *see* her." (343)

This prompts Maria to ask Strether what there is for him to return to in America, and leads to her proposal that he stay with her and his refusal. Before addressing Strether's reasons for rejecting this offer, it is important to consider two points in the above passages, "the image . . . of the figures of the old clock at Berne" and the significance of Strether's being able to "*see*" Mrs. Newsome.

Strether's comparison of himself to the figures of the Bern *Zeitglocken-thurm* (Americans are perhaps more familiar with the somewhat similar timepiece in Munich) is the final instance in the text of the protagonist suggesting his own metaphor for his situation. But now Strether is not imagining a "great romance" à la Hugo (*Amb.* 174) or exotic international fiction—a "typical tale of Paris" (315). Instead, the way he describes both himself and the rotating mechanical figures—"*They* came out, on one side, at their hour, jigged along their little course in the public eye, and went in on the other side. He too had jigged his little course—him too a modest retreat awaited"—expresses futility, something not unlike the famous image of life as "but a walking shadow, a poor player,/That struts and frets his hour upon the stage,/And then is heard no more" in *Macbeth*,[32] but without the same heroic language. Strether's image of himself as one of the mechanical figures from the clock expresses the sense of the futility of his various efforts to accomplish anything for anyone that he had felt after the Cheval Blanc episode: "Verily, verily, his labour had been lost" (*Amb.* 313).[33]

This is the conclusion to the breakdown of the distinction between stage and audience in *The Ambassadors,* of the representation of the drama of the text as actual theatrical drama; the "performance" is not of a romantic melodrama or of a morality play or even of a "typical tale of Paris" full of romantic intrigue but, rather, of a story of despair and failed ambitions. Strether's sojourn in Paris begins with his recollection of his various failures in life: in his first marriage, in fatherhood, "in each relation and in half a dozen trades" (61), and ends with the completion of his newest round of failure. And as he made metaphors, romanticized Mme. de Vionnet, and idealized her relation with Chad, Strether was Macbeth's "idiot" telling his own tale "full of sound and fury."[34]

Strether's emphasized affirmation about Mrs. Newsome, that "I do what I didn't before—I *see* her," is significant because of its relation to his celebrated "Live all you can" speech in Gloriani's garden. In what James called the "germ" of the novel (*LC2* 1305),[35] Strether urges Bilham not to waste his life as he himself has done, but to profit from his example and take advantage of his youth to live life to the utmost.

> It's not too late for *you*, on any side, and you don't strike me as in danger of missing the train; besides which people can be in general pretty well trusted,

of course—with the clock of their freedom ticking as loud as it seems to do here—to keep an eye on the fleeting hour. All the same don't forget that you're young—blessedly young; be glad of it on the contrary and live up to it. Live all you can; it's a mistake not to. It doesn't so much matter what you do in particular, so long as you have your life. If you haven't had that what *have* you had? . . . I haven't done so enough before—and now I'm old; too old at any rate for what I see. Oh I *do* see, at least; and more than you'd believe or I can express. It's too late. And it's as if the train had fairly waited at the station for me without my having had the gumption to know it was there. . . . The affair . . . of life . . . [is] at the best a tin mould, either fluted and embossed, with ornamental excrescences, or else smooth and dreadfully plain, into which, a helpless jelly, one's consciousness is poured—so that one "takes" the form, as the great cook says, and is more or less compactly held by it: one lives in fine as one can. Still, one has the illusion of freedom; therefore don't be, like me, without the memory of that illusion. (*Amb.* 131–32)

The image of having missed the train of life in the speech is in keeping with Strether's many family and career failures, but other parts of the passage are more problematic: Since "it doesn't so much matter what you do in particular," what does it mean to live, to "have your life"? The deterministic image of the mold, either "ornamental" or "dreadfully plain," leads to the resigned conclusion that "one lives in fine as one can," and not to a preference for any particular way of life. This raises a further question: If there is no better or worse way to live, no way that better guarantees having "your life," why does Strether feel that he has not "had" his? Must Strether's belittling of his own life be accepted at face value? Bilham's response to Strether's speech implies quite the contrary, that Strether strikes him as an excellent example of having lived: "Oh but I don't know that I want to be, at your age, too different from you!" (132). Really living, then, is reduced to the importance of having "the illusion of freedom," an illusion of which Strether—with his life as dominated as it seems to have been by Mrs. Newsome—appears to have been deprived.

However, the fact that having "your life" is a matter of having the *illusion* of freedom, and not freedom itself, is problematic.[36] In this text, which represents the process of one character's loss of illusions, can a life be deemed a good one if it is founded on illusion? And how long can an illusion be sustained, at least by characters such as Strether and Bilham? Certainly one of the lessons of the Cheval Blanc episode is that an illusion, such as the theory of the "virtuous attachment," which provides a happy solution to a potentially difficult situation, depends on a narrow view of things, a view that systematically excludes elements that could disrupt the neatness of the happy solution. Finally, the later reference to Madame

Roland questions the value of freedom itself. Since Madame Roland is remembered above all for her famous last words, "O Liberty! What crimes
are committed in your name?" the implication of her final speech—that
freedom, or liberty, has its dark side, its guillotine, too—comments on, and
further undermines, Strether's eulogy of living.

The mention of "the clock of their freedom ticking as loud as it seems
to do here" and of "the fleeting hour" links the "Live all you can" speech
in Gloriani's garden to the image of the figures of the Bern *Zeitglocken-
thurm* jigging "along their little course in the public eye" in Strether's
speech at the end of the novel. In between the two speeches, however,
illusions have been shattered, the value of freedom has been questioned,
and Strether's efforts in any and all directions have proved futile: all he, or
anyone, does is "jig" in the public eye as the "clock" ticks away one's
"fleeting hour." Meanwhile, Bilham has offered another possible way of
understanding life—to equate it to vision. When the artist next speaks to
Strether of the instruction to "live all you can," he uses the verb "to see"
in place of "to live":

> Didn't you adjure me, in accents I shall never forget, to see, while I've a
> chance, everything I can?—and *really* to see, for it must have been that only
> you meant. Well, you did me no end of good, and I'm doing my best. I *do*
> make it out a situation. (165)

Not only does Bilham completely avoid the word "live" and consistently
use "see" where Strether had used "live," but he also gives his own interpretation of the older man's earlier speech—"it must have been that only
you meant." Strether's reply—"So do I!"—could be seen as a sign of his
agreement with Bilham's interpretation of living as seeing and as an affirmation that he, too, had profited from the lesson of his speech in the sculp-
tor's garden; that it was not too late after all; and that despite his age he,
too, was seeing/living. On the other hand, Strether could mean no more
than that he thinks he better understands the particular situation of Chad
and the Vionnet ladies ("I *do* make it out a situation") that formed the
subject of this particular conversation with Bilham. Either way, the text has
raised the question, Does to live fully mean to see fully?

There is one distinctly positive sign at the end of the novel: Strether has
gained at least one thing, he sees Mrs. Newsome now—"I do what I didn't
before—I *see* her." If "see" does indeed mean the same thing as "live" in
The Ambassadors, then the implication of this new ability to "*see*" the ma-
triarch of Woollett is all the greater; it would mean the novel is a moral
lesson that presents Strether traveling abroad and returning to America

having gained something of value—not just the ability to see through his old protector but also a liberation from "the Woollett concept" (Puritan New England morality) she personifies. This would represent a real gain of freedom and would mean that Strether returns to America having learned better how to live. It would mean that *The Ambassadors* represents a world in which breadth of vision and consciousness are valuable qualities. It would also make it simple to resolve the end of *The Ambassadors*.

It would be nice to be able to say that *The Ambassadors* is the story of a man who learns during his trip to Paris to free himself from the restricting moral view that has governed most of his life, that he gains from this important lesson an expanded vision of the world he lives in, and that this liberation from a narrow view of things makes his life fuller and richer. Seen in this light, the significance of the climactic revelation of the Lambinet episode would be that neither the narrow, austere New England morality, which does not try to wish sexuality out of existence but simply transforms it into an evil to be constantly guarded against, nor the idealized belief in "virtuous" intimacy entirely devoid of sexuality alone can make for a fuller vision or enlarged consciousness. Rather, the Cheval Blanc encounter would be a lesson in the natural place of sexuality in a view of society that seeks to understand the world as fully as possible.

Unfortunately, the ending of *The Ambassadors* cannot be resolved in such a neat manner. Because of Strether's refusal of Miss Gostrey at the end of the last chapter, and because of his given names, Lewis Lambert, and the relation to Balzac's *Louis Lambert*, it is not possible to affirm either that Strether has gained a more complete moral view that includes sexuality in its proper place—that sees both sides of the polarity together—or that vision itself, the ability to see, is a purely positive value.

When Strether and Maria meet in the novel's first chapter, he gives the lady his card, and she reads from it: " ' "Mr. Lewis Lambert Strether" '— she sounded it almost as freely as for any stranger. She repeated however that she liked it—'particularly the Lewis Lambert. It's the name of a novel of Balzac's' " (*Amb.* 23). Quentin Anderson has stated that "the name 'Louis [*sic*] Lambert Strether' seems to announce an intention [though] we cannot be sure of this,"[37] but it is impossible to think that Anderson's qualifying "seems" is at all justified and that the explicit allusion to Balzac's novel is gratuitous. The mention of *Louis Lambert* is too explicit to be included without reason; clearly the reader is expected to make a comparison between Balzac's text and James's, and the onus should be on the commentator who ignores—rather than examines—so explicit a reference to justify such a step. Though at first glance *Louis Lambert* is a very different novel from *The Ambassadors* and Balzac's title character seems to have little in common with Lambert Strether, the points of comparison between the two texts and the two protagonists are numerous and striking. Still, only a few commentators on *The Ambassadors* have considered why James's protagonist should be named after Balzac's short novel, and none of them has explored the significance of this naming in much detail.[38]

Balzac's novel traces the life of its metaphysically minded title character through early adolescence at boarding school, where he writes a Swedenborgian-inspired "Treatise on the Will," through his Parisian studies, to his return home, his engagement to the heiress Pauline de Villenoix, and the onset of madness and catalepsy immediately preceding his wedding. The novel concludes with some of the strange sentences that he utters every once in a while and with a quick mention of Louis's early death. While both Strether and Miss Gostrey immediately agree that *Louis Lambert* is "an awfully bad" novel (*Amb.* 24), we do not know why they dislike it. We do know why James himself disliked *Louis Lambert;* he had criticized it in 1877 when he wrote in his review of Balzac's correspondence for the *Galaxy* (included the next year in *French Poets and Novelists*) that " 'Louis Lambert,' as a whole, is now quite unreadable; it contains some admirable descriptions, but the 'scientific' portion is mere fantastic verbiage" (*LC* 2 76). By the " 'scientific' portion" James certainly refers to the involved summaries in Balzac's text of Louis's Swedenborgianism (*Comédie* 11: 616–18) and of the argument of Louis's treatise on the will (11: 622–37), and most likely also to Pauline's notes of Lambert's abstruse sayings (11: 684–91). It is precisely these philosophical passages in which Balzac took pride[39] but that for James were an example of the French novelist's occasional lapses into "self-deceptive charlatanism" (*LC* 2 76).

The irony of James's dislike of the philosophical passages in *Louis Lambert* is that they are the element of Balzac's text that bears the most comparison to *The Ambassadors.* Indeed, James's dislike is perhaps a sign of how pertinent the passages are to his own novel. Lambert's philosophy "attempt[s] to reconcile the seeming antagonism between the material and spiritual sides of man's nature," as James Gargano says;[40] and "[t]his concern with man's dual nature and with the celebration of the inner or spiritual man culminates in Lambert's *Treatise of the Will,* a work inspired by Lambert's trip to a country scene which, he believes, his spirit had already visited while his body slept."[41] The antagonism between the material and the spiritual is played out in a number of passages in *Louis Lambert:* Louis is upset at being reprimanded in school for daydreaming because to him dreaming is part of the life of the mind, which is everything to him (*Comédie* 11: 608); he translates the Latin *vir* (man) as "heart," for the heart, the inside of the man, *is* the man to him (11: 619); and he evolves a Sweden-borgian theory of angels, according to which human nature is divided between the material and the spiritual, the first exterior and the second interior.

The key point, as far as *The Ambassadors* is concerned, in Lambert's philosophy is the relationship between thinking, seeing, and life. Real life starts after the death of the body, but it is not certain to occur; whether or not it does depends on thought and vision. Because thinking is seeing, "Penser, c'est voir!" says Louis (*Comédie* 11: 615), really living depends on both thinking and seeing. Thus "les cinq sens . . . n'en sont qu'un seul, la faculté de voir" [the five senses . . . are really only one, the faculty of seeing] (11: 685).

Lambert's philosophy makes the same connection between living and seeing that Bilham's interpretation of Strether's "Live all you can" speech does (*Amb.* 165). What is more, Lambert's connecting of living, seeing, and thinking helps corroborate a similar relationship of the three faculties—living, seeing, thinking—in *The Ambassadors* that is implied by Bilham's "I *do* make it out a situation" and Strether's "So do I!" (165). The effect of Bilham's speech is to show how much he took to heart the advice Strether gave in Gloriani's garden and how much he intends to follow it: "Well, you did me no end of good, and I'm doing my best" (165). In adding "I *do* make it out a situation" in order to say, "Look how much I've followed your advice and how much good it has done me," Bilham has changed the terms from "Look how well I am living" to "Look how well I am seeing."

Furthermore, when Strether adds "So do I," vision is turned into *inner* vision, for what Strether claims to "make out" is precisely what is visible not to the eye but to the mind, the nature of people's relationships. It is true that Lambert's inner vision differs from Strether's and Bilham's ability to "make it out a situation"; Lambert directs his gaze into his own self, whereas James's characters seek to understand the motivations of others. Nevertheless, Strether's success at "seeing" the invisible in the nature of his acquaintances' relationships depends on self-knowledge, on his ability to see through the illusions he unconsciously invents for himself. Thus *really* seeing is a matter of the inner or intellectual life, which leads to the same conclusion as Lambert's Swedenborgianism: that really living is a matter of cultivating the intellect and inner vision. Balzac's protagonist is a metaphor for James's: both men seek to understand the invisible—metaphysics for Louis Lambert and the hidden truth about human relationships for Strether.

The other significant parallel between the two Lamberts lies in their similar responses to sexual desire. While pursuing his studies in Paris, Lambert is particularly moved by the sight of a beautiful young woman at the theater, an encounter that serves as a preview of the intensity of his later passion for Pauline and significantly foreshadows Strether's response to sexuality:

> La vue de cette femme, jeune et belle, bien mise, décolletée peut-être . . . produisit sur l'âme et sur les sens de Lambert un effet si cruel qu'il fut obligé de sortir de la salle. . . . [P]eut-être aurait-il succombé au désir presque invincible qu'il ressentit alors de tuer le jeune homme auquel s'adressaient les regards de cette femme. N'était-ce pas . . . un éclair de l'amour du Sauvage qui se jette sur la femme comme sur sa proie, un effet d'instinct bestial joint à la rapidité des jets presque lumineux d'une âme comprimée sous la masse de ses pensées?

> [The sight of this woman, who was young and beautiful, well dressed, possibly with a low-cut neckline . . . had so cruel an effect on Lambert's soul and on his senses that he had to leave the hall. . . . (M)aybe he would have given in to the almost invincible desire he then felt to murder the young man who was the object of this young lady's glances. Wasn't this . . . a flash of the love of the Savage who throws himself on a woman as he does on his prey, an effect of a bestial instinct joined with the speed of the almost luminous gushing forth of a soul compressed under the mass of its thoughts?] (*Comédie* 11: 645)

Louis's response to the woman in the theater foreshadows his problems with his eventual fiancée. When Louis Lambert meets Pauline, he immediately recognizes her as the Swedenborgian woman-angel of his dreams, but if the engagement of the young couple promises to realize Lambert's fantasy of pure love, it also promises to realize the sharp desire Louis felt in the theater at the sight of the unnamed young woman. During a walk he refuses to hold Pauline's hand because, as he later admits, he did not know "où m'aurait conduit la violence de mes désirs" [where the violence of my desires would have led me] (*Comédie* 11: 675); he lapses into madness on the eve of his wedding; and after the first cataleptic attack passed, Louis's uncle "le surpri[t] heureusement au moment où il allait pratiquer sur lui-même l'opération à laquelle Origène crut devoir son talent" [fortunately surprised him at the moment when he was about to perform the same operation on himself that Origen believed he owed his talent to] (11: 679).

As Gargano says, "Lambert's pursuit of the ideal is . . . endangered [at the theater] by his experiencing a strong sexual passion";[42] it is a classic case of repressed desire making itself felt. In the theater, Lambert ran away from what provoked his desire, but he was really running away from the desire itself, from the latent bestiality in him (as in any person) that all the metaphysics in the world could not eliminate. Louis's fall into madness is another form of running away from the "Savage," the desiring beast in him. As Gargano says, Lambert's madness is an "escape into an ethereal region where sex does not exist";[43] or, as Tintner puts it, it is the result of "Louis Lambert's *physical* incapacity to tolerate *human* happiness."[44]

Most significant to our understanding of *The Ambassadors* is Louis's attempted self-castration and the reference to Origen. Like Balzac's hero, Origen wrote a treatise and was a visionary and a spiritualist; he practiced allegorical readings of Scripture almost two centuries before Augustine. Like Lambert, Origen, according to the nineteenth-century view, was severely afflicted by temptations, and this is believed to have been what drove him to his famous act of self-mutilation.[45] Balzac's reader is meant to understand Louis Lambert's attempt at self-castration as the young man's effort to escape the same temptations and return to the same sort of predominantly spiritual life Origen led. In both Louis's and Origen's cases, sexual temptation and spiritual insight—the ability to see—are diametrically opposed. Thus, in *Louis Lambert,* the problem of sexuality is related to the metaphysical inner life.

Louis Lambert offers the parallel to *The Ambassadors* of seeing, thinking, and the inner life as life itself, and serves as a *mise en abîme* for a principal concern in both texts: the opposition between the physical and the spiritual and the role of sexuality in that opposition. The metaphysical idealism of Balzac's hero has its parallel in Strether's romantic idealism, and both men at first fit love into their naïve systems in similar ways: the idealization of love (the "woman-angel") in Lambert's case and the belief in the "virtuous attachment" in Strether's. When confronted with the existence of his own latent sexual desire, Louis Lambert's complex response foreshadows Strether's similar reluctance to assimilate the claims of sexuality into his understanding of the world in which he lives. Since *The Ambassadors* never offers Strether's inner thoughts on sexuality, other than the monologue after the encounter at the Cheval Blanc, the parallels between the two protagonists enable the reader to understand Strether's attitude more clearly. When Louis Lambert is seen as a metaphor for Lambert Strether, it is possible to see in Louis's reaction to the woman in the theater and his attempted self-castration on the eve of his nuptials an unequivocal sign of Strether's own response.

Considering the points of comparison between the two protagonists is most valuable to resolving the ending of *The Ambassadors*, an ending that has caused a range of disagreement. Tintner understands Strether's refusal of Miss Gostrey at the end of *The Ambassadors* as an indication of the same sort of problem with sexuality in Strether as in Louis Lambert:

Perhaps, too, Strether's inability to handle a real love affair with a willing woman like Miss Gostrey reflects Louis Lambert's physical incapacity to tolerate human happiness. Strether, though, does not escape through death as did his namesake, but through a transatlantic crossing and a return to his native habitat. Perhaps the war in Strether's personality between his Puritan inheritance and what his Parisian education taught him late in life was symbolically signaled by his parents when they named him after a hero who could cope only with the life of the mind.[46]

Many commentators agree with Tintner's implication in this passage that Strether's refusal of Maria and his return to America indicate his failure to learn and gain from his stay in Paris. Others, such as Gargano, argue that Strether has indeed assimilated the lessons of Paris and returns to America somehow better off (which means that they have to find some explanation for the rejection of Maria).[47] While, as Gargano says, "Strether resembles Lambert in being guided by an idealism which so exalts the spiritual that it denies the existence of the physical"—as when James's protagonist "too readily accept[s] Little Bilham's gentlemanly lie, that Chad's attachment to Madame de Vionnet is a 'virtuous' one"—in the end, "he ultimately achieves a knowledge which recognizes the validity of spiritual values without denying the existence of man's earthy and physical nature."[48]

Gargano recognizes that Strether does not entirely escape from any acknowledgment of the existence of sexuality, "into an ethereal region where sex does not exist,"[49] which is what Tintner suggests. On the other hand, there is no definite sign of Strether's achieving the more complete "knowledge which recognizes the validity of spiritual values without denying the existence of man's earthy and physical nature" that Gargano claims for him.[50] What is certain is that after the revelation of the Lambinet episode, Strether introduces himself into a romantic "typical tale of Paris" and feels for once the attraction of Maria Gostrey's home (*Amb.* 340–41, 344), but this is the closest he comes to recognizing "the existence of man's earthy and physical nature" in himself. The same logic that dictated that Chad should not return to America because Marie deserved a better reward for having "turned a man out so wonderfully" (169) holds true for Maria Gostrey and Strether, for "She had decked him out for others," too (196); but Strether returns to America all the same.

Strether's departure from Europe—like his refusal of Maria in the last chapter—signals that he is still unable to come fully to terms with sexuality. He flees Paris and Maria as if he were fleeing from temptation: "what stood about him there in her offer . . . might well have tempted" (*Amb.* 344). Strether's justification for refusing, " 'That, you see, is my only logic. Not, out of the whole affair, to have got anything for myself' " (344), is his refusal to have any desire for himself. All that he has clearly gained from his stay in Paris is to "see" Mrs. Newsome—in other words, to understand that the idealistically righteous morality of the "Woollett concept" that Mrs. Newsome personifies is an inherently incomplete representation of reality—but it is not clear whether that is a sign that he is better off in other respects. This is how Gargano sums up Strether's evolution in *The Ambassadors:* "James . . . presents the idea-ridden Strether . . . as a deluded romanticist who must be compelled to recognize the complexity of reality before he can become the 'complete man' Miss Gostrey finally pronounces him."[51] But Strether has not become a "complete man"; he understands the world he lives in better—his consciousness is complete—but he is not a more complete *man,* for he does not actively desire.

At the same time, Strether is repulsed by sexuality. That is why, even after the encounter at the Cheval Blanc, he gives the romantic gloss of the "typical tale of Paris" to his final meeting with Mme. de Vionnet. However, even this illusion is not allowed to last; when she breaks down in tears, he sees that the whole affair could just as easily be seen in a less romantic light: "he could see her there as vulgarly troubled, in very truth, as a maidservant crying for her young man" (*Amb.* 323).[52] At this point, Strether has become like his namesake immediately before his wedding; he no longer tries to idealize sexual desire out of existence, but as much as he is attracted to both Marie and Maria, he is also afraid of and repulsed by the attraction.

Paul Rosenzweig argues that Strether has learned to appreciate sexuality: his interest in Maria's melons in the final chapter is in fact associated with his interest in her décolleté at their first meal together, before the theater in London; and his hearty eating of the "small ripe round melon" (*Amb.* 341) is a sign of his giving himself over to sexuality without actually indulging.[53] Rosenzweig sees in this evidence for a positive interpretation of the end of *The Ambassadors:* Strether metaphorically indulges in sex and then returns to America the better for it. In fact, Strether, in returning to America, refuses Maria's offer to continue to indulge; in other words, his response is again twofold: he indulges with pleasure and then flees. Indeed, in leaving for America, he flees his own desire just as Balzac's Lambert at the theater flees his own desire for the beautiful woman in the neighboring box. Thus the end of *The Ambassadors* shows Strether fulfilling the destiny that is implicit in his given names; metaphorically speaking, he, too, tries to castrate himself—he, too, tries to perform the same operation on himself that Origen believed he owed his talent to, just like Louis Lambert.

The complexity with which sexuality can be viewed in *The Ambassadors* is paralleled in the variety of meanings a single word, like "bad," can have. We recall Strether's and Maria Gostrey's negative evaluation of *Louis Lambert* as "awfully bad" (*Amb.* 24). Although we know why James thought Balzac's was a "bad" novel, there is no clue as to why James's characters disapproved of it. However, the word "bad" takes several meanings in *The Ambassadors,* and Maria's and Strether's agreement that *Louis Lambert* is "awfully bad" amounts to more than a simple interpolation of one of James's personal tastes:

> ". . . Lewis Lambert. It's the name of a novel of Balzac's."
> "Oh I know that!" said Strether.
> "But the novel's an awfully bad one."
> "I know that too," Strether smiled. (23–24)

The second "I know that" echoes the first and inaugurates a pattern of repetition that appears in the two other significant instances of the use of the word "bad." When Chad tries to convince Strether to visit Mme. de Vionnet, the conversation ends with the older man's question:

> "Excuse me, but I must really—as I began by telling you—know where I am. Is she bad?"
> " 'Bad'?"—Chad echoed it, but without a shock. "Is that what's implied—"
> "When relations are good?" (144)

In James's personal view of *Louis Lambert* as a bad novel, "bad" means "of poor quality." In the conversation about *Louis Lambert,* Strether and Maria presumably use "bad" in the same sense, although either or both could be understood as using "bad" as it often was in the nineteenth century in relation to French novels. In Chad and Strether's dialogue, though, "bad" in Strether's reference to Mme. de Vionnet means "of easy virtue," just as it does in reference to the "bad woman in a yellow frock" in the play in London (*Amb.* 44). Chad's repetition of "bad" suggests the possibility of more than one meaning to the word, for now there are not only literally two "bad"s on the page but also two meanings of the word in the novel— poor quality and morally reprehensible. Furthermore, Strether's completion of Chad's unfinished question is the first indication that "bad" can also have self-contradictory meanings: a woman is "bad" if she has a "good" relation.

"Bad" is echoed another time, and with even greater equivocation, during a conversation between Strether and Bilham. The young artist is telling his elder friend of how Chad and Mme. de Vionnet met:

"I mean that they first met somehow and somewhere—I believe in some American house—and she, without in the least then intending it, made her impression. Then with time and opportunity he made his; and after *that* she was as bad as he."

Strether vaguely took it up. "As 'bad'?"

"She began, that is, to care—to care very much. . . ." (167)

Bilham uses "bad" here in the sense of "badly gone on someone," but Strether fails at first to understand it that way, as his puzzled question, "As 'bad'?" indicates.

Each of the conversations with Chad and with Bilham teaches that "bad" can mean something good: caring about someone else and having a good relation. The compounding of meanings of this word to the point where it can even mean its opposite is yet another microcosm of the lesson *The Ambassadors* really teaches: that things are not only more than they seem to be, but that in fact they include a contradictory or negating element. Mary is both Mary Stuart and the Madonna at the same time, virtuous attachments involve sex, and there is "good" in "bad." In both of the conversations about Mme. de Vionnet, Strether uses "bad" to mean morally reprehensible, and this gives rise to the equivocations on the word. These conversations present Strether with other possible meanings of "bad" at the same time they suggest that an adulterous relationship can be understood in ways other than Woollett's.

The two ways of reading "bad," as with the two ways of reading "Mary," are paradigmatic of what Strether really learns to "see" in *The Ambassadors:* the paradoxical, heterogeneous nature of reality that James's text presents. Everything can be viewed in a number of ways; the single-minded characters like Sarah Pocock who fail to see this are scarcely better than fools. Those who gain insight into the limits of simplistic, black-and-white moral systems and into the paradoxical, dual nature of reality are rendered impotent by their knowledge. As in the legend of Origen, Strether's gain in insight comes at the cost of his metaphorical castration.

Strether and Bilham are the two characters who claim to have learned to see, but the younger man never does anything but allow himself to be carried off to Switzerland (the land of neutrality) by the Pococks. Strether performs upon himself, metaphorically speaking, the same operation Origen believed he owed his powers to. From such a castration, Strether gains the power—and this is a very questionable gain—to see the clock at Bern as a model for human life. The bear statuettes—reproductions of live bears—on the clock, which every hour revolve in and out of the building that houses the clock, and so please the crowds of tourists and strollers, have at least the "illusion of freedom." But that, too, has its other side in the other great tourist attraction of Bern, the bear pits at the other end of the same street as the *Zeitglockenthurm*, where real bears *live* the most futile lives possible: in total captivity and devoid of any illusion of freedom whatsoever.

Like all the father figures in the "prodigal child" type stories, Strether does leave Babylon with a more complete understanding of the world and society in which he is shown to live. He does see relationships between people in a way that does far more justice to their complexity, but what he gains from that is the understanding symbolized by the Bern bears and his mention of the clock, and it is questionable whether that is truly a positive gain. That is why *The Ambassadors* ends "all comically, all tragically" (345).

The allusions to *Pendennis* and *The Vicar of Wakefield* indicate the trope of the father figure and cast Strether in that role. Since the father figure always departs naïve about the ways of the world and returns much the wiser from his travel (it is conventional in all "journey" narratives since *The Odyssey* that the traveler gains new knowledge of the world before his return), this intertext helps determine the reader's interpretation of the end of *The Ambassadors*. If Strether fits the part in its initial premise—that of the father figure searching in Babylon for the prodigal—then he also fits its conclusion; his illusions have been burst, and he returns to America with new and valuable knowledge about the world he is shown to live in.

At the same time, the Hugo allusion helps show what Strether learns by bringing the reader to terms with the motifs of Mary Stuart and the Virgin Mary, which in turn are a model for the oppositional—or polarized, to use Richard Hocks's term—nature of the world presented in *The Ambassadors*. The opposition between saving and sacrifice and the role of sexuality in *Notre-Dame de Paris* not only are pertinent to *The Ambassadors* but also are referred to by the placement of the allusion to Hugo in the Notre Dame episode. Furthermore, because Strether's fantasy about Marie as a romantic heroine before he recognizes her occurs at the same time as the allusion to Hugo's romance, the polarities of salvation and sacrifice and of Mary as virgin and sexual being are juxtaposed against Strether's tendency to romanticize, and thus are seen as inextricably related to the equally unresolvable opposition between illusion and reality.

Finally, *Louis Lambert* is important for a number of reasons. Sexuality and idealism are opposed in this text much as in *The Ambassadors*, and while the opposition is not unequivocally resolved any more in Balzac's novel than in James's, Balzac's protagonist's attitude toward sexuality is perfectly clear. Louis Lambert's flight from the woman in the theater and the reference to Origen's self-castration are unambiguous signs of the young man's response to the desire within himself, and these responses indicate how to interpret Lewis Lambert Strether's response to sexuality at the end of *The Ambassadors*. At the same time, *Louis Lambert* demonstrates that there are two ways of seeing the world, as spiritual and physical together, and that is what makes it possible to understand that the Mary Stuart/Virgin Mary opposition is more than just a Madonna/whore cliché; it is an aspect of the oppositional, or polarized, nature of reality as it is represented in *The Ambassadors*.

With its use of literary allusions, *The Ambassadors* creates a literary equivalent of the musical theme-and-variations form on the original theme, "Things are more complex than they seem." James's novel presents its reader with a number of correlates to that theme: reality can differ from appearances (as in *The Vicar of Wakefield*), one character can contain several characteristics (Mary Stuart/Virgin Mary), doubling of names (the Marys), multiplicity of meaning (the word "bad"), the refuting of simplistic moral oppositions (the Woollett concept, the virtuous attachment). If we must distill the "theme" or "message" of *The Ambassadors* down to one phrase, it is that people can be and are saving, saved, and sacrificed, virtuous or virginal and sexual, old and young,[54] bad and "bad" all at the same time; but while to see this is to "live," is to recognize better the complexity of human society and psychology, this awareness renders a person impotent. The novel ends—to continue the musical metaphor—with a fugue incorporating all the motifs into an intricate representation of one person's efforts to come to terms with the society he is represented as living in.

5

French Books in *The Awkward Age*

Innocence and Fernande in *The Awkward Age*

In my discussion of *Daisy Miller, The Princess Casamassima,* and *The Ambassadors,* I have traced a progressively more complicated relation between James's text and the other texts (the intertext) to which it refers. Whereas in *Daisy Miller* the purpose of the reference to Cherbuliez's *Paule Méré* was understood simply by virtue of that novel's presentation of a story bearing distinct similarities to James's,[1] in *The Princess Casamassima* the allusion to Octave Feuillet was both less explicit (it did not cite a title) and engaged a series of literary references, including two Feuillet texts and an earlier James novel. *The Ambassadors* weaves allusions to Balzac's *Louis Lambert,* to *Notre-Dame de Paris,* and to Mary Queen of Scots into an evolving complex that suggests how James's reader can resolve the problematic ending of this novel and, more important, shows how complex is the nature of Lambert Strether's ever-evolving perception of reality.

In *The Awkward Age,* we encounter yet another example of James's incorporation of French literature. In one sense, this incorporation is carried out literally, first through a discussion of two "particularly dreadful" unnamed French books, one of which has "A kind of a morbid modernity" (60, chap. 7), and through the placement (as a prop) of a " 'horrid' French novel" as "the focal image of James's plot"[2] in the novel's "climactic scene."[3] The incorporation of French literature is further carried out by references to French texts and fictional characters that, as in *Daisy Miller* and *The Ambassadors,* offer the reader a clearer parallel situation to the more ambiguously presented cruxes in James's text. Many of the critical differences *The Awkward Age* generates can be resolved by attention to references to quintessential literary characterizations of innocence (Goethe's Margaret and Hugo's Esmeralda), to the obvious associations within a French context of the name Fernanda, and to similarities in James's representation of the "problem" of the "modern girl" and the marriage market to the representation of the same problem in the fiction of Gyp, James's model for the dialogue form he adopted for *The Awkward Age*.

Critics of *The Awkward Age* have been, and still are, divided into opposing camps over a number of questions the novel raises, most especially what to make of the novel's protagonist, Nanda Brookenham, and of her mother.[4] According to critics such as Walter Isle, Oscar Cargill, and E. A. Sklepowich, Mrs. Brookenham is another Madame Merle, a heartless, ambitious manipulator who has no scruple about ruining her daughter's happiness rather than lose the man she has set her heart on.[5] For others, like Daniel Schneider, William Hall, Granville Jones, and Jean Blackall (with a few reservations), she is more like Eugenia Münster of *The Europeans*, a brilliant social operator, according to some accounts, whose qualities are so far above those of the people around her that they go unappreciated.[6] The range of perceptions of Nanda is equally wide. Some—Dorothea Krook, Marcia Jacobson, and Isle, for instance—maintain that she is an innocent and "tragic victim"[7] of circumstances beyond her understanding or control,[8] while others, such as Schneider, and to a certain extent Mildred Hartsock and Peggy McCormack, cast her as a younger version of her mother and argue that her social talents—her abilities to manipulate and grasp the motives and intentions of others—are only slightly less accomplished than Mrs. Brook's.[9]

The Awkward Age encourages such differences among its readers first by the nature of its narrative through dialogue form, and second by representing these very diverging views in the characters' own diverging views. Because the novel consists only of dialogue and a few descriptive passages, there is no authoritative voice to offer a source of judgment, nor even a central consciousness against which the reader can weigh perceptions. All interpretations have to be based on what the characters say and do, and of course what the characters say and do in this novel is prompted by motivations too numerous to account for.

The best instance of the problem of interpreting in *The Awkward Age* is the climactic scene of Mrs. Brook's exposure of Nanda's reading of a French novel in front of all the characters at Tishy Grendon's dinner party. The novel compounds the problem of how to view this scene by following it with a parade of characters, each offering his understanding of the French novel scene. Edward Brookenham is utterly unable to understand the undercurrents at play at the dinner party (*AA* 264, chap. 32), a view of the scene that is not reflected in the academic criticism of the novel but certainly is an option for James's reader. Mr. Longdon, who is arguably a surrogate for the reader by virtue of his entering the society of the novel as an outsider, responds to the scene by perceiving Nanda's unhappy future if she continues to reside with her parents (279, chap. 34) and resolving to adopt her. Van expresses his disgust at Mrs. Brook's handling of the scene and blames her for having brought about, as a result, "the smash" of their entire social circle (252–53, chap. 31), while Mitchy shows his admiration for her handling of the situation (267–69, chap. 33).

Van's and Mitchy's views correspond to the range of views offered by the novel's critics, some of whom, like Van, see little reason to approve of Mrs. Brook's brutal exposure of Nanda,[10] while Hall, paralleling Mitchy's praise of Mrs. Brook's manipulation of the French novel scene, claims, "This is a reading—based largely on the Duchess's opinions—that completely distorts the facts that actually occur," and argues that Mrs. Brook's purpose is not to damage Nanda.[11]

The critics have argued over Nanda's innocence because it is important to understanding *The Awkward Age*. However, it is not so much a question of whether there really are grounds to consider her "unmarriageable" but of what attitude the book expects the readers to take toward what happens to Nanda: are readers to blame Nanda as somehow responsible for being who she is or are they to see her as blameless and fundamentally decent and good and attach blame, if blame must be attached, to someone else (Van, Mrs. Brook), or to the age to which she belongs?

Knowing as we do that James could make an obscure and cryptic literary allusion, as he does in the Feuillet reference in *The Princess Casamassima*, and that such an allusion could offer a wealth of interpretive evidence, we have reason to perceive the complex allusion near the end of *The Awkward Age* as a way to resolve the different views on Nanda and her mother and the various interpretive questions the novel raises. During his visit to Nanda, in the first two chapters of the tenth and final book, Vanderbank remarks at the decorations of her room and at his hostess:

> Isn't there some girl in some story—it isn't Scott; what is it?—who had domestic difficulties and a cage in her window and whom one associates with chickweed and virtue? It isn't Esmeralda—Esmeralda had a poodle, hadn't she?—or have I got my heroines mixed? You're up here yourself like a heroine; you're perched in your tower or what do you call it?—your bower. You quite hang over the place, you know—the great wicked city, the wonderful London sky and the monuments looming through: or am I again only muddling up my Zola? (*AA* 283, chap. 35)

Jean Blackall has argued that the passage on the heroine with domestic difficulties refers to Esmeralda from Hugo's *Notre-Dame de Paris* and to

Gretchen from Goethe's *Faust*.[12] The connection to *Notre-Dame de Paris* obviously comes from the explicit mention of Esmeralda; *Faust* is evoked, even though Gretchen herself does not have a pet, because of the poodle who follows Faust and turns out to be Mephistopheles.[13] Comparing Nanda to Esmeralda is appropriate in several respects. As Blackall points out, while Nanda sits "perched in her tower" hanging over "the great wicked city," Esmeralda finds refuge in "an upper room" of Notre Dame Cathedral,[14] the highest point on the skyline of Hugo's medieval Paris. Nanda has flowers, as does Esmeralda, who also has a cage of birds.[15] Furthermore, as Blackall also mentions,[16] Nanda's love for Van and Esmeralda's for Phoebus de Châteaupers have much in common. Both men are identified with Apollo, Hugo's character by his first name and James's metonymically (Mitchy calls him "Apollo in person" [*AA* 85, chap. 10]), and neither returns the love of which he is the object. Phoebus's indifference is partly responsible for Esmeralda's capture and death in the final chapters of *Notre-Dame de Paris*, and it seems that Van's indifference has, at least metaphorically speaking, a corresponding responsibility for Nanda's unhappiness at the end of *The Awkward Age*. That is why Van is called Apollo: not because he is the Greek Apollo but because, like Hugo's Phoebus, he is the unworthy object of a trusting love and a source of the innocent woman's sufferings.

In *Notre-Dame de Paris*, responsibility for Esmeralda's capture and death also belongs to her mother, and in *The Awkward Age*, Esmeralda's mother's role in her daughter's death has its parallel in Mrs. Brook's role in Nanda's unhappiness:

> Unwittingly [Esmeralda's mother] has cursed her own daughter and now, disabused too late, must witness her destruction. So, too, Mrs. Brookenham has raised her voice against Nanda's innocence and is witness to her present sufferings, for which she is herself responsible.[17]

Furthermore, the mother brings about sufferings of her own, in addition to her daughter's, in both novels. Esmeralda's mother dies at the same time and place and at the hands of the same executioners as her daughter, and Mrs. Brookenham's "smash" (*AA* 253, chap. 31) brings her down as well as Nanda. Thus the mother brings the same destruction on herself as on the daughter.

The allusion to Hugo's heroine emphasizes Nanda's victimization, especially at the hands of her mother and Van. That Nanda is a victim is further indicated by the allusion to the poodle and thus to *Faust*. Esmeralda does not have a poodle; she has a goat named Djali. This goat is perfectly harmless, but it is accused and condemned for harboring the devil. The poodle in *Faust is* the devil, thus Van's confusion about Esmeralda and the poodle.

> . . . the goat is the agent of Esmeralda's destruction. The poodle enters this associative complex, I believe, because Faust's poodle like Esmeralda's goat is represented as being an incarnation of the devil. Faust's poodle is Mephistopheles, who is indirectly the agent of Gretchen's destruction. Gretchen like Esmeralda is innocent in heart and capable of selfless love, but also like Esmeralda she is victimized, spoiled, imprisoned, and under a sentence of death. Metaphorically the fate of both these medieval heroines resembles that of Nanda Brookenham.[18]

The problem these allusions to Hugo and Goethe present for James's reader is their apparent uncertainty; maybe, Van says to Nanda, you are comparable to Esmeralda or to Gretchen (or to someone in Zola), or maybe you are not. This uncertainty poses an interpretive problem: What is the point of presenting Van as unsure of which heroine with domestic difficulties characterizes his perception of Nanda? James's reader also needs to consider whether the novel endorses Van's basis for comparison or some other basis. Van's uncertainty over the heroines seems an expression of his own ambiguity toward Nanda herself, being uncertain about whether to represent Nanda to himself as the victimized but innocent Esmeralda or Gretchen or as a Zola heroine—"am I again only muddling up my Zola?"—corresponds to the ambiguousness of Van's thoughts about Nanda, which James's readers can deduce from his behavior subsequent to the French book scene at Tishy's. While Van's expression of disgust with Mrs. Brook for what happened at the dinner party (*AA* 252–53, chap. 31) suggests his sensitivity to Nanda's plight, his avoidance of Nanda after the dinner either is deliberately designed to make it clear that he takes no matrimonial interest in her (which indicates that his scruples overpower whatever tenderness and sensitivity he may have for her) or is a sign that he is insensitive to Nanda's plight. In either case, Van comes out looking too much like the powers in *Faust* and *Notre-Dame de Paris* that condemn Gretchen and Esmeralda.

Blackall's explanation of Van's confusion over whether Gretchen or Esmeralda has a poodle is convincing because it makes sense for Van to displace Esmeralda's goat with Faust's poodle, since the former is thought to be the devil and the latter is the devil.[19] This substitution is a sign of Van's fastidiousness about what he perceives as Nanda's lack of innocence. Esmeralda and her goat are accused and condemned for a serious crime—

sorcery—of which the reader knows both to be completely innocent. Most readers also know that Nanda is unjustly suspected of unspeakable crimes of which she is innocent, yet pays the price.[20] Were Van to think of Esmeralda with her goat, it would indicate his tacit admission of the innocence of Nanda's associations, but by substituting Faust's poodle (the real devil) for the goat (the presumed devil) the text indicates Van's belief that the innocent heroine has, to use a common euphemism of the 1890s, "gone to the devil."

What makes Van's position clear is his mention of Zola, for it is in one of Zola's most famous novels,[21] *Nana,* one that James himself read but disliked, that we do find a heroine with a poodle. Because of the similarity of the two heroines' names, Nana and Nanda, and because *Nana* is probably the first of Zola's novels to come to mind when its author's name is mentioned, Van's mention of a Zola heroine naturally would carry an association to Zola's famous cocotte.[22] This association indicates Van's confusing Nanda with Nana, who is as "bad" as Van could possibly imagine a woman to be, and who has a "griffon écossais," a dog similar to a poodle, named Bijou, whose morning romps under the bedclothes shock the fastidious lover, Comte Muffat, almost as much as Nana's lesbian relationship with Satin and her intrigues with countless other men (*R-M* 2: 1358). This association again shows Van's fastidiousness and how he has resolved his apparent ambivalence toward Nanda, an ambivalence James's reader cannot share, in part because of the references to Hugo's Esmeralda and Goethe's Gretchen, in part because of the reference inherent in Nanda's full name, Fernanda, to several suspected but essentially good "fallen" female literary characters, a reference I shall soon develop.

What strikes the reader of *The Awkward Age* acquainted with *Nana* is that James's Nanda and Zola's Nana have in common that they are both used to personify a fundamental problem at the core of the societies they are represented as belonging to. In Zola's novel, Nana is the emblem of all the corruption of the Second Empire, of the society's rotting from the inside out. When in the last chapter she lies dying of smallpox (*R-M* 2: 1471–85), the Franco-Prussian War is declared, and the rotting away of Nana's body as she lies on her deathbed is juxtaposed to a stereotypical expression in the streets of euphoria and optimism over the outbreak of war. Zola's post-1879 (the year of *Nana*'s publication) readers have the advantage over his characters, who are situated in 1870, for the former know the irony of the latter's cheers: the Franco-Prussian War not only would prove a disaster for France but also would be the downfall of the government and the social order; the same Parisian streets witnessing the celebration of the declaration of war would be the scene of bloody civil war a year later. Thus Zola concludes his novel by juxtaposing the climax of the growth of corruption from the inside out in both his title character and the society of the Second Empire that was his fictional subject, and thereby makes the downfall of his title character symbolic of the downfall of the empire.[23]

James's Nanda is seen to stand for the time and society she is represented as belonging to by virtue of the novel's title: the awkward age refers both to a period in the history of upper-middle-class London society (as contrasted with the time when Mr. Longdon circulated in the same society, a period when that society was quite different) and to adolescence.[24] Thus Nanda's particular problem—how a young woman of exceptional apprehension and awareness, yet limited means and possibilities, tries to find a place for herself in that society—is metaphorically associated with a larger set of problems that is made to stand for the whole modern age. These problems are represented by the pervasiveness of gossip, extramarital affairs among a set of people, and the kind of social and sexual politics Mrs. Brook and the Duchess engage in.

It makes sense, then, to see Van's allusion to Zola as yet another instance of James's own ambivalent response to the value of Zola's contribution to the art of fiction, a point I develop at much greater length in respect to *Washington Square* in the next chapter. James's critical work frequently expresses ambivalence about Zola; on the one hand, Zola and his fellow French naturalists shared, to James's mind, a commitment to the representation of reality. James also shared this commitment and deplored its absence among many practitioners of the novel in the English language. On the other hand, virtually every one of James's critical assessments of Zola contains the caveat that Zola's version of reality is too one-sided; therefore, if Zola is committed to representing reality, he is not committed to representing it, at least to James's satisfaction, in as much of its variety, complexity, and detail as possible. As James puts it in a well-known passage from the 1880 review of *Nana,* a passage that could stand for virtually any critical statement James made about Zola's work: "On what authority does M. Zola represent nature to us as a combination of the cesspool and the house of prostitution? . . . Reality is the object of M. Zola's efforts, and it is because we agree with him in appreciating it highly that we protest against its being discredited" (*LC* 2 866–67).

Van's allusion to Zola is yet another instance of James's making his point about what he saw as the limitations of French naturalist fiction. By having Van confuse Nanda with a Zola heroine, apparently by condemning her as a Nana type, James shows him to be simple minded, as unable to see or look deeply into things. Van does not think nature is only a "cesspool," but he does see things too simplistically; he has categorized Nanda as a "bad" girl, and that is that. Unlike Mr. Longdon, Van is either unable or unwilling to investigate the reasons why Nanda might appear to be a "bad" girl, to question the validity or justice of the social forces that lead to her being so categorized, or to doubt the need to categorize a young, unmarried woman at all. By confusing Nanda and Nana, Van classifies Nanda in a representation of reality that is constrained by as narrow a view as the one James attributes to Zola. The point, which recurs in so much of James's fiction, is one of how to represent.

Part of what is at issue, for both Van and the reader, in Van's allusion to the heroine with domestic difficulties is the question of how to represent the current situation (that is, do we pigeonhole Nanda as Esmeralda and Gretchen or as Nana?). Van's view exemplifies the solution of limiting one's representation to oneself of the current situation to a simplistic vision of things that sees everything as naturally following from the conjunction of a few essential forces such as genetic background (like mother, like child); the other, more enlightening possibility is to view things as James represents them to us: as apparently highly ambiguous and extremely complicated, and as having many ramifications and consequences.

Van's confusion of the poodle with the goat does raise the possibility that his interpretation is right—maybe Nanda should be accompanied by the real devil and not the presumed one, maybe she is Nana. This is why the reader's perception of Gretchen as one of the heroines with "domestic difficulties" is all the more necessary. In order to remove any possible doubt in the reader's mind, the text repeats the motif of victimization by alluding to two innocent victims par excellence, Esmeralda and Gretchen.[25] Thus Van unwittingly provides the objective sign that his own characterization of Nanda is wrong and that she suffers undeservedly at the hands of those around her. In turn this makes it all the more difficult to credit readings such as Hall's or Granville Jones's of Mrs. Brook's treatment of Nanda at Tishy Grendon's party as prompted by the best of motives or in Nanda's own best interests.[26] The disgust Van expressed at Mrs. Brook subsequent to the party is the correct reading, and it is the set of allusions implied by the name Fernanda that enables the reader of *The Awkward Age* to appreciate further that this is the correct view.

Most of the given names of the characters in *The Awkward Age* are either common—Edward, Jane, Harold, Julia—or diminutive—Fanny, Carrie, Tishy. Two other diminutives are taken from far less common names—Aggie, from Agnesina (26, chap. 1), and Nanda, from Fernanda. This last is also Mrs. Brookenham's first name (24, chap. 1), which, along with Vanderbank's first name—Gustavus (25, chap. 1)—is one of the few uncommon given names in the novel. The common names bear little comment, but the unusual ones naturally draw attention to themselves. Aggie's name clearly has its origin in the Agnès type, a cliché of French culture derived from Molière's *L'Ecole des femmes*.[27] In this well-known comedy, in which a guardian raises Agnès in complete ignorance, hoping that when she grows up her ignorance of other wives' tendency to cuckold their husbands will make her an ideal spouse for him, nothing turns out as the guardian expects; in fact, Agnès's ignorance causes his project to fail. James's Agnesina conforms perfectly to this type. Her aunt, the Duchess, had raised her in complete ignorance, hoping that she will make good marriage material. When the wealthy Mitchy marries Aggie, the Duchess's strategy seems to have been successful. However, in our last glimpse of Aggie, she is flirting with her aunt's erstwhile companion, Lord Petherton, which shows that her ignorance has made her all the more susceptible and amenable after her marriage to precisely the sort of relation she was not to know about before.[28]

As the novel is on at least one level a dramatization of the merits of different modes or methods of raising young girls, Aggie's character plays an important thematic role in *The Awkward Age*, exemplifying the drawback of the continental method preferred by her aunt. Aggie and the Duchess's espousal of the continental method also serves another purpose, which is to demonstrate further the limitations of simplistic thinking. The error and the simplicity of the Duchess's idea that raising her ward in ignorance will better suit her to her own (the Duchess's) notion of marriage is precisely what is deconstructed in all the stories of the Agnès type, and Aggie's worldview is certainly simplistic, especially in contrast to Nanda's. The complexity of the various other characters' self-representations of Nanda (as in the confusion in Van's reference to the heroine with domestic difficulties) and of the problem of how to introduce a perceptive young woman into the modern, adult world is at the core of James's representation in the novel of how complex and involved human relations can be. Thus the various interpretations of what happened at Tishy Grendon's dinner party that the various characters express, like Van's confused allusion to Goethe, Hugo, and Zola, is—as in so much of James's fiction—a way of representing problems of epistemology.

While the associations with Aggie's name offer a wealth of interpretive insight, there are no literary associations with Vanderbank's first name;[29] rather, the Latin suffix "-us" and the fact that he is "not even" called "Gussy" (*AA* 25, chap. 1) are indicative of what comes out by the end of the novel: that of all the characters in the novel, Van is the most old-fashioned and fastidious. The novel begins with Van and Mr. Longdon, and contrasts the modern technology in the younger man's apartment building—his elevator and electric lighting—and the loose talk in his social set with Longdon's archaic *"pince-nez"* or "nippers" (21–22, chap. 1) and provincial, old-fashioned astonishment at the elevator (20, chap. 1) and at the looseness of the Brookenham circle (22, chap. 1; 28–29, chap. 2; 36–37, chap. 3). These roles are reversed by the end; Longdon has come to terms with the changing social norms of the awkward age in which the novel takes place, while Van has not. Longdon calls himself "Rip Van Winkle" (136, chap. 17), but in the end Van is the real Rip Van Winkle. This is the reason for his Dutch-sounding family name and the emphasis on the Dutch *particule* in the nickname given him in the Brookenham set.

This leaves the uncommon name Fernanda to account for. There are at least three instances of the use of this name in nineteenth-century French literature: one in Zola's *Nana,* one in a spurious Dumas *père* novel called *Fernande,* and the other in Victorien Sardou's play *Fernande.* The Fernande in *Nana* is a minor character, a theater supernumerary (*R-M* 2: 1097), and the only mention of her comes when the theater director insults her for her behavior on stage. The role Zola's Fernande plays is too limited for her to be perceived as the object of an allusion in *The Awkward Age,* but she is worth citing as an indication of what sort of fictional woman—an actress, presumably one with questionable morals—would have such a name.

In *La Dame aux camélias,* the younger Alexandre Dumas's classic representation of the cocotte or "fallen woman," the narrator comes upon a copy of the eighteenth century's best-known "fallen woman" story, Prévost's *Manon Lescaut,* which makes him muse about the tradition of the courtesan in literature: "Hugo a fait *Marion Delorme,* Musset a fait *Bernerette,* Alexandre Dumas a fait *Fernande,* les penseurs et les poètes de tous les temps ont apporté à la courtisane l'offrande de leur miséricorde" [Hugo did *Marion Delorme,* Musset did *Bernerette* (actually, the tale "Frédéric et Bernerette"), Alexandre Dumas did *Fernande,* thinkers and poets of every age have offered the courtesan their commiseration].[30]

The *Fernande* to which Dumas alludes as by his father was published in 1844 and reprinted several times in the following years until the book's actual author was discovered to be not Dumas but Hippolyte Auger.[31] It tells the story of "la courtisane la plus célèbre de Paris, car . . . c'était le titre que l'on donnait généralement à Fernande" [Paris's most famous courtesan, since . . . that was the title people generally gave Fernande].[32] Regardless of *Fernande*'s authorship, the younger Dumas's reference to this novel makes its title character as emblematic of the type of the "fallen woman" as his own heroine was to become. The way in which Dumas *fils* presents his list of literary courtesans suggests that the characters cited are representative of the type, and the mention of a literary courtesan with the name Fernande in a list including Marion Delorme (after Dumas's own lady of the camellias, undoubtedly the most talked-of and best-known literary courtesan in nineteenth-century French literature) is enough to give a special significance to that name.

Fernande, then, would appear a particularly apt name for a woman of apparently unscrupulous morality like Fernanda Brookenham, but the title character in the novel *Fernande* better bears comparison to Nanda Brookenham, the Fernanda who is mistaken for, but in fact is not, a "bad" woman—which explains why James's mother and daughter could both bear the name. Fernande in the spurious Dumas novel may be known as the most famous courtesan in Paris, but she turns out in the end—like Marguerite Gautier in *La Dame aux camélias* (and like the other heroines mentioned in Dumas's list)—to be a fundamentally good person with a heart of gold. She truly loves Maurice de Barthèle, who reciprocates her feeling, but she dismisses him when she discovers he is married. However, she saves Maurice from dying of a broken heart by visiting him in his own home and then proceeds to save his family from falling apart by convincing Maurice's wife that her husband loves her and Maurice that his first duty is to his wife; by dismissing Maurice's "uncle," whose mistress she has become, which makes possible his marriage to Maurice's mother; and by deciding to leave Paris forever for a quiet country life devoid of lovers. It is in the moral lesson of this story, that the apparently "bad" woman is fundamentally good, that the comparison to *The Awkward Age* lies; *Fernande* is an indictment of a morality that is quick to judge and condemn, and James's novel similarly indicts Van for the same moralistic, judgmental narrow-mindedness.

We cannot positively prove that James read the novel version of *La Dame aux camélias;* although he frequently cites Dumas and mentions several times in his essays on French theater (*SA* 10, 161, 261–81) having seen the play version and owned a set of Dumas's complete dramatic works,[33] there is no mention in James's criticism or published letters of the novel, which alone contains the reference cited above to the spurious elder Dumas's *Fernande*. However, my point is that the name Fernande brought natural associations with a particular type of literary character: first and most generally to a "loose" woman,[34] and second and less obviously to a "loose" woman who in fact was virtuous at heart. The younger Dumas's citing of Auger's Fernande in a list of emblematic courtesans, Zola's choice of the name for one of his "actresses," and Sardou's use of the name for his play *Fernande,* also about an apparently "loose" woman, indicate that in using that name in his novel, James was choosing a name that bore very clear and specific associations. Furthermore, in tracing the similarities between James's Nanda and Sardou's Fernande, we realize that James's young protagonist is related to an entire series of like characters, beginning with Mademoiselle Duquênoi in the Madame de La Pommeraye story from Diderot's *Jacques le fataliste.*

With a few additions and one important alteration, Sardou's *Fernande* is the Madame de La Pommeraye story from *Jacques le fataliste.* This story had been dramatized for the Paris stage by Ancelot as *Léontine* in 1831, thirty-nine years before Sardou's version; and variations on the same basic story, most often with the sexes of the three central characters inverted, had appeared in England and France throughout the nineteenth century.[35] In both Diderot's and Sardou's versions of the story, a woman senses that her lover of several years has lost interest in her, and in order to trick him into admitting his true feelings, she pretends that she herself has lost interest; however, instead of assuring her of his unending love, as she expected, the man avows that he, too, would just as soon end the affair and simply remain friends.

This leads the spurned lover to develop a plan of revenge. She discovers that an old acquaintance and her daughter have fallen into prostitution and are running an illegal gambling house. The plan is to get the ex-lover to fall in love with and marry the daughter, then to reveal to him what kind of wife he has taken. This plan works perfectly, but the revenge backfires when, after the great revelation, the new husband forgives his new wife. In Diderot's version, the mother and daughter are named Duquênoi but have taken the name d'Aisnon, the Marquis des Arcis is the duped husband, and Mme. de La Pommeraye is the spurned lover who masterminds the revenge plot. Mme. de La Pommeraye sets the Duquênois up as *dévotes,* which makes marriage the only way for des Arcis to have Mlle. Duquênoi, and both mother and daughter know what use Mme. de La Pommeraye intends to make of them.

In Sardou's version, Fernande is the daughter and her mother is named Madame Sénéchal (their real name is de la Brière), the marquis is named André, and Mme. de La Pommeraye becomes Clotilde de La Roseraie. The one important difference between Diderot's and Sardou's handling of the story is that in *Fernande,* Sardou contrives to keep his young heroine innocent of the plot for which she is an instrument. Thus, once the marriage between Fernande and André has been arranged, Clotilde leads Fernande to believe that the marquis knows of her squalid past, has forgiven her for it, and would rather that it not be mentioned in his presence. Thus, Sardou manages to keep her consistent and innocent enough at heart, if not in deed, to make her worthy of her husband's pardon at the end. This distinction is important to *The Awkward Age* because Sardou's Fernande can be perceived as an innocent victim while Diderot's Mlle. Duquênoi cannot be.

It is significant that Sardou not only chose to name the title character of his play Fernande but also divided the life of this character into sordid and blameless halves, each with a corresponding given name: Fernande is Fernande only in the first act, which takes place in the gambling house, and when her past is referred to; otherwise, she is Marguerite. Thus Marguerite is the name for innocence and Fernande the one for the sordid past. This contrast is even clearer in French, where, as the author of *Daisy Miller* would have appreciated, a *marguerite* is a daisy—the flower most emblematic of innocence.

The two names of Sardou's title character are the reason that the daughter in James's novel is not called Fernanda but Nanda. Mrs. Brook is Fernanda, and that is because Fernande's earlier life is more appropriate to the mother's, while Nanda is the innocent victim. She should be Marguerite, and in fact she is because of Van's mention of Faust's poodle and the allusion to Gretchen, the diminutive for Margaret.[36]

Sardou was one of the best-known Parisian dramatists of the second half of the nineteenth century,[37] and James knew his work well: "I have thoroughly mastered Dumas, Augier, and Sardou . . . and I know all they know and a great deal more besides" (*HJL* 2: 171).[38] He also knew Francisque Sarcey,[39] a leading Parisian drama critic, who had reviewed *Fernande* for *Le Temps*. Although James makes no mention of *Fernande* specifically,[40] it would have been hard for him or certain types of readers not to be aware of the play or to recognize Sardou's heroine as a conventional type. The fact of the many versions of the Madame de La Pommeraye story is evidence of a considerable familiarity in the nineteenth century with the basic story; this is supported by contemporary reviews of *Fernande*,[41] which generally discuss Diderot as Sardou's source at some length. The surest sign that *Fernande* made its mark on the popular culture of its day is that it inspired a parody by Busnach, Gastineau, and Clairville called *Ferblande, ou l'abonné de Montmartre*, which opened at the Variétés theater in May 1870 and was published that year.[42] The existence of a parody is a clear sign of the prominence in the culture of the parody's subject, and *Ferblande* is strong evidence that *Fernande* was a familiar version of Diderot's story.

Sardou's Fernande is, then, a prominent enough figure for her to be perceived as a conventional type by a reader of *The Awkward Age* having the requisite familiarity with French culture. A familiarity with Fernande means an awareness of this heroine's two lives and two identities; thus a reader would know she has two names, one to correspond with her wicked life and identity and one for the innocent. The innocent life, of course, is identified by the name that stands for innocence: Marguerite.

In the final chapter of *The Awkward Age*, Mr. Longdon visits Nanda in her room, expecting to learn whether she has decided to accept his offer to reside permanently with him. At first he "is nervous in the way a lover would be,"[43] steps out of character, and expresses his anxiety over her decision in the stereotypical vocabulary of an anguished lover: "I felt half an hour ago that, near as I was to relief, I could keep it up no longer; so that though I knew it would bring me much too soon I started at six sharp for our trysting place," he says when he arrives (*AA* 303, chap. 38); admits to "[R]oaming hither and thither in your beautiful Crescent till I could venture to come in"; and tells Nanda of "the absolutely passive thing you've made of me" (304, chap. 38).

As the chapter continues, however, the lover's discourse ceases, and the scene becomes the same as the one that ends *Fernande* and the story of Mme. de La Pommeraye. Longdon's anxiety to know Nanda's decision is replaced by her anxiety as to whether he will accept her as she is. "I'll come if you'll take me as I am—which is, more than I've ever done before, what I must previously explain to you," she says (307, chap. 38).

> "Because, you know," the girl pursued, "I *am* like that."
> "Like what?"
> "Like what [Van] thinks." Then so gravely that it was almost a supplication, "Don't tell me," she added, "that you don't *know* what he thinks. You do know."
> Their eyes, on that strange ground, could meet at last, and the effect of it was presently for Mr. Longdon. "I do know."
> "Well?"
> "Well!" He raised his hands and took her face, which he drew so close to his own that, as she gently let him, he could kiss her with solemnity on the forehead. "Come!" he then very firmly said—quite indeed as if it were a question of their moving on the spot.
> It literally made her smile, which, with a certain compunction, she immediately corrected by doing for him in the pressure of her lips to his cheek what he had just done for herself. (310, chap. 38)

Nanda's stressing that Longdon must take her as she is at this point in the novel is surprising, for Mr. Longdon had accepted that her character was not her grandmother's long before.[44] When he comes to learn whether she will live with him, he is well aware how much she knows of what unmarried girls are not supposed to know. She knows that he knows, and both know that her taking up residence in the country with him will not change the fact of her having known so much about London life. Nanda's being what she is has long ceased to matter to Mr. Longdon, but it matters in the final scene of *The Awkward Age* because it is the crux of the reconciliation scenes at the end of *Fernande* and of the story of Mme. de La Pommeraye.

In the final scene of *The Awkward Age*, Nanda insists on Mr. Longdon's accepting her character so she can complete the role implicit in her name; she acts out the part of Fernande/Marguerite, and Longdon plays the marquis.[45] In both Sardou's and Diderot's versions of the story, the marquis's forgiving his new wife and their living a happy life together depend on his taking her as she is, just as Nanda's and Longdon's life together does. In either version, the marquis's pardon is expressed by his addressing his wife as "madame la marquise" and raising her from her prostrate position at his feet.[46] Both marquis perform an act of absolution that Longdon's taking Nanda's face in his hands and kissing her forehead closely resembles.

James's story resembles the French versions in general as well as in these details, for both *Fernande* and the story of Mme. de La Pommeraye show that a successful marriage does not have to depend on what received opinion considers the requirements for a good bride; as Diderot has his marquis say: "En vérité je crois que je ne me repens de rien; et que cette Pommeraye, au lieu de se venger, m'aura rendu un grand service" [In fact I think that I do not regret a thing, and that Pommeraye, instead of avenging herself, will have done me a great favor].[47] And as Sardou's Pomerol moralizes over the embracing couple in the final speech of *Fernande:* "Ah! mon brave André, va! . . . La raison fait de beaux discours . . . mais un cri du cœur. . . . Eh! qu'est-ce que vous voulez?" [Ah! my good André, carry on! . . . Reason makes pretty speeches . . . but a cry from the heart. . . . Eh! what do you want?].[48] Thus both French stories are about what elements can make for a good marriage, and both come out as protests lodged against the limitations of received opinion.

In modeling its ending on the French stories, *The Awkward Age* makes the same point about marriage. James's novel begins as a study in contrasts between the free-rein English and the restrictive continental methods of raising young girls, introducing them into adult society, and getting them married. Aggie's familiarity with Petherton, her aunt's lover, so soon after her own wedding shows what the reader is supposed to make of the success of the continental method that the Duchess favors; keeping her ignorant does not make her a better wife because it does not make her immune to the dangers of which she is kept ignorant. In casting Nanda as Fernande, the text shows what to make of Mrs. Brook's method of "bringing out" daughters. Despite her awareness of the existence of adulterous relations—in fact, perhaps even because of it—Nanda is more likely than Aggie to contribute to a happy marriage. Unfortunately, the age that James's novel represents is an awkward one; the sort of man who could fill the role of Sardou's André and Diderot's des Arcis does not exist,[49] and Nanda's qualities are obscured by received ideas about a girl's upbringing. Thus *The Awkward Age* differs from the two French texts in that James's story is not just a protest lodged against received opinion but also a representation of the tragic consequences of received opinion.

Only Mr. Longdon can perform the part of the marquis in the novel's final scene; this is why the final chapter opens with him playing the role of an anxious lover: it is a sign that the limits of a strict realistic mimesis are being broken and that conventional roles are being played. At first Longdon is the conventional lover because that is what both Sardou's and Diderot's marquis begin as. Longdon has to be reduced to "the absolutely passive thing you have made me," just like the marquis, before the scene of the pardon can occur. Like the marquis, Longdon is just fastidious enough to care about a woman's reputation but not fastidious enough for it to blind him to her qualities. His long retirement from London life means that at first he subscribes to old-fashioned values; therefore he can find fault with Nanda. However, he is the only man in the novel who can adapt his values to the changing times he encounters when he returns to London life; that is why he can pardon Nanda. Van, not Mr. Longdon, is Rip Van Winkle; as Nanda tells her benefactor, Van is "more old-fashioned than you" and should have married Aggie (311, chap. 38). Since he is the outsider in the novel, Mr. Longdon is the best candidate to be the surrogate for the reader and an example to the reader for how to respond to *The Awkward Age;* he is certainly an example of how best to deal with the awkward age of changing values that the text represents.

James and Gyp: "Autour de" *The Awkward Age*

The Awkward Age is a novel about talk; most of the novel consists of the characters talking, and what the characters talk about is—their own talk. In other words, this is a novel that represents gossip. It also represents the consequences of talk, for one thing that makes Nanda unmarriageable is too much talking in her mother's drawing room. In writing *The Awkward Age,* James appropriately cast this novel *about* talk and about the freedom of talk *as* talk, as a novel in dialogue form.

There is another point to make about the dialogue form of *The Awkward Age,* for it bears immediate comparison to *Jacques le fataliste* and to the French *roman dialogué,* which had a vogue first in France during the 1880s and then in England.[50] Its most eminent practitioner at the time was the Comtesse de Martel, a flamboyant conservative[51] who published under the pen name of Gyp, in the hope that her aristocratic relatives would not find out she was writing novels and making money from it. James says in his 1908 preface to the New York Edition of *The Awkward Age* that he had Gyp consciously in mind as a model when he was writing his novel in 1898–1899:

> What form so familiar, so recognised among alert readers, as that in which the ingenious and inexhaustible, the charming philosophic "Gyp" casts most of her social studies? . . . But that I did, positively and seriously—ah so seriously!—emulate the levity of Gyp . . . is a contribution to the history of "The Awkward Age" that I shall obviously have had to brace myself in order to make. . . . Let me say at once, in extenuation of the too respectful distance at which I may thus have appeared to follow my model, that my first care *had* to be the covering of my tracks—lest I truly should be caught in the act of arranging, of organising dialogue to "speak for itself." (*LC2* 1127–28)[52]

The principal ways James "covered his tracks" in *The Awkward Age* were by retaining the more conventional "he saids" and "she saids" in place of the play-script-style offset speaker's name followed by a colon that Gyp used to introduce a character's speech, and by offering descriptive passages at the beginning of each chapter or new scene in place of the parenthetic stage directions that Gyp favored. In spite of these changes, James expected that the form of *The Awkward Age* would all too clearly appear as an allusion to Gyp's work. I cite the preface to indicate the shame James felt compelled to admit at the idea that his novel would obviously be recognized as homage to his continental counterpart and as an indication of the sort of response James expected from readers of *The Awkward Age,* more than as proof of an authorial intention. James's need to cover his tracks lest he should be too easily caught "organising dialogue to 'speak for itself' " as Gyp did, and his question—"What form so familiar, so recognised among alert readers, as" Gyp's *roman dialogué?*—are evidence that late-nineteenth-century readers should have automatically made the association between the particular form and its best-known practitioner at the time. (That James's readers did not make such an association until long after his preface appeared is a sign that they lacked the partly French perspective James expected of them.)

If turn-of-the-century reviewers did not associate James's novel with Gyp's works, critics in recent decades have more than made up for this oversight. Criticism on *The Awkward Age* so often mentions James's acknowledgment in his preface of Gyp's inspiration[53] that Jacobson argues the point has been worn out:

> What the Preface seems to have done is to have inhibited critics from looking at *The Awkward Age* in the context of other fiction of the nineties. By attributing his form to "Gyp" and his subject matter to a crisis frequently observed in social life, James has deflected such attention.[54]

Jacobson is right that James's preface has overly determined the way subsequent commentators have thought of the relationship between *The Awkward Age* and Gyp, for virtually none of them does more than cite the French author as a source of inspiration for James and rehearse the relevant passages from the preface as evidence. But Jacobson implies that less attention should be paid to the similarity of form between Gyp's fiction and James's. This is wrong, for not only does the dialogue form of *The Awkward Age* naturally suggest an association to Gyp, but it is in one of Gyp's most famous novels[55]—*Autour du mariage,* of which James owned a copy[56]—that we find not only a model for the climactic episode at Tishy Grendon's and the exemplary model for the central character of James's novel, the figure of the modern girl, but also a key to the connection between James's subject in *The Awkward Age*—the marrying of young girls— and his image of "the neat figure of the circle" (*LC2* 1130) to describe the novel's overall structure.[57]

While *The Awkward Age* was one of James's least commercially and critically successful novels, *Autour du mariage,* Gyp's fourth novel (along with her first novel, *Petit Bob*), was instrumental in making its author's reputation. Like James's *The Awkward Age, Autour du mariage* offers an unflattering picture of upper-class morality and manners. Its heroine, Paulette d'Hautretan, is a horribly spoiled, headstrong, and conniving young lady who is introduced to the reader on the eve of her marriage to Joseph d'Alaly. The groom is a *vieux roué* in his mid-thirties,[58] already balding, who expects that in marrying a naïve young girl right out of a convent school he is guaranteeing that his wife will not make him a cuckold and an object of ridicule. Such an innocent bride will, he believes, be satisfied with a quiet life at home. Paulette has very different expectations of marriage, which she sees first and foremost as a liberation from the domination of her parents.

With such illusions about their future, the two principals cannot be expected to live happily together. Paulette flirts with a group of eager men, driving d'Alaly to extremes of jealousy, and she utterly refuses to have any regard, as he sees it, for moderation and propriety. D'Alaly scarcely finds in this marriage the peaceful, retired life he had expected, and Paulette finds his constant scolding and jealous scenes as unbearable as the tight rein of her parents in the days before her wedding. The novel ends with Paulette deciding that if she is going to be treated like an adulteress (she has remained faithful in deed) and put up with all the disadvantages of being thought one, she might as well have some of the advantages of the situation.

A number of details in *Autour du mariage* bear close comparison to *The Awkward Age*. The society and period in which *Autour du mariage* takes place are represented from the beginning as ones where morals and values have fallen considerably. The first scene depicts the signing of the marriage contract and the boredom of one of the guests at the tediousness and length of such a ceremony. The notary disagrees, pointing out that the signing is an occasion for the greatest amusement if one takes a close look at the ladies with their low-cut dresses as they lean over the table to sign the contract. "Quand ces dames se penchent en rapprochant le coude du corps, le corsage s'entr'ouvre comme le calice d'une fleur . . . et l'on entrevoit des horizons. . . . Ah! on plonge à des profondeurs. . . ." [When the ladies lean over and bring their elbows against their sides, their bodices open up like the calyx of a flower . . . and one can make out horizons. . . . Ah! one dives into depths. . . .] (*AM* 2, chap. 1). Thus Gyp's reader is introduced to the immorality of modern Paris in this opening scene just as Van introduces Mr. Longdon—after his long country residence—to the very changed values of modern London in the first book of *The Awkward Age*.

The issue of young girls' upbringing is raised early in Gyp's novel. Paulette's family name, Hautretan, when read phonetically as "autre temps" (another time) is a sign that her parents are old-fashioned and that they have raised her the traditional way. This name makes a contrast in *Autour du mariage* between the past and the present, just as Mr. Longdon's emergence from his rural retirement makes for a similar contrast in *The Awkward Age*. D'Alaly makes the same distinction between English and continental methods of raising girls that James's novel makes in contrasting Mrs. Brook's and the Duchess's approaches to raising their charges. When he assures his friends, at the beginning of the book, that Paulette has had a strict education and that her naiveté will permit him to do as he will with her, he says: "Elle n'a pas été élevée à l'anglaise, la bride sur le cou" [She was not brought up the English way, with the bridle on the neck (that is, given free rein)] (*AM* 11, chap. 1). Like *The Awkward Age*, *Autour du mariage* becomes a case study in the education of young girls, with Paulette, like Aggie, demonstrating how unsuccessful the continental method can be; d'Alaly's mention of an alternative, English method and the subsequent events suggest that Paulette could not have ended up worse if she had been raised the English way.

Though Paulette's character has little in common with Nanda's, there are a number of similar details that show they are both exemplary types of the modern girl. Both young women, for example, surprise their elders by using slang. Mr. Longdon does not like it when Nanda uses expressions like " 'he has come into my life.' . . . 'He called it "mannered modern slang" and came back again to the extraordinary difference between my speech and my grandmother's' " (*AA* 131, chap. 16). Similarly, on the eve of the religious wedding, Paulette's mother scolds her daughter for using such colloquial expressions as " 'Flanquer un abatage!' Mais où a-t-elle appris ces locutions étranges?" ["Get up on your high horse!" Where did she ever learn such strange expressions?] (*AM* 27, chap. 2). Later, an annoyed d'Alaly criticizes Paulette's habitual use of slang: "Vous devriez bien vous déshabituer de parler argot" [You really should break your habit of speaking slang] (*AM* 171, chap. 12).

The emphasis on slang is one means both novels use to cast the two young heroines as typical of the most modern tendencies. Another important similarity that also displays these tendencies is the extent to which these two young ladies' knowledge of adult immorality far exceeds the expected norm. Just as Nanda knows as much as anybody about the various extramarital liaisons in *The Awkward Age,* so Paulette, even before her marriage takes place, has no illusions about fidelity in marriage. She knows, for example, that her father is having an affair with an actress and that when he says he is going to his "Cercle" (social club), he is really visiting his mistress (*AM* 33, chap. 3); she is also more aware of d'Alaly's bachelor days' adventures than her husband thought. When d'Alaly registers his surprise at Paulette's allusion to one of his past flames, she replies, "Parbleu! moi, voyez-vous, je sais toujours ce qu'on ne me dit pas; fourrez-vous bien ça dans la tête" [And how! you see I always know what I'm not told; you might as well get that into your head] (*AM* 252, chap. 16), just like Nanda declaring with assurance, as she does on several occasions: "Oh, I know everything!" (*AA* 208, chap. 25).

Finally, Paulette is aware, like Nanda, that she has not grown up into a conventional, docile young woman, in spite of all everyone did to make her "une petite demoiselle accomplie, baissant les yeux, soumise, douce, banale et insignifiante" [an accomplished, submissive, sweet, banal, insignificant little lady with lowered eyes]. She defies her husband to succeed where her parents failed and urges him to accept her "telle que je suis, avec mes nombreux défauts et mes quelques pauvres petites qualités" [as I am, with my many faults and my few poor, little qualities] (*AM* 300, chap. 18). Nanda expresses virtually the same sentiments in *The Awkward Age.* She is as aware as Paulette that she has not turned out to be a submissive, modest little lady and at times regrets that she was not more like Aggie: "What I don't look like is Aggie, for all I try" (*AA* 188, chap. 23); "If one could be her exactly, absolutely, without the least little mite of change, one would probably do the best thing to close with it" (*AA* 201, chap. 24). Paulette's plea that her husband accept her as she is, is reproduced in Nanda's condition at the end of *The Awkward Age:* that Longdon agree to take her as she is before she agrees to reside with him permanently (307, chap. 38).[59]

While all these details suggest that the reader of *The Awkward Age* could perceive a similarity between James's modern young woman and Gyp's, it would be difficult to argue that James's reader necessarily must see a connection between *Autour du mariage* if it were not for the fact that the scene that more than any other reveals to d'Alaly his illusions about his wife and the extent of her worldly knowledge is so similar to the climactic scene of James's novel. The revelation in *Autour du mariage* comes in the chapter entitled "Mauvaises lectures" (Bad Reading). During one of their stops on their honeymoon, d'Alaly suggests that he and Paulette visit the sights. Paulette, who has already had enough of sightseeing, answers that she would rather stay in and read a book. D'Alaly hints mischievously that he has brought a book that, since she is now married, they can read together. He pulls a volume out of his effects and hands it to Paulette, who makes a face when she sees it.

> Monsieur d'Alaly, étonné. —Le titre ne vous plaît pas? Le livre est charmant, je vous assure . . .
> Paulette. —Je le sais bien, mais je le connais depuis longtemps, et alors . . .
> Monsieur d'Alaly, ahuri. —Vous connaissez *Monsieur, Madame et Bébé*?
> —Mais oui.
> —Vous l'avez lu?
> —A peu près . . . Pas en volume, mais en articles, dans *La Vie parisienne*.
>
> [Monsieur d'Alaly, astonished. —The title doesn't please you? The book is charming, I assure you. . . .
> Paulette. —I know that, but I've known it for a long time, and so. . . .
> Monsieur d'Alaly, horrified. —You know *Monsieur, Madame and Baby*?
> —Of course.
> —You've read it?
> —Pretty much. . . . Not the book, but the serial, in *La Vie parisienne*.]
> (*AM* 103–4, chap. 8)

D'Alaly's astonishment has only just begun, however, for Paulette then tells him she has recently bought a great quantity of similar books. To her husband's considerable consternation, she pulls out of her belongings a number of volumes and discusses perfectly naturally the virtues of *Ma tante en Vénus*, *Choses d'amour*, *Prostitution mondaine*, *Il m'en faudrait deux!*, *Dinah-Samuel*, and *La Vénus rustique* (*AM* 106–10, chap. 8).[60] She also has *Les Liaisons dangereuses,* but it is not saucy enough for her. Sensing her husband's displeasure, Paulette tells him, "Je ne me suis pas mariée pour lire Walter Scott!" [I didn't get married to read Walter Scott!] (*AM* 108, chap. 8). His dismay increases when she mentions that one of her greatest wishes is to read Boccaccio, which the bookstore did not have (*AM* 111, chap. 8).

The revelation of the shocking book at Tishy Grendon's dinner in *The Awkward Age* functions like the "Mauvaises lectures" chapter in *Autour du mariage.* Through her reading material, the heroine in each text is shown not to be the modest girl the husband, or possible husband, expects her to be. Just as d'Alaly realizes his wife is not a *fille bien rangée* when she produces lurid books, neither can Van, nor anyone else, escape the fact that Nanda is not a naïve, dutiful young girl once her mother exposes her reading of the French book. The d'Alaly marriage begins to crumble at this point in *Autour du mariage,* just as the Brookenham circle falls apart after Tishy's dinner.

Not only are Paulette and Nanda similar in representing the "problem of the modern girl," but Paulette—like the protagonists of most of Gyp's fiction of the time—defined the type of the modern girl (and all that was wrong with her and her time) to such an extent that she and *La Vie parisienne,* the journal in which *Autour du mariage* (and *Monsieur, Madame et Bébé*)[61] appeared, were believed to have a considerable negative effect on young ladies' morals at the end of the nineteenth-century.

> *La Vie parisienne* a fait en province un grand mal et de considérables dégâts.
>
> Elle a "défraîchi" quelques jeunes filles. Elle a fait croire à trop de jeunes femmes que le dévergondage, lorsqu'il est élégant et raffiné, est parfaitement acceptable; qu'il faut—pour être chic—admettre certaines libertés, certaines façons de se tenir, de parler et de s'habiller. . . . [V]ers 1880, on a pu constater une sorte de poussée de mauvaise tenue très visible dans la société provinciale, restée jusque-là très correcte, du moins en apparence. Le flirt y est devenu chose courante et normale.
>
> Plus tard, vers 1883, quand j'ai commencé à écrire, je me suis aperçue avec ahurissement, que Paulette, qui n'était à mes yeux qu' "une jolie petite poison" était gobée, admirée et prise pour modèle par les jeunes femmes de ce temps-là.
>
> [*La Vie parisienne* did a lot of evil and considerable damage in the provinces.
>
> It "unfreshened" several young girls. It made too many young girls believe that immorality, provided it is elegant and refined, is perfectly acceptable; that—in order to be chic—one must allow certain liberties, certain ways

of behavior, of speaking, of dressing. . . . [A]round 1880, it was possible to make out a sort of advance of visibly bad manners in provincial society, which until then had remained very proper, at least in appearance. Flirting then became a very common and normal thing.

Later, around 1883, when I started writing, I was horrified to see that Paulette, who to me was nothing other than "a pretty little poison," was relished, admired and used as a model by the young women of that time.][62]

We need not take Gyp's word after the fact that her "pretty little poison" became a stock figure for the decadent upbringing of turn-of-the-century girls and a symbol for what was wrong with the times. The drama critic Henri de Bornier wrote in 1883:

. . . c'est que la femme est [apparemment] la grande coupable, le principal agent de la désorganisation sociale. Mme. de Martel est allée plus avant encore: elle a ouvert, pour chercher le virus social, la chair enflammée et malsaine, et au bout du scalpel impitoyable, elle a trouvé que la gangrène morale avait gagné, après l'épouse et la maîtresse, la jeune fille!

Evidemment, Mme. de Martel n'a voulu peindre qu'une exception; mais cette exception menace de s'étendre, et la lèpre gagnerait bientôt les voisines de Paulette, si on ne coupait court, en l'isolant, aux exploits de cette fantastique héroïne.

[. . . women are (apparently) the guilty ones, the prime agents of this social chaos. Mme. de Martel has gone even farther: in order to find the social virus, she has opened the swollen and unhealthy flesh, and with the tip of her pitiless scalpel, she has found that the moral gangrene, after infecting the wife and the mistress, has reached the young girl!

Obviously, Mme. de Martel only wanted to paint an exception; but this exception threatens to spread, and the leprosy could soon reach Paulette's neighbors unless, by isolating it, an end is put to the exploits of this fantastic heroine.][63]

Firmin Boissin, a critic apparently even more conservative than Gyp, was shocked at *Autour du mariage* and its heroine:

Ainsi, cette Gyp . . . dans *Autour du mariage,* est tout simplement en train de faire . . . le jeu des athées et des jacobins. . . . On donne, pour excuse, que Gyp a voulu tout simplement exposer les déplorables conséquences de l'éducation actuelle des jeunes filles. C'est possible; mais . . . avec les "sous-entendus" et les "naïvetés" brutales de son héroïne, mêlant la "physiologie" à une littérature de parfumeur, Gyp n'en est pas moins une démolisseuse.

> . . . *Autour du mariage* dépasse vraiment les bornes. Le livre est malsain et choquant.

> [Thus, this Gyp . . . in *Autour du mariage,* is quite simply . . . playing into the hands of the atheists and the Jacobins. . . . To excuse her, it is said that Gyp only wanted to expose the deplorable consequences of the upbringing in our age of young girls. That is possible; but . . . with her heroine's "that goes without sayings" and brutal "naivetés," mixing "physiology" with the literature of a perfumer, Gyp is nonetheless a destroyer. . . . *Autour du mariage* really exceeds the limits. The book is unhealthy and shocking.][64]

These passages sufficiently indicate how Paulette represents the figure of the young girl at the turn of the century. Each claims *Autour du mariage* has something to do with a perceived crisis in morality in general and in the behavior of young girls in particular, and Paulette is emphasized as a perfect example of what is supposed to be wrong with young girls.

As much as Paulette and Nanda think they know, they do not know everything. As spoiled and egotistical as she is, Paulette is not a villain; she does not consciously mean to shock and make her husband and admirers miserable—she only wants to enjoy herself and is oblivious of any consequences. What Paulette does not know is that this behavior has consequences; it is judged, and these judgments matter. For all she does understand, she does not comprehend that the society Gyp represents functions as a series of obligations and relationships of dependence and power (that is why, in her efforts to recruit a lawyer to obtain a separation for her, she can hardly understand why the jurists she visits virtually laugh at her explanation of her situation [*AM* 315–32, chap. 19])—she cannot understand the broad picture.[65]

Like Gyp's, James's novel is an indictment of upper-middle-class society (though from a different ideological perspective). But while Gyp's happy ending in the sequel, *Autour du divorce,* with d'Alaly's and Paulette's reconciliation is a reactionary affirmation of traditional family values, Nanda's story is a tragedy. In a sense, *The Awkward Age* itself is the French book in James's text, but one that Nanda has not learned to read, for like Paulette, she does not completely understand the game in which she has been a pawn. Maybe because Longdon has given her a set of "the most standard English works" to read (*AA* 264, chap. 32) instead of Balzac's *Eugénie Grandet,* the book that most clearly parallels her situation, she cannot fully comprehend that her mother has sacrificed her daughter's happiness in a hopeless attempt to retain for herself the man they both covet; she has not entirely realized that she is not the heroine of a traditional English novel.

While she can both read a French novel and be aware of many of the sexual intrigues going on around her just as in the French books, she does not fully understand the effect of the relations and manipulations revolving around her and of which she has been the victim; apparently she has not learned to read her own French book, the one in which she is cast, *The Awkward Age*.

Because it is written in dialogue form and because it has as its central subject the upbringing of young girls, it is natural to see *The Awkward Age* in the context of *Autour du mariage* and its heroine. Within this context, James's text offers a slight variation on the subject, dramatizing the comparison of the English and continental methods of education more completely. (This is why the Paulette figure is divided in two: in Aggie, she becomes the girl whose severe upbringing is guaranteed to bring about the opposite result from the one intended, and in Nanda, she is the girl who cannot help knowing too much.) One other factor (besides the obvious similarity of the dialogue form) makes it difficult to ignore Gyp's heroine as a context for *The Awkward Age*. Paulette is far from unique in the pantheon of Gyp's protagonists; she is in fact so similar to Gyp's other turn-of-the-century protagonists, adolescents of similar temperament, that the redundancy makes one wonder at Gyp's success (by 1900, not only was *Autour du mariage* in its ninety-ninth printing, but Gyp had fifty books in print).

In *Petit Bob*, her first novel and best-known book aside from *Autour du mariage*, Gyp created a bratty little boy who, given petticoats and ten more years, would be Paulette d'Hautretan. So many of Gyp's other novels published before the appearance of *The Awkward Age* in 1899—*Miquette, Les Gens chics, Mademoiselle Loulou, Mademoiselle Ève, Le Mariage de Chiffon,* and *Ohé les psychologues,* for example—are also about adolescent girls and the problems of their marriage games. All of these young heroines share the same characteristics as Paulette or Bob; they are self-indulgent, independent-minded, spoiled and bratty, but essentially well-meaning deep down. To say that Paulette or Bob represented a type would not be enough; everything Gyp had written when James wrote *The Awkward Age* represented a type.

This was the view of contemporary critics of Gyp: according to Jules Lemaître, the young girl in Gyp's fiction "est un type *national*" [is a *national* type];[66] and according to Anatole France, Gyp's Loulou is the modern girl: "D'ailleurs, où ne rencontre-t-on pas Loulou? Loulou, c'est la petite fille moderne" [Where does one not meet Loulou? Loulou is the little modern girl].[67] The conventional French view of the Gyp protagonist is the same today: "un caractère garçonnier, une verve narquoise, impertinente, effrontée, une insubordination d'écolière sans discipline" [a boyish character, a sardonic verve, impertinent, affronted, the insubordination of an undisciplined schoolgirl].[68]

Because the type of the Gyp girl is so clear-cut, and in spite of Marcia Jacobson, James's commentators are right to talk about *The Awkward Age* in relation to Gyp. In fact, because none of them seems to have read Gyp, preferring to summarize what James himself said about Gyp in the preface to *The Awkward Age*, they rarely know how right they are. What these commentators would doubtless recognize, were they to read Gyp closely, is that it is natural for James to have cast his novel about the upbringing of young women and their entrance into modern society in the *roman dialogué* form that one would naturally associate with Gyp.

Gyp is careful that the impossible personalities of her "pretty little poison" protagonists are not understood as isolated phenomena but as logical products of the moral laxness of a corrupted society (the natural view of such an archconservative). James in his novel makes a related point: society—not Nanda—is to blame for her knowing all she does, and her tragedy is that she pays the price despite her innocence. This implies that Gyp was an important fixture in the cultural context at a point in James's career when his fiction focused exclusively on the English social scene and used children and adolescents as central characters, as a means of representing the corruption of that social milieu. Gyp, as James well knew, had been doing the same thing in respect to French society for over a decade, and it is far less of a coincidence than has been suggested before by anyone, other than Tintner,[69] that at the end of the 1890s, James set the last of his series of fictions featuring children in the dialogue form Gyp had been using for fifteen years in her novels about children and adolescents.

In his preface to the revised edition of *The Awkward Age*, James recalled a diagram he had sent the editor of *Harper's Weekly* (where *The Awkward Age* first appeared) to describe the novel's division into ten books, each with a character's name as its title. James visualized

> . . . the neat figure of a circle consisting of a number of small rounds disposed at equal distance about a central object. The central object was my situation, my subject in itself, to which the thing would owe its title, and the small rounds represented so many distinct lamps, as I liked to call them, the function of each of which would be to light with all due intensity one of its aspects. (*LC2* 1130)

Many critics of *The Awkward Age* have commented on this passage, often emphasizing the image of "the neat figure of a circle" and the significance of circularity throughout the novel. Daniel Fogel, for example, makes a parallel between the diagram and "the pattern of the spiral dialectic, rounding back on its point of origin," which he sees as the central thematic structure of the novel.[70] Similarly, Isle connects the diagram and the individual book structure to the novel's overall circularity: "The direction of the whole, from [Book] I to [Book] X, is from old conceptions of innocence to new innocence. . . ."[71] What becomes apparent to the reader of *The Awkward Age* aware of *Autour du mariage* is that the fundamental circularity of James's novel derives from the double meaning of Gyp's title.

Translated into English, Gyp's title would best be rendered either as "About Marriage" or "On Marriage." However, such translations would lose the more usual meaning of the French word *autour*, meaning around, which Gyp uses to show that her investigation of marriage functions like a reconnaissance flight *around* the subject. Just as Stendhal entitled his treatise on love *De l'amour* (literally, "*of* love," as in "we are speaking *of* love"), so Gyp could have called her novel "Du Mariage." When James constructed his story as a series of scenes, each with a character's name for a title and each casting its light on the subject of "the awkward age" (in both meanings, the awkward age of late adolescence and a particular awkward epoch in the history of English upper-class society), he was fulfilling the prescription of Gyp's title *Autour du mariage* (around marriage), for what James created was a guided tour *around* the core subject of the "awkward age," which is marriage and sexual politics.

Suggesting that *The Awkward Age* is quite literally James's version of *Autour du mariage* obviously flies in the face of both Jacobson's warning about James's preface overdetermining the interpretation of his novel and the warning implicit in an influential trend in recent Jamesian criticism to deconstruct the degree to which James, through various means, created a construct of himself as "the Master" that has always had a powerful aftereffect on his own critical legacy.[72] The injunction to break the bounds of this construct is valid, and not just in respect to *The Awkward Age,* or even to all of the Jamesian canon, for few texts exist in a space entirely void of a powerfully overdetermining commentary. Nevertheless, this does not mean that readers and commentators of *The Awkward Age* should want to avoid considering that novel's relation to Gyp's fiction; Jacobson's warning to take James's preface with a grain of salt is made for the sake of a more complete and better understanding of James's novel and is a natural consequence of the great quantity of commentary on *The Awkward Age* that simply paraphrases James's references to Gyp in his preface. Nevertheless, Jacobson's warning should not serve as an excuse to turn a blind eye to the importance of Gyp's portrayals of unruly children and adolescents as a context for James's own interest in and portrayal of young people in his fiction of the late 1890s.

6

The Experimental and
Sentimental Novels in
Washington Square

*J*ames's incorporation of French literature and culture into his fiction did not solely take the form of allusions to specific literary texts. In *Washington Square,* James created one character as a personification of an entire mode of French fiction when he had Dr. Sloper base his behavior and his view of life on the same model—that of medicine—that Zola used as his basis for the procedure of the naturalist novelist. *Washington Square* has its most immediate impact as the tragedy of a young woman caught in an impossible bind; she would please both her father and the man she loves, but she can please her father only by rejecting her suitor, and the only possible result of whatever happens is for her to suffer.[1] Underlying this portrayal of domestic life as essentially tragic is another plot, a battle between fictional modes of representation, modes characterized by the heroine's father and aunt. This battle corresponds to the struggle in the mind of James as a critic and commentator on the contemporary novel and his struggle as a novelist for his own unique fictional voice. James apparently saw these struggles as binary oppositions, with the one side French and serious, the other English-language and sentimental. In dramatizing these struggles in the fictional form of *Washington Square,* James had to cast "serious, contemporary French fiction"—the French naturalists—as one of his characters, and in so doing, he made *Washington Square* one of his most obvious fictional investigations into the nature of representation.[2]

At the end of the 1870s, recent fiction writing provided no model to James's satisfaction for the uniquely American realist fictional voice he was searching for. The craft of the two realist novelists James admired most, Balzac and Turgenev, was too closely tied to the society each author represented to be a sufficient model for the would-be American realist. On the other hand, in his 1878 publication, *Hawthorne,* in a Bloomian wrestling with his strong precursor, James had turned Hawthorne, the one American author he could admire, into a writer whose faults were only too manifest. Contemporary models were even less satisfactory to James; to his way of thinking, narrative fiction as it was practiced around the beginning of the 1880s consisted primarily of the predominantly sentimental novels appearing in England and the United States and the experimental novels of Zola and other French writers most often referred to as the children of Flaubert. Neither type of fiction provided a happy alternative, as James saw it, and this concern is expressed in virtually all of his criticism published between 1878, when *Hawthorne* appeared, and 1886, the high point of what Powers has called James's "Naturalist Period."[3]

Washington Square is a fictional expression of James's ambivalence toward these two contemporary fictional forms and of his search for the uniquely American realist fictional voice. This novel portrays two conflicting approaches to the representation of the events it presents that correspond to the binary view James had at the time as a critic of the state of the contemporary novel. The siblings, Mrs. Penniman and Dr. Sloper, understand *Washington Square*'s central situation—the courtship of Catherine Sloper and Morris Townsend—in radically different ways, and these ways correspond to fictional modes: Mrs. Penniman's to sentimental fiction and Dr. Sloper's to the experimental or naturalist novel. As a result, *Washington Square* is a representation and dramatization of James's preoccupation throughout his career, and especially during the late 1870s and early 1880s, with forging a realistic fiction that was uniquely his own, or as Millicent Bell puts it, "to establish a distinctive voice";[4] the novel is about what fictional form to adopt for the understanding and representing of the central events of the plot and of events in general.[5]

James's critical writings between the appearance of *Hawthorne* in 1878 and the publication in *Longman's Magazine* of "The Art of Fiction" in 1884 testify to the importance of Zola and his fellow French naturalists to James's thinking about the craft of fiction.[6] The majority of James's critical writing during this period is concerned with continental European literature, and much of that—the 1880 review of Zola's *Nana,* two articles on Daudet, and "The Art of Fiction," the culminating critical work of the period—directly concerns itself with French naturalism and its leading proponent and practitioner.[7] The problem of how to create a uniquely American realistic fiction is the underlying theme in these four articles; James dramatized the problem in fiction in *Washington Square* through his portrayal of Dr. Sloper and Mrs. Penniman, and their personification of the extremes of naturalist and sentimental fiction.

Since much of James's 1880 review of *Nana* is devoted to criticizing Zola for representing "nature to us as a combination of the cesspool and the house of prostitution" (*LC2* 866), it is generally seen as a testimony of James's prudish side. However, the review is really a typical example of James's career-long ambivalence toward the value of Zola's fiction: at least "[r]eality is the object of M. Zola's efforts" (*LC2* 867), says James, which is more than he can say for his fellow English-language novelists:

> A novelist with a system, a passionate conviction, a great plan—incontestable attributes of M. Zola—is not now to be easily found in England or the United States. . . . The novel, moreover . . . is almost always addressed to young unmarried ladies, or at least always assumes them to be a large part of the novelist's public. This fact, to a French storyteller, appears, of course, a damnable restriction. . . . Half of life is a sealed book to young unmarried ladies, and how can a novel be worth anything that deals only with half of life? (*LC2* 868–69)

James expresses much the same sentiments four years later in "The Art of Fiction":

> In France today we see a prodigious effort (that of Emile Zola, to whose solid and serious work no explorer of the capacity of the novel can allude without respect), we see an extraordinary effort vitiated by a spirit of pessimism on a narrow basis. M. Zola is magnificent, but he strikes an English reader as ignorant; he has an air of working in the dark; if he had as much light as energy, his results would be of the highest value. As for the aberrations of a shallow optimism, the ground (of English fiction especially) is strewn with their brittle particles as with broken glass. (*LC1* 65)

Both these passages show James thinking in either/or terms; on the one hand there is Zola, on the other hand the English and American sentimentalists. James presents these two sides as the only two contemporary approaches to the craft of novel writing, but both sides have serious faults. Zola is faithful in theory to Balzac's ideal of representing reality as much as possible in all its complexity, although in practice he represents only a particular, negative version of reality; and the "aberrations of a shallow optimism" currently produced in England and the United States lack the merit of a commitment to reality.

In *Washington Square,* James reproduced this opposition between the naturalist and sentimental ways of viewing reality in the characters of the highly unlikely siblings Dr. Sloper and Mrs. Penniman. At the center of the story is the painfully shy Catherine, and the novel presents its readers with Dr. Sloper's and Aunt Penniman's particular ways of viewing her situation. While the problem James was working out in his criticism was how to transcend the shortcomings of both of his contemporary models of fiction writing, in *Washington Square* he shows his heroine to be tragically done in by the lack of an alternative to her aunt's and her father's forms of representation.

These forms correspond to the sentimental and naturalist novels, and what James says in "The Art of Fiction" about Zola and the English-language novelists could be applied to Mrs. Penniman and Dr. Sloper. The doctor can hardly "take *au sérieux*" his sister's "shallow optimism" and romantic sentimentality, and his view of the world is "vitiated by a spirit of pessimism on a narrow basis." Claude Bernard's experimental method was the model for Zola and his novelist in "Le Roman experimental," and Dr. Sloper is similar in using medical procedure as his model for life in general. At the same time, the narrator makes clear from the beginning of *Washington Square* that Mrs. Penniman is the personification of melodramatic sentimentality: "She was romantic, she was sentimental, she had a passion for little secrets and mysteries. . . . She would have liked to have a lover, and to correspond with him under an assumed name in letters left at a shop" (*WS* 9). Morris's entrance into the Slopers' world is a great event for Mrs. Penniman, who takes "much satisfaction in the sentimental shadings of this little drama" (81).

In every way that she is connected to Catherine and Morris's relationship, Mrs. Penniman demonstrates a will to make it conform to the conventions of a sentimental melodrama; the text displays this through her responses to the young couple's encounters and through the conventional rhetoric the narrative voice uses to portray her thoughts. When Catherine prefers that Morris visit her at home, her aunt cannot understand why Catherine declines "a sentimental tryst beside a fountain sheeted with dead leaves" (*WS* 52) in the park. Aunt Penniman imagines innumerable possibilities for her own part in what she views as a romantic melodrama: "She . . . expected to figure in the performance—to be the confidante, the Chorus, to speak the epilogue" (53). Her hope is for "the plot to thicken" (81), and she has a vision of a clandestine marriage in "some subterranean chapel" (82) that results in her making ludicrous arrangements to meet Morris secretly in an out-of-the-way oyster bar (82–83). After Catherine has an emotional scene with her father, Mrs. Penniman thinks Catherine should stay in bed for three days and is "in despair" over her niece's normal behavior the next day—and annoyed that "the trace of the night's tears had completely vanished from Catherine's eyes" (102).[8]

Catherine and Morris's ultimate separation does not disturb Mrs. Penniman at all, for a separation has as many romantic possibilities as an engagement. When Aunt Penniman returns home one day to find Catherine gone from the house, she is overjoyed at the thought that Catherine's absence fits in with her own romantic notions for a spurned heroine: " 'She has followed him to his own door—she has burst upon him in his own apartment!'. . . To visit one's lover, with tears and reproaches, at his own residence, was an image so agreeable to Mrs. Penniman's mind . . ." (WS 159). The only problem is that the backdrop for the scene does not correspond perfectly to her image of what the situation requires; Mrs. Penniman "felt a sort of aesthetic disappointment at its lacking, in this case, the harmonious accompaniments of darkness and storm" (159).

While Aunt Penniman sees all the romantic possibilities in Morris and Catherine's affair, her brother, Dr. Sloper, views the matter with the cold, scientific eye he turns on everything. The doctor takes pride in the length of his experience, in the keenness of his observation, and in the validity of the diagnoses he derives from his observations. His experience at making diagnoses on the basis of his observational skill may be a fine quality in a man of medicine, but the doctor applies the same formula to everything in life. This formula is most conspicuous to the plot of the novel in the doctor's negative first impression of Morris, an impression that is the assessment of a "physiognomist" (39) and "the result of thirty years of observation" (41).

Dr. Sloper approaches all of life as clinically as he would a patient's illness, and the brutality of this is most apparent during the doctor's call on Mrs. Montgomery, Morris Townsend's sister. The doctor lectures Mrs. Montgomery on young men who take advantage of the sacrifices of the women who are nearest and dearest to them, then finishes by exclaiming abruptly: " 'You have suffered immensely for your brother!' " (75). This "perfectly calculated" exclamation makes Morris's sister burst into tears (75–76). When she asks him how he figured her out, the doctor replies as though he were fielding a question from an observer of a scientific experiment: " 'By a philosophic trick—by what they call induction' " (76).

The doctor treats personal matters as though they were scientific experiments, and the situation between his daughter and her suitor takes on precisely the interest of an experiment in progress. After an emotional scene between father and daughter that ends with the doctor pushing Catherine out of his study, Dr. Sloper exclaims to himself: " 'By Jove . . . I believe she will stick—I believe she will stick!' " (99).[9] Instead of feeling any sympathy for his daughter's unhappiness, Dr. Sloper adopts the position of an observer. Catherine is caught between the desire to please her suitor and the desire to please her father, and like a psychologist studying laboratory rats in a cage, the doctor observes her behavior with complete detachment.

Twenty-five years after the publication of *Washington Square*, in "The Lesson of Balzac," James contrasted the *Rougon-Macquart* novels to *La Comédie humaine*, "the monument . . . without the example of which . . . Zola's work would not have existed" (*LC2* 130). While James praised Balzac for the extent to which he could "get into the constituted consciousness" of his characters, to see their situation "from their point of vision . . . from their point of pressing consciousness or sensation" (*LC2* 132), he took Zola to task for not being able to enter convincingly into his characters' consciousness: it is in his "knowing, and . . . showing, of life, only what his 'notes' would account for" (*LC2* 129–30) and his "mechanical side" (*LC2* 130) that Zola shows himself to be inferior to Balzac, who got "into the very skin and bones, of the habited, featured, colored, articulated form of life that he desired to present" (*LC2* 132). James criticizes Zola for his detachment from his subjects as he praises Balzac for his immersion.

What we see in James's presentation here of Zola is the same objective distance Dr. Sloper shows in *Washington Square;* if Zola relied too heavily, to James's way of thinking, on his notes and could not "enter convincingly into his characters' consciousness," so Dr. Sloper, who "made notes of everything, and . . . regularly consulted his notes" (*WS* 34), has (according to his other sister, Mrs. Almond) "no sympathy . . . that was never your strong point" (*WS* 170). And just as Zola creates novels on the medical model of Claude Bernard, presenting situations with the objective distance of a scientist, so Dr. Sloper uses his medical knowledge and training as his model for life in general and views the life around him with the same detachment.

Dr. Sloper admits the scientific detachment in his observation of his daughter to Mrs. Almond when he tells her of his conclusion that Catherine will "stick." He refers to himself as "a geometrical proposition" and says that "Catherine and her young man are my surfaces; I have taken their measure." The doctor adds that "there will be a great deal to observe." Mrs. Almond, who represents a happy medium between the romantic Mrs. Penniman and her scientific brother, scolds him: "You are shockingly cold-blooded!... I don't see why it should be such a joke that your daughter adores you" (*WS* 109). The doctor's reply again reveals his scientific disinterestedness in his daughter's situation:

> It is the point where the adoration stops that I find it interesting to fix. . . . The two [affections, for Morris and for Dr. Sloper,] are extremely mixed up,

> and the mixture is extremely odd. It will produce some third element, and
> that's what I am waiting to see. (109)

To the doctor, the situation is a chemical experiment: mix together a good-
looking fortune hunter and a domineering father; add a timid, unprepos-
sessing girl to whom the handsome young man pays unexpected attention,
and what new element is produced? As Richard Poirier says, "the word
'experiment' . . . is descriptive of Dr. Sloper's relationship with his daughter
in *Washington Square*."[10]

If this description of the doctor observing Morris and Catherine sounds
like Zola's description of the experimental novelist and his material in "Le
Roman experimental," it is not just because Zola's idea of creating novels
and Dr. Sloper's outlook on life are both extended metaphors on a medical
model but also because Dr. Sloper dramatizes naturalistic fictional representation.[11] As a result, readers of *Washington Square* have the same ambivalent response to Dr. Sloper that James shows to Zola's work.[12] The doctor
is concerned with reality, pragmatic observation, and the results of experiments, like Zola's novelist, and he is right in attempting to prevent a fortune hunter from taking advantage of his daughter. But his blunt realism
leaves the same bitter aftertaste that James found in Zola's.

When he learns from Mrs. Penniman of his daughter's final separation
from her suitor, the doctor cares only for the "great pleasure" he derives
from having been "in the right" (158). When Catherine tells her father of
the breakup, he is "disappointed" and unable to resist cruelly teasing her
so as to have "his revenge after all" (168). Mrs. Almond scolds Dr. Sloper
for his heartless treatment of his daughter's separation from her lover. "You
have no sympathy," she tells her brother, and if (as they both presume)
Catherine has not dismissed Morris but has been abandoned by him, it is
" 'All the more reason you should be gentle with her' " (170). But the
doctor never shows such delicacy; when he catches pneumonia, he bluntly
apprises his daughter of the situation:

> "It is congestion of the lungs," he said to Catherine; "I shall need very good
> nursing. It will make no difference, for I shall not recover; but I wish every-
> thing to be done, to the smallest detail, as if I should. I hate an ill-conducted
> sick-room; and you will be so good as to nurse me on the hypothesis that I
> shall get well." . . . But he had never been wrong in his life, and he was not
> wrong now. (177)

After the doctor's death, his will is read along with the codicil that disinher-
its his daughter in language so indelicate that it prompts Catherine to complain—one of the few times she ever does—not about being disinherited

but about the terseness of the language: "I wish it had been expressed a little differently!" (178).

Catherine's complaint against her father's lack of delicacy is exactly the same complaint James made about Zola's *Nana* during the same year he was writing *Washington Square:* "The human note is completely absent. . . . It is not his choice of subject that has shocked us; it is the melancholy dryness of his execution, which gives us all the bad taste of a disagreeable dish and none of the nourishment" (*LC2* 870). A concern with realism, argues James in the same pages, is no excuse for a want of taste:

> Taste, in its intellectual applications, is the most human faculty we possess, and as the novel may be said to be the most human form of art, it is a poor speculation to put the two things out of conceit of each other. Calling it naturalism will never make it profitable. It is perfectly easy to agree with M. Zola . . . for the matter reduces itself to a question of application. It is impossible to see why the question of application is less urgent in naturalism than at any other point of the scale, or why, if naturalism is, as M. Zola claims, a method of observation, it can be followed without delicacy or tact. (*LC2* 868)

These remarks can be applied verbatim to Dr. Sloper. Like Mrs. Almond, who tells the doctor he is cold-blooded and has no sympathy, we can see that the "human note is completely absent" in Dr. Sloper, and we can complain of "the melancholy dryness of his execution" just as Catherine complains of the way he expresses himself in the codicil. Dr. Sloper is concerned with "the question of application" and the "method of observation," just as Zola is; but just as James complains of the excessiveness of the application and the observation in Zola,[13] so the characters in *Washington Square* complain of the doctor's equal excessiveness. In both Zola's and Dr. Sloper's cases, the excessiveness is the cause of the want of delicacy, and the want of delicacy is the principal fault in each man's clinical representation of reality.

A pivotal moment in the novel comes when the doctor gleefully reports to his sister his impression that "the scoundrel has backed out!" Mrs. Penniman retorts, "It seems to make you very happy that your daughter's affections have been trifled with," and the doctor replies, "It does. . . . It's a great pleasure to be in the right." This is one of the more glaring examples of the doctor's lack of delicacy, and when his sister responds, "Your pleasures make one shudder," the reader ceases to laugh at Mrs. Penniman and shudders with her at the absence of the human note in her brother (*WS* 158).

This moment is important, for here Mrs. Penniman's romantic sentimentality gets the better of her brother's clinical detachment. After that moment, neither of the alternatives that the two siblings represent can be seen as superior. Both the romantic and the scientific modes of representation are unsatisfactory, and the other characters in the novel do not offer any better forms of expression. Morris dissimulates, Catherine barely knows how to express herself at all,[14] and Mrs. Almond, the reasonable medium between her brother and her sister, is not developed enough to be seen as a third alternative.

Just as Mrs. Penniman looks better by virtue of her contrast to her brother, so the critique of Zola's lack of delicacy and taste in *Nana* leads James to a better appreciation of English fiction, in spite of all its weaknesses.

> The human note . . . is what saves us in England . . . this fact . . . that we have . . . a deeper, more delicate perception of the play of character and the state of the soul. This is what often gives an interest to works conceived on a much narrower program than those of M. Zola. (*LC* 2 870)

When James complained about the lack of taste in *Nana,* it was not just out of Victorian prudishness. The fictional example of Dr. Sloper illustrates what James meant by the absence of "delicacy and taste" and the "human note." James's reservations in the 1880s about Zola's fiction derive not so much from its indecency as from how clinically it characterizes human life. As much as he agreed with the naturalists' ideal of realistic representation, James obviously had difficulty with the naturalists' perception of human society as a Darwinian world. This implies that he was even less sympathetic to the naturalist school's Darwinian, Marxist-based ideology than has been suggested, and if after 1884, in his "Naturalist Period,"[15] James still grappled with the problem of how to forge a realistic fiction of his own, it is perhaps because he did not see how to represent reality in a way that did not lead readers to the conclusion that this represented reality was Darwinian.

If in *Hawthorne* James set his American precursor up as a straw man in order to enable his own fictional accomplishments to transcend Hawthorne's, then *Washington Square* and the criticism of the early 1880s serve the same purpose with respect to the contemporary fiction scene. In both *Washington Square* and the critical essays of the period, James defined his views of the limitations of contemporary novel writing in England, America, and France in his attempt to transcend them in his search for his own distinctive fictional voice. Bell argues that James found his "true voice, an authentic and original being," which he denied Catherine Sloper, in Isabel Archer.[16] It is very much to the point that James cast female protagonists as emblematic of his own search for a voice, especially at a time when women were first raising their voices to demand the vote (the French use the word *voix* to mean both "voice" and "vote"), and just a few years before he was to write a long novel about women's efforts to secure a vote/voice.

However, a skeptical view of the novels following *The Portrait of a Lady* suggests that James had not resolved the problem of voice and was still struggling with it: *A London Life* shows another young woman's ineffectiveness to speak or act against the situation she finds herself in; *The Bostonians* treats the movement of women attempting to make their collective voice heard and portrays one young woman in particular who *can* speak, and brilliantly at that, showing the questionable fate this ability to speak nevertheless brings her;[17] and *The Reverberator* tells of the consequences of a young woman's mistake in speaking too much to a reporter. The last two long novels of the 1880s both have women as their title characters, and while both Miriam Rooth and the Princess Casamassima use their voices to eloquent effect,[18] James still isolates their unique voices through a narrative point of view that (with the exception of the Princess in the last chapter of *The Princess Casamassima*) presents these two women only through the eyes of others and primarily through men's. The problem of voice remained with James through the end of the decade, and in *The Tragic Muse* he dramatized the related issue of representation again in fictional form.

7

Mountebanks, Artists, Representation, and *The Tragic Muse*

At the apartment of Mme. Carré, in the same scene in which Peter Sherringham hears Miriam Rooth recite from *King John* and is struck by the young aspirant's progress, Basil Dashwood, Miriam's eventual husband, makes his first appearance in *The Tragic Muse*. Peter had first heard of Dashwood in the novel's preceding chapter, when Miriam's mother told him that "Dashwood" was a "*nom de théâtre*" (*TM* 928). When Miriam finishes her recital from *King John* and Peter admires her ability to hide her self-consciousness as she performs, Dashwood quotes (inaccurately) the Latin proverb "*Ars [est] celare artem*" [art consists in concealing art] (937). This proverb makes the point so central to understanding *The Tragic Muse:* that at the root of art and its appeal is the paradox that art is inherently deceitful, and the better art is at concealing how deceitful or false it is (which in itself constitutes a deception), the more truthful it seems. Thus representation always threatens to be misrepresentation (and to convey this potential appropriately, I use the neologism, [mis]representation).[1]

It is particularly appropriate that in a novel about this paradox of realistic art, a character with a false name (indeed, we never learn Dashwood's real name) should utter the proverb expressing that paradox. Ovid's *Ars amatoria* is perhaps the source for the proverb (if it is not, it expresses the same point): "Si latet, ars prodest" [Art, if concealed, succeeds].[2] This injunction is the conclusion to a series of admonitions to men interested in keeping the heart of their beloved. It is the secret to a lasting seductive power, and the point is related to the appeal (or seductive power) of art, which is based on fiction masquerading as truth. For fiction to masquerade successfully as truth, it must conceal the artifice, just as Ovid's lover must conceal the artifice in order to remain appealing to his beloved.

This is precisely the grounds for Miriam's admiration of Mlle. Voisin, the actress from the Comédie Française: "The grace of [Miriam's] new acquaintance was the greater as the becoming bloom which she alluded to as artificial was the result of a science so consummate that it had none of the grossness of a mask" (*TM* 953). James's contemporary, the painter James Whistler, expressed the same paradox at the very same time that James was working on *The Tragic Muse:* "Industry in Art is a necessity—not a virtue—and any evidence of the same, in the production, is a blemish, not a quality; a proof, not of achievement, but of absolutely insufficient work, for work alone will efface the footsteps of work."[3] Much the same point is also made in *Wilhelm Meister's Apprenticeship,* a text to which *The Tragic Muse* alludes specifically (1046), in a passage praising the actor Serlo: "the intellectual style, in which he could so easily and gracefully express the finest shadings of his part, excited more delight, *as he could conceal the art* which, by long-continued practice, he had made his own."[4]

Most interpreters of *The Tragic Muse*[5] follow James's comment in his 1908 preface to the novel that it is about "the conflict between art and 'the world' " (*LC2* 1103) and read this novel as James's novelistic reflection on the nature and demands of art and the life of the artist—as opposed to those of the "world." Typically they have concluded that the novel emphatically privileges the idealized world of the artist—"art"—over the ordinary, material "world."[6] Such readings of the novel, many of which rely on a biographical approach, see Nick Dormer's spurning of a promising career in Parliament for solitary hours in his painter's studio as a fictional representation of what was long held to be James's own belief in the "true" artist as dedicated to his craft and above material and commercial considerations.[7]

The Tragic Muse is about the conflict between art and the world, but it is not a manifesto favoring an idealized artist's world above and removed from the material, ordinary world. Rather, the novel suggests that conflict and paradoxical opposition are central to art and being an artist; art is not the result of choosing "art" over the "world" but a constant juggling of the conflict between art as an ideal, on the one hand, and the material, the "real," "the world," on the other. Furthermore, *The Tragic Muse* shows that the task of the producing, serious artist involves negotiating a space between the opposites of the ideal and the practical.

Because critics have neglected *The Tragic Muse* (compared with James's other novels), and because so much of what critics have written about *The*

Tragic Muse has necessarily had to be devoted to explicitly making a case for the novel's being considered at all,[8] analysis of the formal ways the novel reinforces its treatment of art has not been as exhaustive as with other James novels. Commentators have not mentioned the way this text uses references to other—mostly French—texts, almost always in pairs, in relation to a pervading motif of charlatanism and hypocrisy and an equally pervasive theater metaphor. These three formal features (the intertextual references, the motif of charlatanism and hypocrisy, and the theater metaphor) reinforce the view that *The Tragic Muse* does not treat artistic representation and the artist's life as a conflict between the material world and a transcendental world of art; rather, *The Tragic Muse* is about the complexity of pursuing an artistic vocation, the appeal of art, and the paradox of fictional truth inherent in artistic representation. Art, the novel suggests, makes human life meaningful, but it is fictional, unreal in nature; yet in spite of being fictional, art's appeal derives from its apparent realism. *The Tragic Muse* "is *about* representation"—"representation is . . . its primary subject-matter," as William R. Goetz says,[9] and about how representation's paradoxical nature is at the heart of the power and attraction of artistic representation.

In *The Tragic Muse,* the theater is a recurrent metaphor for the characters' "real" lives; the novel persistently presents other walks of life than the theater world as theater, thus reminding readers that life is like art and vice versa. Gabriel Nash, on being introduced to Peter Sherringham, comments that social life is "like a procession at the theatre" (*TM* 736), and he implies that parliamentary politics is another form of theater when he asks Lady Agnes Dormer if "comedian for comedian, isn't the actor more honest" than the politician (741); Peter argues that the dramatic art is all-inclusive: "it seems to me to include all others" (740); and when Nick Dormer complains of his inability not to appear bored with politicians, he supposes that "apparently I'm not enough of a comedian" (963).

Characters in the novel make frequent accusations or self-accusations of hypocrisy (these accusations—what I call the motif of charlatanism—are usually indicated by words like "mountebank" or "humbug," which are repeated twenty-one times in the novel),[10] thus pointing out what the theater metaphor already indicates: that pretending and (mis)representation are at the heart of all the professions portrayed in the novel. Finally, *The Tragic Muse* alludes to a series of texts, mostly French theatrical ones, and mostly in pairs of titles. Virtually all of them are texts in which duplicity and acting in the general sense of performing and pretending play a significant role.

Given the importance of the theater world in *The Tragic Muse,* it is appropriate for the theater to provide one of the novel's dominant metaphors and for most of the literary allusions to be to dramatic literature. In the novel's fourth chapter, Nash and Peter Sherringham contrast Balzac's *La Cousine Bette* with Emile Augier's play *Les Lionnes pauvres* (*TM* 748); two chapters later, the Dallow party sees Musset's *Il ne faut jurer de rien* and Jules Sandeau's *Mademoiselle de la Seiglière* at the Comédie Française (769); and in the following chapter, Miriam performs for Madame Carré from Augier's *L'Aventurière* (787–88), a play about an actress who poses as an "honest" woman in order to snare a wealthy husband (following which she recites one of Musset's poems [789]).[11]

The appropriateness of alluding to so many dramatic texts in a novel set partly in the theater should not obscure the fact that these allusions bear considerable significance. In some of the works referred to, such as *Wilhelm Meister* and *L'Aventurière*, actors or the theater world plays a significant role; in *La Cousine Bette*, as in *The Tragic Muse* itself, the theater is a central metaphor; and in virtually all of them, deceitful role-playing is central to the plot and to characterization. The consistency with which deceit appears in the literary allusions and the frequency with which the allusions are made in pairs[12] are too much to be coincidental; obviously something is going on.[13]

The allusion to Augier's *L'Aventurière* is typical of such references in *The Tragic Muse*, most obviously because it is to a play with a plot centering on the deceitful scheme of a former actress to marry into a wealthy family. The allusion also plays a complex role in the scene in which it appears and in relation to the novel's treatment of the questions of art and representation. It cites chapter and verse precisely, making clear that the first piece Miriam recites for Madame Carré consists of "the lines of Clorinde, in the fine interview with Célie, in the third act of the play" (*TM* 788). This scene, the fifth of act 3 of *L'Aventurière*, is a dialogue between Célie and the former actress and fortune hunter, Clorinde, who, while masquerading as a respectable woman, has succeeded in gaining the affection of Célie's father and expects to obtain his hand and fortune. Miriam performs Clorinde's lines, and Mme. Carré, who generally played "bad" women, including the role of Clorinde, recites Célie's speeches. This is an ironic reversal, for the innocent, naïve, young Miriam here plays the role of the experienced woman while the older and experienced Mme. Carré performs that of the innocent girl.

This reversal is not inappropriate to either Augier's or James's scene, for the principal function of Augier's scene is for Célie to give Clorinde the lesson in conventional virtue she sorely needs. Mme. Carré also gives a lesson, although in a different kind of virtue. Intertwined with the preparations for reciting Augier's scene is a discussion between Mme. Carré and

Mrs. Rooth on the subject of virtue. Miriam's mother had expressed concern over the sort of life—the "standards... the... tone... the conduct" (*TM* 785)—Miriam would encounter if she worked in the theater, eliciting Mme. Carré's scorn of middle-class British prudery. Referring to the English bowdlerizing of French plays for the London stage, Mme. Carré tells her guests: "I know what you [English] do with our pieces—to show your superior virtue!... Bad women? *Je n'ai joué que ça, madame.* 'Really' bad? I tried to make them real!" (785–86). At this moment, Miriam breaks into the conversation to state that she "can say 'L'Aventurière' " (786). The recital does not begin immediately, though, for "instead of beginning the scene, Madame Carré turn[s] to" Mrs. Rooth and lectures her on virtue and artistic achievement: "to go where things are done best . . . [t]o do them well is virtue enough, and not to make a mess of it the only respectability" (786).[14]

What James's text accomplishes here is the juxtaposition of two lectures on virtue and conventional manners. In having Mme. Carré recite Célie while Miriam recites Clorinde, rather than the opposite, *The Tragic Muse* answers Miriam's mother's scruples in two ways. First, the text plays a joke on Mrs. Rooth in having Miriam recite exactly the kind of part she does not want Miriam to play. Second, and equally important, because Mme. Carré is known for playing precisely the "bad" roles Mrs. Rooth hopes her daughter will avoid, her taking Célie's part serves as a concrete example that the role one plays hardly matters, which in turn raises the question of representation. Mrs. Rooth's scruples about the roles Miriam might be expected to play—"I shouldn't like to see her represent a very bad woman—a *really* bad one" (*TM* 785)—in conjunction with her fear about the sort of behavior Miriam would encounter in the profession rely on Mrs. Rooth's making too literal a connection between the actress's role and her character off the stage.

Miriam's mother fails to recognize that there can be a difference between the role and the player; in other words, she fails to see that representation is illusion (which is perhaps the result of her passion for novel reading [853]). With Miriam acting the "bad" woman and Mme. Carré the innocent and "virtuous" one, the scene shows that such roles can be interchanged and thus rebuts Mrs. Rooth's assumption about the connection between role and actor. Mrs. Rooth has fallen into the representational fallacy, and one of the roles of the conversation about virtue and of the allusion to the encounter between Clorinde and Célie in *L'Aventurière* is to point out the distinction between the representer and the represented.

A further aspect of the allusion to *L'Aventurière* raises at least one other issue about representation, about the relationship between the representing and the represented, between the signifier and the signified: the potential social danger of the absence of the kind of connection between representer and represented that Mrs. Rooth believes in. Clorinde's part, the one Miriam recites, is a straightforward example of (mis)representation, of the inherent danger in representation, for Clorinde's misrepresentation of herself as a respectable lady has potential social consequences that are tangible and damaging: Clorinde manages, at least at first, to lure Célie's father toward an unwise marriage. This threatens to destroy the family, as Célie and her brother attempt to prevent the marriage; and after the scheme is discovered, Célie's rich father suffers considerably at having been so taken in by Clorinde's performance.

This aspect of *L'Aventurière* demonstrates the power and danger of (mis)representation, and its dramatization of a character who is more than she appears to be has something in common with James's portrayal of such characters as Madame Merle, Eugenia Münster, Mrs. Brookenham, and Kate Croy. Like these characters, Augier's Clorinde suggests the social complexity, indeed the social chaos and anarchy, that a duplicitous, playacting person can give rise to, and thus demonstrates some of the inherent dangers of (mis)representation.

Another way the play suggests the power of (mis)representation is through Célie's father, who *wants* to believe Clorinde is honest and in love with him; he would prefer to believe the illusion, the representation. This preference is repeated in another text *The Tragic Muse* alludes to, Balzac's *La Cousine Bette,* and it is also an important point in *The Tragic Muse* itself. There are several instances in James's novel where fiction, representation, or lies are seen as preferable to reality. As Peter tells Nick in their discussion about drama and painting, "I am fond of representation—the representation of life: I like it better, I think, than the real thing. You like it, too, so you have no right to cast the stone. You like it best done one way and I another" (*TM* 756).

These two are not the only ones who feel the power of creative representation; there is Mrs. Rooth, who "delighted in novels, poems, perversions, misrepresentations and evasions, and had a capacity for smooth, superfluous fascination" (853), and there are Nick and Nash, who enthusiastically discuss "the mysteries and miracles of reproduction and representation" over dinner (977). The alternative to representation is "a fifth-rate world . . . a bedimmed, star-punctured nature which had no consolation—the bleared, irresponsive eyes of the London heaven" (1199) that Peter envisions when he is obliged to confront life without Miriam.[15]

While artistic representation can be a consolation for or an alternative to the meaninglessness of human existence, it is also a fantasy. This is why

James has Miriam recite Tennyson's "The Lotos-Eaters" after the Augier performance, for the chorus in Tennyson's poem characterizes human life as "Trouble on trouble, pain on pain,/Long labor unto aged breath";[16] therefore, rather than struggling and suffering, how much more appealing it is to rest and dream the lotus-induced dream: "How sweet it were, hearing the downward stream,/With half-shut eyes ever to seem/Falling asleep in a half-dream!/To dream and dream, like yonder amber light."[17] The drug-induced dream is more attractive than ordinary life even if the dream is but a fantasy, much as figurative (representational) art, which is fiction masquerading as truth, is the more appealing alternative to a meaningless universe.

Because representation is fiction, though, one must question its value. The ability to represent implies the ability to misrepresent—which is why Kenneth Graham speaks of "the dangerously protean adaptability of the imagination"[18]—and misrepresentation can have damaging consequences. In *The Tragic Muse*, it is Peter who questions the value of representation— even though it is he who speaks so clearly to Nick in favor of representation—and he does so by considering the possible dishonesty and the potential danger of Miriam's ability to represent anything and everything. Miriam seems to have no character of her own—"she positively had no countenance of her own"—only the ability, albeit a talented one, to represent other personalities—her "only being was to 'make believe,' to make believe that she had any and every being that you liked" (*TM* 832).

Miriam is an infinity of potential representations, and although the danger of her capacity for representation has far less tangible consequences than, say, Mrs. Brookenham's or Augier's Clorinde's, at least in Peter's mind, Miriam's ability to represent anything is dangerous and dishonest. Peter paradoxically describes the "artistic character" as a pillaging army that is welcome: "You must forage and ravage and leave a track behind you; you must live upon the country you occupy. And you give such delight that, after all, you are welcome—you are infinitely welcome!" (949). And "the artistic character," as represented by Miriam, is "bad, perverse, dangerous . . . an abyss of ruin" (948). Paradoxically, the better Miriam is at representing—the more truthful she is to her role—the more dishonest she seems: "She sometimes said things with such perfection that they seemed dishonest" (958). Other than in remarks such as these, (mis)representation does not appear to have tangible negative social consequences in *The Tragic Muse* (except perhaps to Peter's heart), as it does, for example, in *L'Aventurière* or in *La Cousine Bette* or to Isabel Archer and Nanda Brookenham.

Nevertheless, *The Tragic Muse* persistently alludes to literary texts that more or less melodramatically dramatize deceit, misrepresentation, and their dangers in order that the reader may see Peter's concerns as not resulting just from his growing amorous attachment to Miriam. The allusions remind the reader that representation is dangerous and essentially dishonest, and this is necessary because *The Tragic Muse* is a reflection on the paradoxical nature of art; because of this the novel does not glorify the artist's calling but presents the artist and the work as both painful and satisfying and as involving compromises. Also because of this, the novel presents the pictorial and narrative arts that purport to be realistic as themselves fundamentally paradoxical—these arts masquerade as truth (and derive much of their power from this masquerade) at the same time that they are acknowledged as fiction; this is why Peter can be so "fond of representation" and "like it better . . . than the real thing" at the same time he finds Miriam dangerous and dishonest.

Peter's image of the artist as a pillaging army presents the artist as preying off his or her public, but the image also suggests a mutually necessary though painful symbiosis between public and artist. From Peter's point of view, that of the spectator and connoisseur of art, the artist is a source of both pain and pleasure. From the perspective of the artist, the act of creation works in the same way; artistic creation is both painful and pleasurable. *The Tragic Muse* suggests something of these concerns by having Miriam offer to "recite the 'Nights' of Alfred de Musset" (789) once she has finished her recitation of Clorinde in *L'Aventurière*. Once again, James indulges in a joke at his characters' expense, for Musset's "Nights" consists of four poems ("La Nuit de mai," "La Nuit de décembre," "La Nuit d'août," and "La Nuit d'octobre") plus a four-line fragment ("La Nuit de juin"). The aggregate length of the "Nuit" poems would certainly tax the speaker's memory and endurance, and any audience's patience, which is why Miriam's offer to recite them elicits Mme. Carré's reply: "Diable! . . . that's more than I can!" (789).

Whereas James's text was specific about exactly what passages Miriam recites from *L'Aventurière* and from Shakespeare's *King John*, it is vague about what Miriam recites from Musset's "Nuit" poems, saying only that she "rolled out a fragment of one of the splendid conversations of Musset's poet with his muse" (789). But it hardly matters which of the poems Miriam recites, for they all express the pain involved in poetic creation. The most famous passage in the "Nuit" poems, and the one that most specifically relates pain to artistic creation, is the image of the pelican that offers its own breast to appease the hunger of its young in "La Nuit de mai"; this, Musset's muse tells the poet, is an image for the creation of poetry:

> Poète, c'est ainsi que font les grands poètes.
> Ils laissent s'égayer ceux qui vivent un temps;

Mais les festins humains qu'ils servent à leurs fêtes
Ressemblent la plupart à ceux des pélicans.

[Poet, this is the way of great poets.
They allow joy to those who live a while;
But the human feasts they serve at their festivals
For the most part resemble the pelicans'.][19]

The image of the pelican feeding its young with its own breast is emblematic to Musset's muse of the pain of poetic creation, but it is different from Peter's image of the artist as a pillaging army: for Musset, the poet is the prey of his or her readers; for Peter in *The Tragic Muse*, the artist preys off his or her public.

Musset's "Nuit" poems bear comparison with *The Tragic Muse* in a number of respects. These poems plot a relationship between suffering and artistic creation, and as such show art to be essentially paradoxical. The paradox in Musset's vision—that artistic creation is both painful and a source of pleasure—is different from the paradox being developed in *The Tragic Muse*, in which art is a *source* of pleasure to *both* audience and artist at the same time as it is grounded in fantasy and is potentially dangerous to the spectator and a difficult vocation, demanding compromises of the artist. This difference is paradigmatic of the high Romantic and late realist views of art that Musset and James, respectively, espouse. It is yet another example of the ironic use of literary allusions in *The Tragic Muse* to have Miriam recite from this group of Romantic poems early in her career, when she has no idea, as she will later, of the conflicts and problems she will encounter as a working artist. This irony suggests that real experience working in the theater will alter any romantic views about being a performer that Miriam has at the beginning.

The issue of virtue that was raised in the conversation between Mme. Carré and Mrs. Rooth appears again in relation to the two plays the Dormer party sees at the Comédie Française—*Mademoiselle de la Seiglière* and *Il ne faut jurer de rien*—plays that also further pursue the themes of deceit and representation. Sandeau's and Musset's plays have in common the issue of interclass marriages, which is not an entirely irrelevant one to James's novel, given the attraction between Peter and Miriam. More important for the purposes of *The Tragic Muse*, though, the plots of both French texts are structured around characters who dissemble by playing roles, pretending to be different from who they really are. In Musset's *Il ne faut jurer de rien*, in order to convince him to get married, the retired merchant Van Buck permits his nephew and heir, Valentin, to masquerade as an anonymous admirer of Cécile de Mantes, the young lady Van Buck projected for his nephew's wife. Valentin does not want to marry and hopes that his advances to Cécile will succeed, thus proving to his uncle that the young lady is not a dutiful daughter and therefore not likely to prove a faithful wife; Van Buck hopes that Cécile will withstand her pretended admirer's overtures and thus help convince Valentin to agree to the marriage. Valentin introduces himself into the de Mantes household under false pretenses, his uncle pretends not to know the young man, and Cécile, who is far more resourceful than her naïve and innocent demeanor suggests, feigns fainting in order to escape to a rendezvous with Valentin and eventually wins his heart and hand.

While Cécile de Mantes is only apparently an ingenue, her counterpart, the title character of *Mademoiselle de la Seiglière,* has all the requisite characteristics of the ingenue: she is good through and through, and she is completely incapable of conceiving of deception and ulterior motives on the part of her acquaintances. Nevertheless, she is surrounded by deceit. *Mademoiselle de la Seiglière* tells of two aristocratic émigré families during and after the French Revolution. One family, the Seiglières, emigrated and forfeited their estate; it eventually falls into the hands of their former farmer, Stamply. The Seiglières' neighbors, the widowed Mme. de Vaubert and her son, had saved a remnant of their property, and the novel and the play based on it tell primarily of the efforts of Mme. de Vaubert to recover the neighboring Seiglière property for the Seiglières and to marry her son, Raoul, to Mlle. de la Seiglière. To this end she wages a hypocritical campaign, first for Stamply's affection and trust, which succeeds in persuading the old farmer to give the property back to the Seiglières and drives him to a lonely death, and then to distract Stamply's son, Bernard, from his legal claim to the property. The play ends happily when Bernard abandons his claim and young Raoul de Vaubert suddenly—and equally unbelievably—renounces his claim to Mlle. de la Seiglière's hand, making it possible for her to marry Bernard.[20]

Deceit is central to Sandeau's plot, for unless Mme. de Vaubert (who also merits comparison to James's Madame Merle–type characters) can play a role that wins the trust of the gullible Stamply, there is no story. Deceit is also central to Musset's play: first, the play tests Valentin's assumption that his future wife will naturally prove deceitful sooner or later, and second, it renders Valentin's mistrust all the more problematic by having him use deceit and disguise to prove his belief in the generality of falseness. In any case, characters pretending and playing deceitful roles are central to both plays.

The centrality of deceit in *Il ne faut jurer de rien* and *Mademoiselle de la Seiglière* explains in part why they are mentioned in *The Tragic Muse*. They are also mentioned as examples of French theater that are acceptable for an unmarried Englishwoman's viewing: "just the thing for the cheek of the young person" (*TM* 769). These two plays are to be understood as not offensive to a genteel young lady's virtue, even if they are full of deceit. There is yet another comment here on the matter of virtue, similar to the conversation on the subject between Mrs. Rooth and Mme. Carré. If the deceit in Musset's and Sandeau's plays is not offensive to conventions of virtue, the deceit in the first pair of literary allusions in *The Tragic Muse*—to Augier's *Les Lionnes pauvres* and Balzac's *La Cousine Bette*—certainly is: as Lady Agnes says on hearing Balzac and Augier mentioned, "What dreadful authors!" (748).

However, there is not much beyond convention to distinguish Balzac's Valérie Marneffe's giving her pretended love for the Baron Hulot's fortune from Sandeau's Mme. de Vaubert's offering her pretended affection and consideration in return for the deed to Stamply's property. In fact, the deceivers in all four of these French texts are characterized by their seeking to take advantage of someone's innocence and gullibility. Thus these two pairs of allusions bear contrast to each other, the one—to the Musset and Sandeau plays—showing a socially acceptable deceit and thus suggesting to James's reader just how hypocritical "virtue" can be, and the other—to *La Cousine Bette* and *Les Lionnes pauvres*—showing deceit in a much harsher light.

James's novel has already related the issue of virtue to the issue of representation in Mme. Carré's speech to Mrs. Rooth: "To do [things] well is virtue enough, and not to make a mess of it the only respectability" (*TM* 786). Conventional virtue would have things be as they should *appear*, while according to Mme. Carré's definition (which is the ancient definition of virtue, the Aristotelian notion of *virtù* or excellence), virtue lies in representing things, as much as possible, as they *are*. The running commentary in *The Tragic Muse* on virtue underscores the hypocrisy in the conventional notion of virtue; this is Mme. Carré's point, and this is what comes of contrasting *La Cousine Bette* to *Mademoiselle de la Seiglière*. Both texts can be read as cautionary tales moralizing against deceit: Mlle. de la Seiglière is honest and true in an exemplary way, and it is her honesty and faithfulness that save the day in Sandeau's story, not Mme. de Vaubert's machinations; Balzac's novel demonstrates the ravages of Valérie Marneffe's intrigues upon a family.

Mme. Carré would no doubt argue that *La Cousine Bette* represents deceit better than *Mademoiselle de la Seiglière* does, and that Balzac's text makes a more convincing case to avoid the evils of deceit. However, the theater version of Sandeau's novel is "just the thing for the cheek of the young person," while Balzac's novel is not. The conventional notions of virtue as they are reflected in the preference for the Sandeau and Musset plays over the Balzac and Augier texts are as hypocritical and false as the ability of Valérie Marneffe, Cécile de Mantes, Mme. de Vaubert, and Séraphine Pommeau (the deceitful wife in Augier's *Les Lionnes pauvres*) to represent one thing as another, namely, deceit as virtue.

The emphasis on the hypocrisy of virtue in *The Tragic Muse* is part of the novel's attention to acting, pretending, and representation, and to its presentation of acting and pretending as pervading all realms of society; in pointing out the hypocrisy of conventional virtue, the novel finds one of several ways to show the pervasiveness of pretense—what I call the motif of charlatanism. Since the English "hypocrisy" derives from the Greek *(hypokrisis)*, meaning playacting, the emphasis on the hypocrisy in conventional virtue, along with the reminders of the impact of conventional virtue on society (through, for example, the discussions of what is suitable for young women to view) is another way for the novel to show that playacting is fundamental to social manners and norms.

The reference to *La Cousine Bette* and *Les Lionnes pauvres* is the first literary allusion in *The Tragic Muse,* and more than any of the others in the novel is presented as an opposed pair. Nash speaks admiringly of Balzac's "magnificent portrait of Valérie Marneffe, in 'La Cousine Bette,' " and Peter supposes that Nash contrasts this portrait with "the poverty of Emile Augier's Séraphine in 'Les Lionnes Pauvres' " (*TM* 748).[21] On the most immediate level, the contrast is about literary merit. Nash's admiration of the representation of Mme. Marneffe in *La Cousine Bette* is an example of Nash sharing James's own critical views: *La Cousine Bette,* as we know from James's criticism, was one of the novels, and Valérie one of the characters, James admired most in Balzac's work.[22] *Les Lionnes pauvres* is in fact a shallow representation of a married woman gone astray, providing little sense of what drives Séraphine to take and ruin a lover, while *La Cousine Bette* quite powerfully renders what prompts Valérie's schemes. As a result, we might be tempted to see in this exchange an instance of James making Nash a mouthpiece for his own artistic views, for on the surface this double allusion seems only to provide contrasting examples of a gripping and an unconvincing character portrayal.[23]

But to see these allusions to *La Cousine Bette* and *Les Lionnes pauvres* only as good and bad examples of portraits of ladies who are anything but ladies is to miss much of what resonates between *The Tragic Muse, Les Lionnes pauvres, La Cousine Bette,* and the issue of (mis)representation. For one, James's reference is once again humorous; there is a joke in comparing the titles of these two French texts about ruthless courtesans, for as *La Cousine Bette* is the first part of a diptych called *Les Parents pauvres,* the titles of Balzac's and Augier's works are almost identical *(Les Parents pauvres, Les Lionnes pauvres);* the irony is that Balzac's Valérie (who in her pursuit of an income of forty thousand francs a year [*Comédie* 7: 400] disgraces and ruins an entire family, causing one uncle's suicide, another's premature death, and driving the father, Baron Hulot, to defrauding the government) comes off as the lioness of Augier's title far more than Séraphine (who hopes to get either her present or her future admirer to pay off the comparatively small ten-thousand-franc debt she has incurred for the sake of her wardrobe).

More significantly, though Valérie Marneffe and Séraphine Pommeau both use adultery for personal gain, they are far from representative of the cocotte or courtesan type. They are not actresses, singers, or dancers, as courtesans usually are in French nineteenth-century depictions of this type;[24] they are both, in fact, apparently respectably married, middle-class women. What makes them so singular is that they hide their ambitions and adventures behind the facade of their supposedly respectable bourgeois marriages. Valérie Marneffe actually uses this pretense of respectability as a tool to get what she wants from the men she preys on. Because both women are apparently respectable middle-class wives, citing these two texts is particularly appropriate to the theme of representation in *The Tragic Muse.* Once again, the texts alluded to are about the danger of deceit, pretending, and playacting, for the conventional cocotte is not the threat Valérie and Séraphine are, as at least one critic of the late nineteenth century stated:

> Mais il y a pis encore que Clorinde [of *L'Aventurière*] et qu'Olympe [Taverny of Augier's *Le Mariage d'Olympe*]: celle-là, en effet, est la courtisane romantique, assez inoffensive dans le fond; celle-ci est la fille grossière et stupide dont il ne semble pas très malaisé de préserver la famille. Infiniment plus dangereuse est Séraphine Pommeau, qui appartient à une troisième espèce, celle des lionnes pauvres.

> [There is even worse than Clorinde or Olympe: the one is, in fact, the romantic courtesan, essentially inoffensive; the other is the vulgar and stupid girl from whom it should not seem difficult to preserve the family. Infinitely more dangerous is Séraphine Pommeau, who belongs to a third species, that of the impoverished lionesses.][25]

Séraphine, like her sister Valérie, is more dangerous than the real courtesan because the demimonde to which the conventional courtesan belongs is governed by rules. Thus one does not know where one stands with a Valérie or a Séraphine, as one does with a typical courtesan. When the seemingly respectable *bourgeoise* can misrepresent herself as successfully as Valérie Marneffe does, then the structure of "acceptable" society is threatened far more seriously, as Balzac's novel makes it a point to demonstrate. It is no coincidence, implies Paul Morillot, that *Les Lionnes pauvres* was rejected by the censorship commission (it was published only after the personal intercession of Napoleon III) at the same time that *Madame Bovary* was a succès de scandale.[26]

While both Valérie and Séraphine are false to their husbands and lovers, and rely on duplicity to achieve their ends, *La Cousine Bette* resonates particularly with *The Tragic Muse* in using the theater as the dominant metaphor for this duplicity. The language used to describe Valérie and her actions constantly compares her to an actress. In fact, theatrical imagery, allusions to plays, quotations from plays, and references to the actor's craft pervade Balzac's novel, turning the courtesan as actress into an extended metaphor. The narrative voice and several characters in *La Cousine Bette* either quote or parody lines from classic plays by Racine (five times), Corneille (twice), Voltaire, Molière, and Shakespeare (once each), and from operas by Rossini and Adam (once each).[27] The novel alludes twice each to *Othello* and *The Tempest*, and there are references to two Rossini characters. By contrast, there are only two allusions to novelists (one to Laclos, one to Rousseau).

In addition to the theatrical allusions or quotations, either the narrator or a character in *La Cousine Bette* frequently casts the plot of the novel as theater. Four of the chapter titles from the 1847 Chlandowski-Pétion edition (which Balzac suppressed in the 1848 Furne edition) have theatrical references: "Une Première Scène de haute comédie féminine" [First Scene of High Feminine Comedy], "Scène digne des loges" [Scene Worthy of Actors' Dressing Rooms], "Deuxième Scène de haute comédie féminine" [Second Scene of High Feminine Comedy] (*Comédie* 7: 1301), "Une Belle Entrée" [A Beautiful Entrance] (7: 1312).[28] In summarizing the early years of the Hulot marriage, the narrator states that Adeline Hulot had held the role of *"prima donna assoluta"* for twelve years (7: 77), and in another context, Adeline talks about playing her *role* badly (7: 330). Josépha, Hulot's previous mistress, speaks of Adeline as having "le rôle opposé au mien" [the role opposite mine] (7: 337), and during her meeting with Adeline points out that "Cette scène se joue aussi souvent dans la vie qu'au théâtre" [This scene is played as often in real life as in the theater] (7: 381). Once Valérie allows herself to succumb to Hulot's advances, the narrator states that the story so far is only the introduction to what follows: "Ce

récit est au drame qui le complète ce que sont les prémisses à une proposition, ce qu'est toute exposition à toute tragédie classique" [This narrative
is to the drama that completes it what the premises are to a proposition,
what all exposition is to all classical tragedy] (7: 186).[29]

The theatrical imagery in *La Cousine Bette* appears most frequently in
respect to Valérie and her deceitfulness. The novel makes no secret of her
hypocritical, deceitful character. She is one of "Ces Machiavels en jupon"
[those Machiavellis in a petticoat] (*Comédie* 7: 188), "faux comme des
programmes d'Hôtel de Ville" [false like a town hall program] (7: 235).
However, what is most important is that the novel presents her "hypocrisie
sociale" [social hypocrisy] (7: 189) in theatrical terms.

> En présence du monde, elle offrait la réunion enchanteresse de la candeur
> pudique et rêveuse, de la décence irréprochable . . . mais, dans le tête-à-tête,
> elle dépassait les courtisanes. . . . Crevel . . . est flatté d'être l'unique auteur
> de cette comédie, il la croit jouée à son seul profit, et il rit de cette délicieuse
> hypocrisie, en admirant la comédienne.

> [Publicly she presented the enchanting union of dreamy, modest candor, of
> irreproachable decency . . . but, in private, she surpassed even courtesans. . . .
> Crevel . . . is flattered to be the sole author of this comedy, he believes it
> played only for his benefit, and he laughs at this delicious hypocrisy, while
> admiring the comedienne.] (7: 192)[30]

Valérie presents her lovers with a paradox that they acknowledge but do
not care to analyze. She pretends to the credulous Hulot and Crevel that
she is sacrificing her honesty and reputation at great cost for their sakes;
incredibly, both men are delighted to learn that she does not conduct herself in the bedroom like the prude she appears to be in public. For Crevel,
"elle dépassait les courtisanes"; Hulot is thrilled to find Valérie "la jeune
fille la plus innocente et le diable le plus consommé" [the most innocent
young girl and the most complete devil] (7: 185); and in a fleeting moment
of introspection, the two men admit that "Le mensonge vaut souvent
mieux que la vérité" [Lies are often better than the truth] (7: 235).

Balzac's novel is acknowledging here the same paradox that both *The
Tragic Muse* and at least one recent theorist of novelistic representation
examine: the power of fiction is that it masquerades as truth; indeed, fiction-masquerading-as-truth is more powerful, more enticing, more affect-
ive than truth itself.[31] The power of fictional representation is evident, for
example, in Peter's response to Miriam's performance on her second opening night:

> Miriam was a beautiful, actual, fictive, impossible young woman, of a past age and undiscoverable country, who spoke in blank verse and overflowed with metaphor, who was exalted and heroic beyond all human convenience, and who yet was irresistibly real and related to one's own affairs. But that reality was a part of her spectator's joy, and she was not changed back to the common by his perception of the magnificent trick of art with which it was connected. (*TM* 1180)

This passage expresses the same paradoxical power of fiction-masquerading-as-truth that Balzac's Hulot and Crevel acknowledge. Miriam is "fictive, impossible," of a different age and from no real place (of an "undiscoverable country"); she is transcendent, "exalted," and "beyond all human convenience," but at the same time she is "real," indeed "irresistibly" so. Her reality is part of her appeal, and the mixture of "reality" and the "fictive" is "the magnificent trick of art." That the very next thing Peter does in the novel is to propose marriage to Miriam shows the power of this "magnificent trick."

Crevel and Hulot, on the one hand, and Peter Sherringham, on the other, are indeed seduced by the paradoxical power of (mis)representation, of fiction-masquerading-as-truth. Because of this, *La Cousine Bette* is not just a cautionary tale about the ruin of a family; it is an examination of the power of fictional representation, an investigation into the paradoxical and complex nature of art and artistic truth. For the same reason—and this is why James's novel mentions Balzac's—*The Tragic Muse* is not just about "art" and the "world"; it is also a reflection on the paradoxical nature of art and artistic representation.[32]

In *The Tragic Muse* all the possible professions pursued or abandoned by the principal characters in the novel have in common the related characteristics of pretending, performing, acting, and faking.[33] This is partly because the theater is a recurrent metaphor, as in *La Cousine Bette,* for realms of human activity outside the theater. In *La Cousine Bette* the theater metaphor points to Valérie as an actress, a pretender, a performer, a fake. Her success and her danger are possible because of the paradoxical power of (mis)representation, as Hulot and Crevel fleetingly recognize when they admit preferring lies to truth. Representation has the same paradoxical nature in *The Tragic Muse* it has in *La Cousine Bette*—it is both compelling and fake—which is why charlatanism is so central a motif to James's novel. *The Tragic Muse* takes the central device of the play—the actor pretending to be someone else—and develops it into what I call the motif of charlatanism.[34] The theater metaphor and the motif of charlatanism are related and pervade the novel. *The Tragic Muse* metaphorically treats all professions as theater and shows everyone to be a pretender or charlatan as a result. Among other things, this explains the running commentary on virtue as hypocritical; since the word "hypocrisy" derives from the Greek for play-acting, the novel shows that pretense and the theater are integral to society.

The Tragic Muse makes Nash the most explicit voice of the pervasiveness of the charlatan motif. In his conversation with the much annoyed Julia Dallow,

> Gabriel Nash asked her if she had not been struck with the main sign of the time, the preponderance of the mountebank, the glory and renown, the personal favour, that he enjoyed. . . . "Aren't they under your feet wherever you turn—their performances, their portraits, their speeches, their autobiographies, their names, their manners, their ugly mugs, as the people say, and their idiotic pretensions?" (*TM* 804–5)

As if to illustrate Nash's remark, *The Tragic Muse* proceeds to associate virtually everything with the mountebank and its correlates—the humbug, pretending, falsity, deceitful representations.

Since the actor is by definition a pretender, the words "humbug" and "mountebank" and other indicators of charlatanism appear in reference to Miriam and the theater. Peter sees the actress in general as "a female gymnast, a mountebank at higher wages" (832), Madame Carré calls the world of the London stage "your mountebanks' booths" (941), and Nick speaks of Peter's passion for drama as his going "in for mountebanks and mimes" (980). It is no surprise that *The Tragic Muse* makes the charlatan the metaphor for an art form in which people pretend to be other people; what is perhaps more significant is that because the theater serves as a metaphor for so many other realms of human activity, in *The Tragic Muse* the metaphor of charlatanism carries over from the theater world into other realms of life. The talented Comédie Française actress Mlle. Dunoyer plays only the ingenue or innocent young girl, but "with all her talent [she] could not have represented a woman of her actual age" (*TM* 946). Her colleague, Mlle. Voisin, plays the proper lady so well that "She shows them [*femmes du monde*] how to act in society" (943). There is an irony in "proper" ladies learning from an actress how to behave in their own world, and the text shows the depth of this irony in the choice of the word "act," as opposed to "behave," in the phrase "how to act in society," for it is precisely the point of *The Tragic Muse* that pretending, acting, performing, and representation are not limited to the stage but are in all walks of life. This is why, for example, the text calls Julia, who apparently despises all the arts, "a sort of leading woman" (1081), just as Adeline Hulot was a *"prima donna assoluta"* in *La Cousine Bette* (*Comédie* 7: 77). It is also why Nash speaks to Nick of his struggling to choose between politics and art and to establish himself as an artist as "your engagement at your own theatre" (*TM* 981), and to a certain extent it is why in her confrontation with Peter before her second London opening night, Miriam "began to listen to herself, to speak dramatically, to represent. She uttered the things she felt as if they were snatches of old playbooks" (1129). Virtually no person or thing in *The Tragic Muse* escapes comparison to the drama.

As part of the motif of charlatanism, acting, the theater, and the basis of theater acting—pretending—are metaphors for every realm of human society in *The Tragic Muse*. This is certainly true of diplomacy, Peter Sherringham's profession. Peter claims that he has "no talent" for acting (*TM* 1197), but of course performing—maintaining a facade, in this case one of "imperturbable, urbane scepticism most appropriate to a secretary of embassy" (1090)—is as inherent in his profession as it is in Miriam's. Peter admits that the embassy is as much a stage as the theater when he tries to convince Miriam that her talents would find as much of an outlet and be just as valuable as an ambassador's wife as in stage productions, and Miriam concurs when she urges Peter to "Stay on *my* stage; come off your own" (1190). Peter's argument is that all the world is a stage—and this is indeed a metaphor the novel endorses—"The stage is great, no doubt, but the world is greater. It's a bigger theatre than any of those places on the Strand" (1189). "You were made to charm and console," Peter tells Miriam, "to represent beauty and harmony and variety to miserable human beings [art is again a consolation]; and the daily life of man is the theatre for that—not a vulgar shop with a turnstile, that's open only once in twenty-four hours" (1190). The stage and the embassy are also conflated in Miriam's admiration of the Comédie Française actress Mlle. Voisin, who, receiving Miriam and Peter in her dressing room, "might have been the charming young wife of a secretary of state receiving a pair of strangers of distinction" (955).

For Nick, misrepresentation is the principal characteristic of the political world in *The Tragic Muse*—a characteristic of politics not surprising to the late-twentieth-century reader. Nick complains a number of times to Julia about the deceit inherent in politics. He details the kinds of things a candidate is required to say in a stump speech: "Do men who respect each other or themselves talk to each other that way? They know they would deserve kicking if they were to attempt it" (773). Yet, while campaigning, he is "surprised at the airs he could play; and often when the last thing at night he shut the door of his room he mentally exclaimed that he had had no idea he was such a mountebank" (882). He wonders whether constituents expect their members of Parliament to *pretend* to have read articles like Mr. Hoppus's (885); he complains to Julia of "all the appearances and imitations, the pretences and hypocrisies in which I've steeped myself to the eyes" (963); and he tells Mr. Carteret: " 'I'm such a humbug . . . I deceive people without in the least intending it' " (915).

If the motif of charlatanism pervades Nick's aborted political career, it is nevertheless not entirely absent from his artistic one. Late in the novel, Nick's reflections on his choosing a career as a painter appear in a long passage in which he recognizes that, on the one hand, he would like to justify his becoming an artist to those most upset by his having abandoned politics: his mother, Julia, and his former constituents. On the other hand, he "mistrust[s] . . . the superficiality of performance into which the desire to justify himself might hurry him" (1206). In other words, Nick would like to produce some paintings for exhibition and admiration, but anything produced in the near future would not be of a high enough quality to match a truly exacting standard: "Cheap and easy results would dangle before him" (1207). The few who had seen his present productions "pronounced [them] wonderfully clever. That they were wonderfully clever was just the detestable thing in them, so active had that cleverness been in making them seem better than they were" (1206). This prompts Nick to the "ugly revelation" that "the lesson of his life" was "that nature had cursed him with an odious facility" (1207). It was precisely because of this facility that he had been successful as a political speaker, and it was precisely because he pleased so easily as a speaker that he had been tempted by a potential career in politics. Nick realizes that "his humbugging genius" (1207) is just as much a menace to him in his new profession as in his old, that he is capable of being just as untrue to himself as a painter as he was as a politician.[35]

This means that even an artist can be a charlatan; he can produce clever things—"Cheap and easy results"—or he can struggle to produce works of art that, by implication, are not fakes but the "real thing."[36] That is why when Miriam tells Nick, " 'I'm too clever—I'm a humbug,' " we must read his answer, " 'That's the way I used to be' " (*TM* 1226), very skeptically, for Nick's battle with facile cleverness and humbugging is far from over. Miriam faces a similar battle; when she regrets not being able to hone her craft during an apprenticeship in a repertory company, she tells Nick, "For want of it I shall never really be good. However, if you don't tell people I've said so, they'll never know" (1225). In other words, Miriam does not consider herself a "real" artist, but only a fake, although no one knows it.[37]

Although it is tempting to see them as diverging at the end of the novel,

Miriam's and Nick's artistic careers have developed along very similar lines. Nick's struggle with the danger of being "wonderfully clever" is Miriam's struggle, too. The two artists share a desire not to be precipitated into action and production, but rather to devote themselves to "the principle of quiet growth" (1207–8). In their last involved conversation in the novel, Miriam laments a future of "play[ing] the stuff I'm acting now" (1226) and tells Nick of her envy "that I haven't before me a period of the same sort of unsociable pegging away that you have. . . . What I want most I never shall have had—five quiet years of hard, all-around work, in a perfect company" (1225–26). However we may be tempted to see a suggestion here that Nick is the "real" artist, dedicated to a higher standard, and Miriam only the "Philistine" she twice admits to being in this scene (1225, 1227), we must not fail to notice that Nick envies Miriam. Realizing the length and loneliness of "his own battle," viewing the "wofully [*sic*] cold and gray and mean" studio in which he must fight it, Nick thinks of the benefits of success: "He cared enough for it [a fruition] . . . to feel that his pertinacity might enter into comparison even with such a productive force as Miriam's" (1220–21).

Thus, while one artist envies the other's opportunity to "plug away," the other envies the first one's dogged persistence. Both desire to perfect their art so that when they present their work, there is no danger of its being mistaken for anything but the "real thing." However, the impulse to perfect this work before subjecting it to public judgment can lead to never producing at all (as with Nash), which means that these artists would never be able to justify themselves—and thus would always seem a sham—in the eyes of the Julias and the Lady Agneses. The artist, then, is in a bind and, whatever he or she does, will appear a charlatan to someone. This is not the same pain Musset's poet and muse have in mind in the "Nuit" poems, but James's artists' bind is nonetheless not an easy situation. Indeed, this bind is an appropriate late-nineteenth-century rewriting of Musset's Romantic version of the crucible of poetic creation. In the Romantic version, the poet creates beauty out of suffering and pain, and in the version of the realist novelist, significant artistic achievement is the result of hard work—"pegging away"—in less than ideal conditions, the "wofully cold and gray and mean" studio.[38]

The Tragic Muse does not limit its reflection on art to the more general problems of the paradox of artistic representation and the nature of the appeal of such representation. It also addresses more practical concerns of the artist's craft. In the same conversation in which Miriam regrets not being able to work in a repertory company, Nick and Miriam discuss Gabriel Nash, the aesthete who makes it his "business to take for granted an interest in the beautiful" (*TM* 821), the artist whose medium is "life" itself (806), who does not believe in doing, only in being (975), who is himself the "fine consequence" of his art (724). At the time of his conversation with Miriam, Nick has come to realize that Nash does not care for "The applications, the consequences, the vulgar little effects [which] belong to a lower plane" (1225), and agrees with Miriam that "The simplifications of practice . . . are just precisely the most blessed things on earth" (1225).

What we should note about these two working artists extolling the practical problems of their art is their search for a space between the facile success they both fear and the entirely ideal philosophy of art expressed by Nash. On the one hand, the two artists struggle to avoid falling into the semblance of a career as a serious artist—to produce "Cheap and easy results," as Nick puts it, or to "be condemned for . . . the rest of my days . . . to play the stuff I'm acting now" (1226), as Miriam fears; on the other hand, they find no satisfaction in the opposite extreme, that represented by Nash's not producing anything at all.

Edel argues that "the true artist" in *The Tragic Muse* "must be prepared to sacrifice everything to his commitment; that one cannot be half artist and half something else; that he must strip himself of all worldliness, or accept the easy compromises society exacts."[39] But to be such an artist in this novel would mean being like the uncompromising Gabriel Nash, who finds "Real art . . . depresses him by the little compromises on which it is dependent."[40] Nick and Miriam—the two artists the text holds up as models—stand on a middle ground between the extremes of the nonproducing Nash and the "Cheap and easy results," working hard not to be a poor sham of an artist but nevertheless producing results—consequences, to use Nash's term—and submitting those results to the propagating mechanisms (all of which Gabriel Nash would frown on) appropriate to their particular art form: the "*cheval de bataille*" (*TM* 1226); the audiences with their suburban trains (748); the provincial theater tours in Miriam's case; the salon where the novel begins; the Royal Academy; or the exhibition where, at the end of the novel, Nick exhibits the portrait of Julia (1255).[41]

James recognized that the serious artist is always compromising: "there is no art at all . . . that is not on too many sides an abject compromise. The element of compromise is always there; it is of the essence; we live with it, and it may serve to keep us humble" (*LC2* 134).[42] If the artists sacrifice in *The Tragic Muse*, they do not sacrifice the material world, as Edel and Krook would have it,[43] but *to* the demands of the material world. "The only alternative to such realistic compromise," as Graham points out, "is to be a Peter Sherringham or a Gabriel Nash . . . [both of whom are] menaced by inanition and impotence through refusing to risk the imperfect."[44]

Because of such worldly constraints upon the artist to compromise, Nash has abandoned his own promising career as a writer. In one light, his renunciation is admirable, for by making his life his art, he is never a charlatan or pretender: the materials from which Nash receives his artistic sensations—the fig tree in a Spanish city wall (823), "the subtle sadness" of the Breton landscape (1230), Samarkand, the "drama" of Nick's career choice, "a bank of flowers in the vale of Cashmere" (1241)—are real; they are not fakes or (mis)representations. In another light, though, they are unreal: Samarkand, the vale of Cashmere, and Spain are as exotic as can be to the late-nineteenth-century English or American reader and correspondingly unreal, and the art/life that Nash leads is possible only to someone of independent means (in spite of Nash's insistence that he does "it very cheap" [823]). It is no wonder, then, that Nash's portrait unrealistically—indeed surrealistically—fades away "as in some delicate Hawthorne tale" (1236), the tale perhaps being Hawthorne's fictional reflection on the impossibility of artistic ideals, "The Artist of the Beautiful."[45]

The Tragic Muse is not about the "true" artist sacrificing the worldly but about the fundamental paradoxes of artistic life. Art makes life meaningful because it is the only alternative to a meaningless, "fifth-rate world" (*TM* 1199), but art's power and appeal derive from and in spite of its inherent falseness: it is fake, pretense, and misrepresentation. As Nash says, becoming an artist is "choosing a life of shams" (985), but as the novel so persistently shows, choosing any other profession also amounts to choosing a life of shams. Art may be the alternative to a "nature which had no consolation" (1199), but its pursuit is painful, as in Musset's "Nuit" poems, and lonely, as in Nick's studio. The artist is constrained by material and commercial concerns, as Nash points out, but to pursue art to its idealistic extreme, as Nash attempts to do, is to lose touch with the "simplifications of practice" that Miriam calls "the most blessed things on earth" (1225) and, through the absence of production, to risk no longer being an artist of consequence. Thus the successful artist has the further problem of staking out a ground between this extreme and the other of "[c]heap and easy results" (1207), where the artist—already a master of representation and pretense—is but the simulacrum of an artist. Because artists of high standards like Miriam and Nick aspire to transcend the worldly constraints Nash criticizes, they follow an artistic ideal,[46] but in following this ideal, the satisfaction of such artists comes from handling the practical problems they encounter.

Art and the artist's life are, in sum, based on irreconcilable opposites; there are fundamental paradoxes between artistry and craftsmanship, reality and fiction, the practical and the ideal, the public and the private, and "choosing a life of shams" and living a life that is a sham. This is why James uses the oxymoron "the cold passion of art" when Miriam recites from *King John* (*TM* 932), for, as Graham says, the actress is "the meeting-point of heat and coolness," and her performance fuses "mind and feeling, abstraction and substance, art and life."[47] Such a fusion of opposites is appropriate in a novel in which the major characters are themselves a fusion of contradictions; as William Macnaughton points out, the principals, especially Nick and Peter, are all "deeply divided." Nick is divided in the first half between the parliamentary and artistic careers, and Peter is practically a schizophrenic, torn between his career ambitions and his love of Miriam; "his 'liberal' attitude toward women . . . as opposed to his wish for females to support his manly point of view; his tolerance of those belonging to inferior social classes and his feeling that they are inferior"; and his passion for the drama and "his strong distaste for aspects of the theater."[48]

This prevalence in everything and everyone in *The Tragic Muse* of divisions and oppositions explains the consistency with which James's text makes its literary allusions in pairs, some in opposed pairs; two seems to be the magic number of this novel, because the novel posits that the characters involved in artistic pursuits are themselves perpetually facing binary oppositions. The prevalence of such oppositions in this novel about art is understandable, though, since art is the product of the mixture of the opposites fantasy and truth, and the root of art's power to affect is based in the paradox that art is fake at the same time it claims to be true. The literary allusions in *The Tragic Muse* are essential to our understanding because they are so often allusions to stories of deceit, playacting, and pretending; it is the foregrounding in texts such as *La Cousine Bette, Mademoiselle de la Seiglière, Il ne faut jurer de rien, L'Aventurière,* and *Les Lionnes pauvres* of deceitful, dissimulating characters that leads us to pay attention to deceit, pretending, falseness, acting, humbuggery, and dissimulation in all the walks of life James's novel represents. And this in turn makes it difficult to ignore the centrality of the art/artifice paradox to the treatment of artistic representation in James's novel.

Conclusion

*I*n her many tracings of literary references in Henry James, Adeline Tintner has repeatedly argued that James rewrote other writers' works. James felt "compelled," says Tintner, "to redo the classic works of literature . . . to improve them and to revise them in *his* way . . . his adaptation turned the original into his own thing."[1] In the preceding chapters, I have argued from a theoretical perspective more concerned with how to read a text than with Tintner's primary perspective, which is how James's text came to be written. It is possible to reconcile Tintner's biographical view, which theorizes about how James's imagination worked, with my own emphasis on the effects on the reader of James's text's invocations of aspects of French culture. James, says Tintner, "desir[ed] to induce the reader to participate in the immediate writing of his tale through recognition of the work drawn from the imagination of another. . . . He uses as a measure of his own intention a literary model and expects his reader to be almost as thoroughly familiar with it as he is himself." James "intends us to recognize his analogues"; these "analogues" are not hidden to his reader, for James provides "liberal clues and factual signposts," and their recognition "illuminates the meaning of his work."[2]

The preceding chapters have shown that James's novels are certainly sprinkled "with liberal clues and factual signposts" to French novels and plays and to French conventions and stereotypes, that these clues and signs are recognizable, and that the extent to which they are recognizable implies that James's reader is familiar with what they indicate. I have a problem with Tintner's claim that the references in James's texts are signs of intention because it is a circular argument: Tintner claims on the one hand that the "analogue" is what inspired the story James tells, and on the other, she claims that the references to the appropriated analogue are the "clues" that help the reader understand James's inspiration.[3]

Tintner could circumvent such reasoning by claiming that the references to French texts themselves become references to conventions, stereotypes, and clichés embedded in French culture; that it is these conventions, stereotypes, and clichés that constitute James's "analogues"; and that their recognition illuminates the meaning of James's fictional texts. Specific allusions to *Notre-Dame de Paris* and to *Louis Lambert* are not to stories that parallel the plot of *The Ambassadors;* rather, they invoke parallel motifs in the French texts that are conveyed through an understanding, for example, of what Mary Stuart or Origen stands for—sensuality, the scaffold, and salvation on the one hand, seeing, spiritual insight, and spiritual salvation at the cost of sexuality on the other—and these in turn are connected to significant features in James's novel: the metaphor of salvation, which in turn is connected and opposed to the role of sexuality and to the opposition between the physical and the spiritual, which is connected to the significance of "seeing" and of freedom.

I have argued that allusions in *The Tragic Muse* serve to bombard the reader with examples of stories involving deceit; deceit is not explicitly apparent in any of the dealings among the characters in *The Tragic Muse,* but it is nonetheless tremendously important to understanding what *The Tragic Muse* has to say about art and artistic representation. In this case, the "analogues" are not "parallels" to James's text, as Tintner would have it,[4] but provide what is missing in *The Tragic Muse*. *La Cousine Bette, Il ne faut jurer de rien, L'Aventurière,* and *Mademoiselle de la Seiglière* do not tell a parallel, simpler, more straightforward version of the story told in *The Tragic Muse*. Rather, they tell precisely what is left out of James's plot but is central to his theme. In this case, the allusion in James functions like an allusion in Hemingway, by serving as a clue not for what is said but for what is left out. The same is to an extent true of the allusion in *The Princess Casamassima* to *Roderick Hudson* and the princess's illegitimate birth; the fact of Christina's illegitimacy is the great "secret" of *The Princess Casamassima* just as the nature of Jake Barnes's war wound is the "secret" of *The Sun Also Rises*. It is not something that can be stated explicitly in the novel, but it is nevertheless expressed through the reference to another text.[5]

James's texts allude to other literary texts, and through them to conventions and stereotypes in French culture. Thus the mention of Cherbuliez's *Paule Méré* in *Daisy Miller* is to a conventional view of Geneva and the Swiss personality; the constant titillation of expectations and the conventional meeting at the theater scene in *The Princess Casamassima* invoke a tradition of texts about ambitious young outsiders that James's novel plays against; the name Fernanda in *The Awkward Age* invokes a French convention of a character who seems bad but is in fact good and innocent; and the use of the dialogue form in a novel about an adolescent girl's marriage prospects is not just homage to Gyp but a means of invoking a contemporary literary discussion about upbringing and limited career paths for upper-middle-class young women.

My point is that James's novels invoke connections that in turn invoke other connections, that the second level of connections is more readily apparent when James's novels are read from a partly French perspective, and that reading James from that partly French perspective determines the sense we give his novels. If authorial intention illuminates meaning for Tintner, for me context constitutes meaning; these two views of the locus of meaning in literary texts have equally long traditions, but if the utility and value of criticism lie in its ability to make literature resonate for readers, then locating meaning in contexts should be more rewarding, for it is not so much how James made the texts *his* own but how modern-day readers make them *their* own that keeps James's novels, stories, and novellas interesting to later generations of readers.

Notes

Introduction

1. James did have an English tutor when the Jameses lived in London during the winter of 1855–1856, and he studied the German language—in how formal a setting is not clear—in Bonn during the summer of 1860. See Leon Edel's *The Life of Henry James,* vol. 1, *The Untried Years, 1843–1870* (Philadelphia: Lippincott, 1953), 125, 154–55; and Fred Kaplan's *Henry James: The Imagination of Genius: A Biography* (New York: William Morrow, 1992), 28–29, 43–44.

2. All of James's translations were from the French—in addition to the Daudet novel, he translated an article by Daudet, another by Maurice Barrès, and a short prose poem from the French by Turgenev. See Leon Edel and Dan H. Laurence's *A Bibliography of Henry James,* 3rd ed. (Oxford: Clarendon Press, 1982), 210–11.

3. The Library of America volumes of James's critical essays contain nine hundred pages on French authors, slightly over one hundred on other European writers (*LC2* 1–899, 901–1034), a little more than five hundred pages on American writers, and about seven hundred pages on English writers (*LC1* 183–702, 705–1413).

4. *The French Side of Henry James* (New York: Columbia University Press, 1990).

5. Many of these articles have been compiled (with some significant revisions) in Tintner's recent books: *The Book World of Henry James: Appropriating the Classics* (Ann Arbor, Mich.: UMI Research Press, 1987), *The Pop World of Henry James: From Fairy Tales to Science Fiction* (Ann Arbor, Mich.: UMI Research Press, 1989), and *The Cosmopolitan World of Henry James: An Intertextual Study* (Baton Rouge: Louisiana State University Press, 1991).

6. *Henry James and the French Novel: A Study in Inspiration* (New York: Barnes and Noble, 1973).

7. *Henry James and the Naturalist Movement* ([East Lansing]: Michigan State University Press, 1971). Sergio Perosa's *Henry James and the Experimental Novel* also makes a significant contribution to the discussion of the comparison of James's novels of the 1880s and the French naturalist or experimental novel (1978; reprint, New York: New York University Press, Gotham Library, 1983), 11–44.

8. *The Melodramatic Imagination: Balzac, Henry James, Melodrama, and the Mode of Excess* (1976; reprint, New York: Columbia University Press, 1984).

9. *Balzac, James, and the Realistic Novel* (Princeton: Princeton University Press, 1983).

10. *Melodramatic Imagination*, 198.

11. F. R. Leavis, *The Great Tradition: George Eliot, Henry James, Joseph Conrad* (reprint, New York: New York University Press, Gotham Library, 1967); Robert Emmet Long, *The Great Succession: Henry James and the Legacy of Hawthorne* (Pittsburgh: University of Pittsburgh Press, 1979); Richard Brodhead, *The School of Hawthorne* (New York: Oxford University Press, 1986).

12. *The French Side of Henry James* is entirely devoted to the Gallicisms, French dialogue, and French settings in James's fiction. My study complements Fussell's by examining a different aspect of James's "French side": the allusions in James's fiction to French literature and cultural motifs.

13. *French Side of Henry James*, 119.

14. Ibid., 120.

15. The most complex study of James's relation to Hawthorne is probably Brodhead's (see 104–200, esp. 134–39).

16. The extent to which James found both his French and his Anglo-American literary models inadequate is perhaps best expressed in (and probably best known from) his review of Zola's novel *Nana:*

> To us English readers . . . *[Nana]* raises questions which no one apparently has the energy or the good faith to raise among ourselves. . . . [A Zola] is not now to be easily found in England or the United States, where the storyteller's art is almost exclusively feminine. . . . The novel, moreover, among ourselves, is almost always addressed to young unmarried ladies, or at least always assumes them to be a large part of the novelist's public. This fact, to a French storyteller, appears, of course, a damnable restriction, and M. Zola would probably decline to take *au sérieux* any work produced under such unnatural conditions. Half of life is a sealed book to young unmarried ladies, and how can a novel be worth anything that deals only with half of life? . . .
>
> The human note is completely absent [from *Nana*], the perception of character, of the way that people feel and think and act, is helplessly, hopelessly at fault; . . . This is what saves us in England, in spite of our artistic levity and the presence of the young ladies. . . . It is not [Zola's] choice of subject that has shocked us; it is the melancholy dryness of his execution, which gives us all the bad taste of a disagreeable dish and none of the nourishment. (*LC* 2 868–70)

I discuss the ambivalence James expresses in this passage about Zola and French naturalism in general in the chapter on *Washington Square*.

17. The one obvious exception is in Adeline Tintner's work, which often

discusses forgotten French writers; as Tintner says, "James not only took 'liberties with the greatest' but also took them with the least" (*Cosmopolitan World*, xiii).

18. *Henry James—the Lessons of the Master: Popular Fiction and Personal Style in the Nineteenth Century* (Chicago: University of Chicago Press, 1975).

19. *Henry James and the Mass Market* (University: University of Alabama Press, 1983).

20. Ibid., 13.

21. Ibid., 143, 1.

22. Ibid., 1–19; Marcia Jacobson, "Literary Convention and Social Criticism in Henry James's *The Awkward Age*," *Philological Quarterly* 54 (1975): 633.

23. *The Theoretical Dimensions of Henry James* (Madison: University of Wisconsin Press, 1984).

24. Anne T. Margolis, *Henry James and the Problem of Audience: An International Act* (Ann Arbor, Mich.: UMI Research Press, 1985). Michael Anesko, *"Friction with the Market": Henry James and the Profession of Authorship* (New York: Oxford University Press, 1986).

25. Sarah Daugherty in *The Literary Criticism of Henry James* ([Athens]: Ohio University Press, 1982) (43-50) seems alone among Jamesian critics in understanding the relevance of the *Revue des Deux Mondes* writers to James's fiction. I agree completely with Daugherty's statements that "Since the minor French novelists have passed into oblivion, scholars have underestimated their influence on James" and that James's "reading of *La Revue des Deux Mondes* was probably of cardinal importance to his own career" (48).

26. For a survey of intertextual theory and its variants, see Jonathan Culler's *The Pursuit of Signs: Semiotics, Literature, Deconstruction* (Ithaca, N.Y.: Cornell University Press, 1981), esp. 47–135. For a more specific and rigorous application of intertextual theory, see Michael Riffaterre's "Interpretation and Undecidability," *New Literary History* 12 (1981): 227–42, and "Intertextual Representation: On Mimesis as Interpretive Discourse," *Critical Inquiry* 11 (1984): 141–62.

27. The calls for an end to interpretation in literary criticism over the last twenty years are too numerous to cite; what I believe clear (and it would require an entirely different book to catalogue the evidence behind this belief) is that each new school of criticism since the heyday of the New Criticism has claimed to replace interpretation in some form or other, and itself has been replaced with a subsequent school that claims to replace the dominance of the interpretive model in literary study, because each new school either consists of or—as it gains adherents throughout the profession—turns into (which amounts in the end to the same thing) yet another variant on the interpretive model.

28. If (as in, say, Balzac's *Comédie humaine*) high realism is the effort to reproduce reality as faithfully as possible in as much of its complexity and detail as possible, and Modernism "casts doubt on the very existence of any reality independent of human perception, and . . . questions whether individual perception can yield an understanding of the world that has more than subjective validity," as Julia Bader puts it in "The Dissolving Vision: Realism in Jewett, Freeman, and Gilman" (in *American Realism: New Essays*, ed. Eric J. Sundquist [Baltimore: Johns Hopkins

University Press, 1982], 177), then James's fiction occupies a middle ground where there is still an attempt to represent the complexity of reality at the same time that this representation cannot be separated from the representation of the perception of that reality.

29. Stanley Fish, "What Is Stylistics and Why Are They Saying Such Terrible Things About It?" in his *Is There a Text in This Class? The Authority of Interpretive Communities* (Cambridge: Harvard University Press, 1980), 68–96; see esp. 68–69, 71–72.

30. Ibid., 172, 356.

31. *Cold War Criticism and the Politics of Skepticism* (New York: Oxford University Press, 1993), 121.

32. Tobin Siebers, *Morals and Stories* (New York: Columbia University Press, 1992), 208.

Chapter 1: Cherbuliez's Geneva in *Daisy Miller*

1. The valuable but not comprehensive notes to the Library of America volumes of James's novels (which include to date *Watch and Ward, Roderick Hudson, The American, The Europeans, Confidence, Washington Square, The Portrait of a Lady, The Bostonians, The Princess Casamassima, The Reverberator,* and *The Tragic Muse*) offer the following incomplete list of literary allusions:

Watch and Ward: "Child's Own Book" (24), Jemima Tautphoeus's "The Initials: A Story of Modern Life" (39), Charlotte Mary Yonge's "The Heir of Redcliffe" (62).

Roderick Hudson: Tennyson's "The Princess" (211) and "Daydream" (291), Goethe's *Faust* (229), Thomas à Kempis's *De imitatione Christi* (346), Browning's "A Lover's Quarrel" (371), Mme. de Staël's *Corinne* and Sismondi's *History of the Italian Republics* (380), William Roscoe's *Life of Leo X* (381).

The American: Couvrai's *Les Amours du Chevalier de Faublas* (769).

The Europeans: Keats's "Ode to a Nightingale" (880).

Confidence: Hamlet (1147)

Washington Square: Longfellow's "Excelsior" (26), *Macbeth* (160).

The Portrait of a Lady: The Tempest (314), "a volume of Ampère" (506).

The Bostonians: Esmeralda, from Hugo's *Notre-Dame de Paris* (854), Goethe's *Faust* (879–80), Milton's "L'Allegro" and/or Carlyle's *The French Revolution* (1050).

The Princess Casamassima: Lamartine, "the spurious memoirs of the Marquise de Créqui," Marmontel, Madame de Genlis, M. J. T. de Saint-Germain, Balzac (221), Sheridan's *Lydia Languish* (271), *The Aeneid* (341), Dante's *Inferno* (368), *David Copperfield* (375).

The Tragic Muse: Musset's *Il ne faut jurer de rien* and Jules Sandeau's *Mademoiselle de la Seiglière* (769), Molière's *Le Misanthrope* (781), Emile Augier's "L'Aventurière" (786), *The Arabian Nights* (805), Browning's "How They Brought the Good News from Ghent to Aix" (863), *Othello* (866), Corneille's

Horace (936), Molière's *Les Femmes savantes* (965), Dickens's *Nicholas Nickleby* (1042), Goethe's *Wilhelm Meister's Apprenticeship* (1046).

2. Many of James's fictions establish the same situation, for example, *The Princess Casamassima,* which casts Hyacinth Robinson in a position, with respect to its title character, similar to Winterbourne's position to Daisy.

3. *Meaning in Henry James* (Cambridge: Harvard University Press, 1991), 60. Bell further adds that *Daisy Miller* is really about "Winterbourne's typological compulsion" (61) to categorize people, that the novella "exhibits the desperation underlying the need of category generally," and that "Daisy seems engaged in the defense of her own indeterminacy" (59).

4. Cathy N. Davidson, " 'Circumsexualocution' in Henry James's *Daisy Miller*," *Arizona Quarterly* 32 (1976): 357.

5. Paul Lukacs, "Unambiguous Ambiguity: The International Theme of *Daisy Miller,*" *Studies in American Fiction* 16 (1988): 209–16.

6. Lukacs partially attributes this difference to style—"James's style was much more direct in 1878 than in 1904" ("Unambiguous Ambiguity," 210)—but I do not agree that the evolution of James's written style is the cause of this change in clarity as much as a result of it.

7. As Lukacs concludes:

> While the story [of *Daisy Miller*] is filtered through a character's consciousness, that character's interpretation is never obscure. Put simply, Frederick Winterbourne's opinion of Miss Daisy Miller changes over the course of her story, but what occasions the change always seems perfectly clear. (Ibid.)

8. Ibid., 211.

9. Ibid., 212. Leslie Fiedler's remarks on Daisy are probably the best-known reading of this type, and his view that she is "the prototype of the blasphemous portraits of the Fair Goddess as bitch" (*Love and Death in the American Novel* [New York: Stein and Day, 1966], 310–13) has been echoed by Judith Fryer in *The Faces of Eve: Women in the Nineteenth Century American Novel* (New York: Oxford University Press, 1976), 100–101.

10. Lukacs, "Unambiguous Ambiguity," 212.

11. The proponents of the first reading appear more numerous in recent decades than those of the second. James Gargano offers a strong critique of Winterbourne and the other Europeanized Americans in "Daisy Miller: An Abortive Quest for Innocence," *South Atlantic Quarterly* 59 (1960): 114–20. Edward Wagenknecht emphasizes Daisy's innocence (*Eve and Henry James: Portraits of Women and Girls in His Fiction* [Norman: University of Oklahoma Press, 1978]), as do Susan Koprince ("The Clue from *Manfred* in *Daisy Miller,*" *Arizona Quarterly* 42 [1986]: 293–304); Jeffrey Meyers ("Velázquez and 'Daisy Miller,' " *Studies in Short Fiction* 16 [1979]: 171–78); and Adeline Tintner ("Two Innocents in Rome: Daisy Miller and Innocent the Tenth," *Essays in Literature* 6 [1979]: 71–78), for example.

No recent critics advocate the second reading, which is probably why Lukacs does not cite any (he cites Leslie Fiedler; James Kraft [*The Early Tales of Henry James* (Carbondale: Southern Illinois University Press, 1969)]; and Judith Fryer as examples of the first reading ["Unambiguous Ambiguity," 215, nn. 6, 7]). The second reading was that of many of James's contemporaries (beginning with the editor of *Lippincott's* who, according to James, rejected *Daisy Miller* as "an outrage on American girlhood" [*LC2* 1269]) but has gone out of fashion (at least for the time being).

Some critics in recent decades do qualify the general view of Daisy as innocent and misunderstood. F. W. Dupee, for example, is highly critical of Daisy:

> Like that of the field flower she is named for, her very prettiness is more generic than individual. Extremely imprudent and somewhat callow, even on occasion rude by any standard. . . . Her love can find expression only in flirting or in defiance. Inadequate manners afflict her in the weightier as in the more trivial affairs of life. . . . Daisy inhabits a human vacuum created equally by a large fortune and no commitments, much freedom and little use for it.
>
> The story is not, then, altogether a tribute to the American girl. (*Henry James* [1951; reprint, New York: Delta, 1965], 94–95)

Carol Ohmann also provides a qualified assessment of Daisy's innocence:

> As Winterbourne judges Daisy, judges her unfairly, and completes her expulsion from the American set in Rome, our sympathy for her naturally increases. But I think James does not . . . guide us to any such simple intellectual alignment with his heroine. . . . James hints from time to time at a possible richness of aesthetic experience that is beyond Daisy's capabilities—a richness that would include an appreciation of the artificial, or the cultivated, not as it is represented by the mores of Geneva but by the "splendid chants and organ-tones" of St. Peter's and by the "superb portrait of Innocent X. by Velasquez." ("*Daisy Miller:* A Study of Changing Intentions," *American Literature* 36 [1964]: 1, 5–6)

12. In one of the most recent scholarly commentaries on *Daisy Miller,* Bell has diligently tried to tread a ground between both schools of interpretation of the novella: while Daisy "is one of those feminine characters . . . whose capacity for love is unperceived or unvalued," like Tina Bordereau of "The Aspern Papers" and May Bartram of "The Beast in the Jungle," and her "death-defying extravagance" of visiting the Colosseum "is itself a romantic expression of the passion of a character who desires, at whatever cost, to preserve the potentiality of her own being," at the same time "James undermines our readiness" to see Daisy as the romantic "martyr to her own faith in an unconfined selfhood . . . by making her literally the victim of imprudence." However, at the same time, Daisy's "posture in the arena where

Christian martyrs had died before her is not entirely an ironic touch. Her individuality, such as it is, is doomed by Winterbourne's decision to 'cut her dead' and the stiff box into which his categorical mind has thrust her is in effect a coffin" (*Meaning in Henry James*, 64–65).

13. Critics have debated the question of which is the central character of *Daisy Miller*, Winterbourne or Daisy. James Gargano, for example, has argued for Winterbourne: "He, I believe, is the subject of the novel and not merely the lens through which Daisy's career is seen" ("Daisy Miller," 114–15). Edward Wagenknecht responds:

> James does tell the story from Winterbourne's point of view, and what Winterbourne does not understand about Daisy is very large. . . . None of this, however, can reasonably be taken to justify us in . . . arguing that the real subject is not Daisy Miller but the effect she has on others or that Winterbourne, not Daisy, is the principal character. (*Eve and Henry James*, 9)

14. As Carl Wood has written:

> By omitting after Daisy's death the careful recording and analysis of Winterbourne's mental processes that he has consistently presented beforehand, James challenges his readers with some subtle ambiguity about the impact of Daisy's death on Winterbourne and about the Europeanized American's psychological state at the work's close. ("Frederick Winterbourne, James's Prisoner of Chillon," *Studies in the Novel* 9 [1977]: 40)

15. Ibid.

16. *The Sense of an Ending: Studies in the Theory of Fiction* (New York: Oxford University Press, 1967); *The Genesis of Secrecy: On the Interpretation of Narrative* (Cambridge: Harvard University Press, 1979); *The Art of Telling: Essays on Fiction* (Cambridge: Harvard University Press, 1983).

17. John Randall, "The Genteel Reader and *Daisy Miller*," *American Quarterly* 17 (1965): 568–81; Koprince, "The Clue from *Manfred* in *Daisy Miller*."

18. "James's Prisoner of Chillon," 33. Adeline Tintner argues that both the reference to *Manfred* and the presence of Chillon in *Daisy Miller* demonstrate that Daisy is " 'a Byron in petticoats,' " who "overrides the opinions of others as Byron did before her," and who "dies as Byron had died, of a fever, he for the independence of others, she for the independence of the American girl" (*Book World*, 97–98).

19. Tintner, "Two Innocents in Rome"; Meyers, "Velázquez and 'Daisy Miller.' "

20. *The Battle and the Books: Some Aspects of Henry James* (Athens: Ohio University Press, 1964), 88–93, 120–22.

21. The third expatriate, Mrs. Costello, is Genevan in spirit: by association with her nephew and by sharing the same values and reactions to the Millers as Mrs. Walker, she demonstrates the same moral obtuseness. It is not clear whether Mrs.

Costello is as much an expatriate as her nephew or Mrs. Walker; her permanent residence is apparently in the United States (*DM* 62, chap. 2), but she is clearly not a tourist like the Millers.

22. Pierre Larousse, *Grand dictionnaire universel du dix-neuvième siècle*, 15 vols. (Paris: Administration du Grand Dictionnaire Universel, 1866–1876), 8: 1145 (emphasis added).

23. Contemporary Baedekers, for example, in their discussions of Switzerland and the Swiss make no mention of this stereotypical view, though less prosaic travel writing, such as James's own "Swiss Notes" chapter in *Transatlantic Sketches*, certainly does (see *TS* 626–27).

24. Viola Dunbar, "A Note on the Genesis of *Daisy Miller*," *Philological Quarterly* 27 (1948): 184–86.

25. *The Battle and the Books*, 120.

26. Ibid., 121.

27. Ibid., 120.

28. Ibid., 120, 122.

29. Ibid., 88–89.

30. Ibid, 89.

31. Ibid.

32. Victor Cherbuliez, *Paule Méré* (1866; reprint, Paris: Hachette, 1906), 352, part 4. All subsequent references will be cited parenthetically as *PM* in the text.

33. *The Battle and the Books*, 89.

34. "Genesis of *Daisy Miller*," 184.

35. Dunbar says:

> . . . it seems probable that when James came to develop into a story the anecdote which he heard in Rome in 1877, his recollection of the moral atmosphere of Switzerland and his familiarity with Cherbuliez's novel on the same theme caused him to place the first half of his story in Switzerland. He had already identified this country as a place where one could become the victim of rigid social conventions. ("Genesis of *Daisy Miller*," 184)

Edward Stone repeats this argument in his earlier article on *Paule Méré* and *Daisy Miller*, "A Further Note on *Daisy Miller* and Cherbuliez" (*Philological Quarterly* 29 [1950]: 215): "What is much more likely is that *Paule Méré* remained in his memory until the account given him in 1877 inspired him to adapt the Swiss novelist's story." In fairness to Stone, I should point out that he does consider the effect of this allusion on the reader of *Daisy Miller*, although he puts it in terms of speculation on the effect James must have wished to have had on his reader: "And we can add that so far from concealing his source, James counted on having his readers recognize it—literally led them to it, no doubt hopefully as well as playfully" (*The Battle and the Books*, 122).

Motley Deakin, in seeking to define the tradition of European fictive heroines (including *Paule Méré*) in which James intended to situate his title character, has also stressed authorial intention in "Daisy Miller, Tradition, and the European Heroine," *Comparative Literature Studies* 6 (1969): 45–59. In a similar vein, Jörg Hasler (in *Switzerland in the Life and Work of Henry James* [Cooper Monographs 10; Bern: Francke, 1966], 65–71, 105–8) discusses the sentiments James expressed about Geneva and its inhabitants in "Swiss Notes"—they are virtually the same as those Cherbuliez's characters describe in the passages I have cited above—and tries to relate them to an interpretation of *Daisy Miller*. In this article, James alludes to *Paule Méré* (without mentioning it by name) and thoroughly confirms his agreement with Cherbuliez's representation of the repressiveness of Geneva:

> The moral tone of Geneva, as I imagine it, is epigrammatically, but on the whole justly, indicated by the fact, recently related to me by a discriminating friend, that, meeting one day in the street a placard of the theatre, superscribed *Bouffes-Genevois*, he burst into irrepressible laughter. To appreciate the irony of the phrase one must have lived long enough in Geneva to suffer from the want of humor in the local atmosphere, and the absence, as well, of that aesthetic character which is begotten of a generous view of life. (*TS* 627)

Dunbar mentions "Swiss Notes," and other critics cite this very passage, but while this instance of James's travel writing is an appropriate example of the image of Geneva in nineteenth-century culture, the article itself does not specifically bear on the actual reading of *Daisy Miller* in the way *Paule Méré*—with the direct allusion to it in Mrs. Costello's letter—imposes on the reader's consciousness.

36. Stone, *The Battle and the Books*, 121; Bell, *Meaning in Henry James*, 62. The fact that T. S. Perry published a lengthy article on Cherbuliez in *The Atlantic Monthly* (Mar. 1876, 279–87) two years before *Daisy Miller*'s first appearance suggests that at least a certain kind of American readership knew, or could be expected to know, of Cherbuliez.

37. Wood writes: "Winterbourne understands Daisy's message and also comprehends that he has lost her because of the obtuse and vicious mental habits formed in him by overlong residence in Geneva . . ." ("James's Prisoner of Chillon," 42).

Chapter 2: Princess Casamassima and Octave Feuillet

1. Powers, *Henry James and the Naturalist Movement*, 1.

2. Ibid., 2.

3. Ibid., 169.

4. Leon Edel, *The Life of Henry James*, vol. 3, *The Middle Years, 1882–1895* (Philadelphia: Lippincott, 1962), 95–96, 55–56.

5. *LHJ* 1, 102–3; *HJL* 3, 27–29.

6. Millicent Bell is the one recent critic who has written persuasively against the view of Powers and Grover that the 1880s was James's naturalist- or French-influenced period; indeed, she sees *The Princess Casamassima* as a fictional testing

and subversion of the naturalist fictional plot (*Meaning in Henry James*, 152–84), not unlike the function I describe for Dr. Sloper in the sixth chapter of this volume.

7. See the essay by that title on Flaubert and Charles de Bernard, which first appeared in *Galaxy* (*LC2* 159–83).

8. See the review of *Nana*, published in 1880 (*LC2* 864–70).

9. See, for example, the final paragraph of "The Art of Fiction" (*LC1* 63–65).

10. "Emile Zola," first published in 1903 (*LC2* 871–99).

11. See "Honoré de Balzac," published in 1902 (*LC2* 90–114, esp. 106), and "The Lesson of Balzac" (*LC2* 115–38, esp. 129–30).

12. Tintner's articles on *The Princess Casamassima* are characteristic: "Arsène Houssaye's 'Capricieuse' and James's 'Capricciosa' " (*Revue de la littérature comparée* 50 [1976]: 478–81) and "Octave Feuillet: *La Petite Comtesse* and Henry James" (*Revue de la littérature comparée* 48 [1974]: 218–32), which are included in slightly different form in *Cosmopolitan World of Henry James* (61–79); "Hyacinth at Play: The Play Within the Play as a Novelistic Device in James" (*Journal of Narrative Technique* 2 [1972]: 171–85), "Keats and James and *The Princess Casamassima*" (*Nineteenth-Century Fiction* 28 [1973]: 179–93), and "Vanda de Margi and Rose Muniment" (*Revue de la littérature comparée* 55 [1981]: 110–12), which are included in revised form in *Book World of Henry James* (10–13, 82–93, 273–75).

13. In "Octave Feuillet: *La Petite Comtesse* and Henry James"; see next note.

14. Patricia Crick, in her notes to the latest Penguin edition of *The Princess Casamassima*, does acknowledge that the Feuillet story Hyacinth reads is *Histoire d'une parisienne*, and adds:

> Feuillet's story tells of a virtuous woman, Jeanne de Maurescamp, and of how she is eventually corrupted by her husband's unjustified suspicions and cruel behavior. James may have seen a parallel between Jeanne and Christina, but we really know too little about the married life of the Casamassimas for it to be very obvious. (*The Princess Casamassima* [Harmondsworth: Penguin, 1987], 603 n. 175)

My argument is that the allusion to Feuillet's heroine necessarily leads James's reader to make a comparison between her and the Princess Casamassima, and that the reader knows enough from James's text to make this comparison. Tintner's "Octave Feuillet: *La Petite Comtesse* and Henry James" is the only piece I have found that is devoted entirely to the Princess Casamassima's "incarnation" as Feuillet's heroine. Jane Barstow does mention the "incarnation" in passing in her Deleuze-inspired reading of *The Princess Casamassima* ("Originality and Conventionality in *The Princess Casamassima*," *Genre* 11 [1978]: 450). And John Carlos Rowe considers the allusion a significant marker of what he sees as *The Princess Casamassima*'s "deconstruction of 'the romance of realism' ": "at the high-water mark of Christina's conversation with Hyacinth about revolutionary matters, she asks his opinion of a new story by M. Octave Feuillet, a popular romancer of the nineteenth century whose works clearly serve the ideology's romance" (*Theoretical Dimensions of Henry James*, 188, 185).

15. "Octave Feuillet," 218–19, 226–31, 231–32, 229. Tintner repeats some but not all of these arguments in *Cosmopolitan World* (68–73).

16. Tintner cites Madame Grandoni not only in "Octave Feuillet" but also in "Arsène Houssaye's 'Capricieuse' and James's 'Capricciosa.' " Virtually all the critics agree with Tintner's and Dove's description of the Princess's personality, for example, Powers (*Henry James and the Naturalist Movement*, 90); John L. Kimmey: "capriciousness is the one steady quality she possesses" (" *The Princess Casamassima* and the Quality of Bewilderment," *Nineteenth-Century Fiction* 22 [1967]: 60); and Clinton Oliver: "Madame Grandoni, who comprehends her more completely than anyone else in the novel, with the possible exception of Paul Muniment, calls her a *capricciosa*" ("Henry James as Social Critic," *Antioch Review* 7 [1947]: 250), to cite just a few.

17. John Roland Dove, "The Alienated Hero in *Le Rouge et le noir* and *The Princess Casamassima*," *Studies in Comparative Literature*, ed. Waldo F. McNeir, Louisiana State University Studies, Humanities Series, 11 (Baton Rouge: Louisiana State University Press, 1962), 150.

18. *The Princess Casamassima* carefully avoids distinguishing among specific labels of contemporary political movements, such as "socialist," "communist," "anarchist," and "nihilist," distinctions W. H. Tilley has clearly delineated in *The Background of "The Princess Casamassima,"* University of Florida Monographs, Humanities, 5 (Gainesville: University of Florida Press, 1960), 22–29. Since these differences are not very significant here, for the sake of convenience I consistently use the term "anarchist" throughout, as it is the one that appears most frequently in the novel.

19. These passages do not represent all that is to be noticed in Feuillet's fiction, or indeed all that James noticed. Feuillet's "marquises and countesses" may inhabit an "elegant and superfine" world, but that world is far from morally perfect, and the tales always teach a lesson in morality. The problem here—and this is James's second most recurrent complaint about Feuillet—is one of degree and depth; the moral dilemmas that Feuillet's protagonists find themselves in—while often ostensibly similar to situations in James's own fiction—are either shallow, characterized by a choice between obviously opposed extremes, or both. See, for example, "Camors" (*LC2* 285–86) and "Pierre Loti" (*LC2* 485–86).

20. Larousse's article on Feuillet (1872) suggests that James the critic held a typical view of this author; for example, according to Larousse, in *Monsieur de Camors* "se rencontrent . . . les délicates études de la vie mondaine, si familières à l'auteur" [are found . . . the delicate studies of worldly life, so familiar to the author]. In support, Larousse quotes G. Vattier:

M. Octave Feuillet est un esprit délicat, fin, aimable, dont l'observation est plus ingénieuse que profonde; . . . ses personnages . . . ce sont des ombres élégantes et gracieuses, vivant dans l'atmosphère raréfiée des Champs Elysées antiques. Chez lui dominent le joli, la distinction, le goût (non pas le grand, mais celui dont se contentent les salons), l'habileté, le soin du détail, la toilette du style. . . .

[Monsieur Octave Feuillet has a delicate, subtle, and amiable mind, whose power of observation is more ingenious than profound; . . . his characters . . . are elegant and gracious shadows who live in the rarefied atmosphere of the old Champs Elysées. In his fiction, prettiness, distinction, taste (not the grand, but that which pleases the salons), cleverness, care for detail, a fashionable toilette . . . dominate.] (*Grand dictionnaire universel* 8: 310)

21. Jacobson, *Henry James and the Mass Market,* 57.

22. *L'Education sentimentale: Histoire d'un jeune homme,* vol. 2 of Flaubert's *Oeuvres,* ed. André Thibaudet and René Dumesnil (Paris: Gallimard, Pléiade, 1952), 267. Larousse's explanation of reasons for the success of the *Revue des Deux Mondes* is another indication of the sort of readership the journal was associated with. After the revolution of 1848, "elle rallia les partis monarchiques en désarroi, tous les intérêts alarmés" [it rallied the disarrayed monarchists and all the alarmed interest groups]. After Napoleon III came to power in 1852, "elle se tint sur la défensive, pour affirmer de plus en plus ses tendances constitutionnelles, ses aspirations libérales" [it stayed on the defensive in order to affirm all the more its constitutional tendencies and its liberal aspirations]. According to Larousse, these opportunistic policies followed during the politically treacherous years of the mid–nineteenth century assured the *Revue des Deux Mondes* its upper-class readership: "Cette conduite habile assura à la *Revue* le concours des classes riches ou aisées, les seules qui puissent s'abonner à une publication d'un prix assez élevé. . . . (50 fr. par an)" [This clever maneuvering assured the *Revue* the support of the rich or financially comfortable classes, the only ones who could subscribe to such a high-priced periodical. . . . (Fifty francs a year)] (*Grand dictionnaire* 13:1130).

23. Mention of the *Revue des Deux Mondes* is also a sign of the intellectual stimulus that Hyacinth thinks he would receive in the ideal, upper-class milieu he fantasizes living in.

24. "Alienated Hero," 148–53.

25. Ibid., 148.

26. *The Middle Years,* 188.

27. Georges Bourgin, *La Commune,* rev. ed., ed. Paul Chauvet (Paris: Presses Universitaires de France, 1969), 123; [Prosper Olivier] Lissagaray, *Histoire de la Commune de 1871,* rev. ed. (Paris: Marcel Rivière, 1947), 388.

28. The two most frequently cited pieces of evidence for the period of James's composing of *The Princess Casamassima* are his 12 Dec. 1884 letter to T. S. Perry, which speaks of James's having visited Millbank prison that morning (*HJL* 3: 61), and the 10 Aug. 1885 notebook entry, in which James asserts that he must work out the details of the future evolution of *The Princess Casamassima* and complains of having "never yet become engaged in a novel in which, after I had begun to write and send off my MS., the details had remained so vague" (*CN* 31).

29. The *Revue des Deux Mondes* published Feuillet's one-act play *Le Voyageur: Scènes dialoguées* in 1884 and his short novel *La Morte* in Dec. 1885 and Jan. 1886 (the serialization of the latter was exactly contemporary with that of *The Princess Casamassima* in *Atlantic Monthly*). Feuillet also had four short novels in the *Revue des Deux Mondes* during the 1870s: *Julia de Trécoeur* (1872), *Un Mariage dans le monde* (1875), *Les Amours de Philippe* (1877), and *Le Journal d'une femme* (1878). If the princess's reference to Feuillet in the *Revue des Deux Mondes* is indeed to an actual novel but not historically accurate, it is conceivable that one of these novels is referred to. None of them, however, offers the abundance of similarities to *The Princess Casamassima* that *Histoire d'une parisienne* and *La Veuve* do, which provides additional evidence for the historical accuracy of the allusion.

30. The twelfth volume (1874) of Larousse's dictionary cites several now-forgotten plays entitled either *The Parisian* or *The Parisians,* all of which amply demonstrate that French playwrights both before and during the nineteenth century consistently represented libertinage as a common characteristic of natives of the French capital. Arsène Houssaye's 1869 *Les Parisiennes* features "une série de parisiennes du grand monde qui se livrent à la débauche" [a series of high society Parisian women who go in for debauchery]. In Champmeslé's 1682 *Les Parisiens,* "l'auteur . . . n'a mis en scène que des vauriens, des libertins, et des avares" [the author has presented nothing but good-for-nothings, libertines, and misers]. The heroine of Dancourt's 1691 *La Parisienne* "est une petite personne qui sort du couvent et qui passe pour une Agnès. La voilà bientôt avec trois amants . . . cette abondance est gênante, et la parisienne a besoin de tout son esprit pour se tirer de l'affaire" [(she) is a little thing just out of the convent, and she passes for an Agnès (the heroine of Molière's *L'Ecole des femmes* is the typical innocent). Soon she has three lovers . . . this abundance is troublesome, and the Parisian requires all her wit to get out of the situation]. The title alone of Théodore Barrière's 1854 *Les Parisiens de la décadence,* which is about "l'âme loyale et honnête" [the loyal, honest soul] who falls into a Paris of Balzacian intrigue, shows this play's attitude toward Parisians (*Grand dictionnaire* 12: 292–93). Henri Becque's *La Parisienne* is the best-known play by that title. It was first produced in 1885, the year *The Princess Casamassima* began to appear in serial form, and its heroine "plays elegant acrobatics with a husband, a lover who is jealous of the husband, and a second lover brought in to maintain equilibrium" (Paul Harvey and J. E. Heseltine, eds., *The Oxford Companion to French Literature* [Oxford: Clarendon Press, 1959], 538). Against the background of this traditional representation of Parisian women we distinguish the Princess Casamassima and Feuillet's *Parisienne.*

31. Octave Feuillet, "Histoire d'une parisienne," *Revue des Deux Mondes,* 15 Apr. 1881, 762.

32. For clarification on Hyacinth's perceptions of the world around him, James's oft-cited remarks on the "mirror" (*LC2* 1095–97) and on his own "perceptions" of London (*LC2* 1101) in his preface to *The Princess Casamassima* should be examined.

33. Oliver, "Henry James as Social Critic," 250.

34. Edel, *The Middle Years,* 182.

35. William Stowe's belief that representation constitutes the primary function or process of *The Princess Casamassima* (*Balzac, James, and the Realistic Novel*, 98) presents only part of the picture; his argument that the heroes of *The American* and Balzac's *Le Père Goriot* learn a "set of lessons—on social and moral interpretation" (21) and comprehension of the "system of behavior, of social relations, and of communication" (37) of the societies they are trying to break into is equally applicable to *The Princess Casamassima*. The protagonist's struggle to interpret a complex world of people not always easy to interpret or willing to be understood is a prime characteristic of every James fiction.

36. Both Lionel Trilling ("*The Princess Casamassima,*" in his *The Liberal Imagination: Essays on Literature and Society* [1950; reprint New York: Anchor-Doubleday, 1954], 94) and John Carlos Rowe (*Theoretical Dimensions,* 167) quote this speech by Madame Grandoni and derive from it rare examples of analyses of the Princess's personality that do some justice to the complexity of the character James represents for us. Trilling's psychological interpretation presents the Princess as dominated by a guilt-ridden superego, as someone who engages in philanthropic and prorevolutionary altruism out of horror at the inclination of her own will: "She is, in short, the very embodiment of the modern will which masks itself in virtue, making itself appear harmless, the will that hates itself and finds its manifestations guilty and is able to exist only if it operates in the name of virtue" (95). Rowe, in his neo-Marxist interpretation of *The Princess Casamassima,* argues that the Princess is consumed by a "self-hatred" resulting from the "essential contradiction in the Princess's life" between "the choice she made to commodify herself" (to sell herself for a title and a fortune) and "her economic worth as objet d'art" and "her individualism, her womanhood, her familial role as wife, her social role as princess" which is "an indication of what draws the Princess and Hyacinth together" (168).

37. Kimmey, "*The Princess Casamassima* and the Quality of Bewilderment," 60.

38. Frederick J. Hoffman, *The Mortal No: Death and the Modern Imagination* (Princeton: Princeton University Press, 1964), 47, n. 12.

39. *Henry James and the Mass Market,* 53.

40. *Theoretical Dimensions of Henry James,* 167.

41. "Histoire d'une parisienne," 15 Apr. 1881, 762; emphasis added.

42. Ibid., 1 Apr. 1881, 487–88.

43. Ibid., 15 Apr. 1881, 762.

44. Although John Carlos Rowe agrees that "the binding [of the Tennyson volume] expresses Hyacinth's love as a longing for the ideal, both in the woman and the art" (*Theoretical Dimensions of Henry James,* 178), rather than seeing the gift as metonymically associated to the later binding of the Princess's books, he offers an "account of the morphological associations among Hyacinth's gift of the volume of Tennyson's poems, the Princess's visit to a duke in the country, and the Princess's ultimate identification of Hyacinth's target as the 'Duke' " (181). He concludes, "The gift . . . is the sign that art has been transformed from its principal functions of communication and social consolidation to an aspect of the will to

power and of the sociological consequence of such psychology: class hierarchies" (179).

45. An additional reading of the name Hyacinth, emphasizing the Greek myth of Hyacinthus, is Reid Badger's in "The Character and Myth of Hyacinth: A Key to *The Princess Casamassima*," *Arizona Quarterly* 32 (1976): 316–26.

46. *Henry James and the Naturalist Movement,* 110.

47. Ibid., 116.

48. *The Novels of Henry James* (New York: Macmillan, 1961), 163–64. D. G. Halliburton offers a similar explanation:

> In killing the Duke—thereby annihilating a surrogate of his father and of himself—he would revive his mother's shame . . . even as he would destroy the hero of a vision to which he deeply aspires; and Hyacinth could not exist without his dream. It is his tragedy that even if he did go on living his aspirations would be meaningless, for he has been rejected by both halves of his self—by the Princess, who seemed a viaticum conducting to an elevation in class, and by those class peers who, by accusing him of losing faith, rob him of the closest approximation to identity he has ever known. ("Self and Secularization in *The Princess Casamassima*," *Modern Fiction Studies* 11 [1965]: 121)

49. John Colmer, *Coleridge to "Catch-22": Images of Society* (London: Macmillan, 1978), 103, 102. In addition to Powers, Cargill, and Halliburton, Philip Page (who sees the suicide as the logical conclusion to Hyacinth's attempts to project light into the unknown, to penetrate "the darkest mystery" ["*The Princess Casamassima:* Suicide and 'the Penetrating Imagination,'" *Tennessee Studies in Literature* 22 {1977}: 167–68]) and Kimmey (who relates the suicide to Hyacinth's loss of his illusions ["*The Princess Casamassima* and the Quality of Bewilderment," 61]) offer stimulating interpretations of Hyacinth's suicide. Jane Barstow briefly summarizes, without attributing, many of the interpretations offered ("Originality and Conventionality in *The Princess Casamassima*," 447, 457); and Mildred E. Hartsock gives a useful synopsis of the leading positions up to 1969 on Hyacinth's death ("*The Princess Casamassima:* The Politics of Power," *Studies in the Novel* 1 [1969]: 305).

50. I again rule out *La Morte,* both on historical grounds—its serialization occurred when chapter 22 of *The Princess Casamassima* was being written—and because nothing in it would justify Hyacinth's perceiving Christina as its heroine's "incarnation."

51. *Henry James and the Naturalist Movement,* 90–93.

52. "The Influence of Turgenev on Henry James," *Slavonic and East European Review* 20 (1941): 46–51; see also Cargill, *Novels of Henry James,* 147–49.

53. *The Background of "The Princess Casamassima,"* 34.

54. "Henry James's *The Princess Casamassima* and Ivan Turgenev's *Virgin Soil*," *South Atlantic Quarterly* 61 (1962): 354–64.

55. "Henry James's Divergences from His Russian Model in *The Princess Casamassima*," *Revue des langues vivantes* 37 (1971): 535–44.

56. Powers, *Henry James and the Naturalist Movement*, 92.

57. In 1877, James wrote a lengthy and positive review of Turgenev's novel for the *Nation* when it first appeared in French translation *LC2* 1000–6.

58. "La Veuve," *Revue des Deux Mondes*, 1 Dec. 1883, 481.

59. In no other novel of James's that comes to mind are the heights of the various characters not only so clearly emphasized but also so neatly divided into tall or short. With the interesting exception of the Princess and Madame Grandoni, every important character's height is divulged as soon as the character appears, and nobody is of average height. Millicent Henning forgets that Miss Pynsent, "the little dressmaker" (*PC* 68), is so small (40). Young Hyacinth "was exceedingly diminutive" (13) and, as an adult, "was as small as he had threatened" (55). "Mr. Vetch was short, fat, and bald" (17), Madame Poupin is "a small, fat lady" (67), her husband—like Hyacinth—is called "the little bookbinder" (67), and Rosy Muniment—Paul's invalid sister—is "a small figure" (85). On the other hand, Mrs. Bowerbank is a "towering woman" (5), Millicent has such a "tall young figure" (42) that Miss Pynsent calls her "[t]oo tall for a woman" (42). Paul Muniment is tall (79, 84). Lady Aurora—the philanthropist who looks after Rosy and who is infatuated with Paul—has a "high, lean figure" (87); Sholto is "tall and lean" (133), "at least six feet high" (136); and the Prince is a "high, lean person" (188).

60. "La Veuve," *Revue des Deux Mondes*, 1 Dec. 1883, 489.

61. Ibid., 490–91.

62. Ibid., 493.

63. "La Veuve," *Revue des Deux Mondes*, 15 Dec. 1883, 743–44.

64. Ibid., 738–39.

65. Ibid., 747.

66. Ibid.

67. Ibid.

68. *Henry James and the Naturalist Movement*, 116.

69. *Novels of Henry James*, 157–58.

70. See chap. 3, note 36, of this volume.

71. "James on a Revolutionary Theme," *Nation*, 23 Apr. 1938, 474.

72. "Henry James's *Capricciosa*: Christina Light in *Roderick Hudson* and *The Princess Casamassima*," *PMLA* 75 (1960): 310.

73. "Self and Secularization in *The Princess Casamassima*," 121.

74. *Person, Place, and Thing in Henry James's Novels* (Durham, N.C.: Duke University Press, 1977) 159.

75. Actually, Bell only hypothesizes that Christina is illegitimate (*Meaning in Henry James*, 177). Nevertheless, she still insists that Christina "is a *capricciosa* by nature—and she has always been one" (179).

76. "James on a Revolutionary Theme," 474.

77. *Person, Place, and Thing in Henry James's Novels*, 159.

78. There is no doubt that by the end of the novel, Christina knows Hyacinth intimately: just before she and Schinkel discover Hyacinth's body, they climb

the stairs to his room and see light coming from underneath his door; Christina is alarmed at the sight of this light (since Hyacinth has not responded to the knocking on his door), but Schinkel rationalizes that their young friend "very likely may have left it." The Princess vehemently responds that Hyacinth "doesn't leave candles!" (*PC* 551). While someone of Hyacinth's slender means would most likely not be wasteful with his candles (although his voracious reading habits must have made him quite a consumer of candles), the fact that Christina is so certain Hyacinth does not waste candles suggests how well she knows her friend's habits. In the modern world, people vary in being wasteful or careful consumers of electric lighting, but how often do we notice if our acquaintances belong to one extreme or another? I submit that we notice and remember only whether our friends are in the habit of unnecessarily leaving lights on, or of carefully turning them off, when we know them well, and Christina's claim to know that her friend is not in the habit of wasting candles is a sign either that she knows his habits well or that she is willing to pass for doing so.

79. Tintner has suggested yet another way of linking *The Princess Casamassima* to *Roderick Hudson,* involving the scene at the theater when Hyacinth and the Princess at last meet. The performance is of the fictitious *The Pearl of Paraguay,* and Tintner sees in that play a *mise en abîme* of both Roderick's earlier death and Hyacinth's later suicide: "*The Pearl of Paraguay* contains both a repetition of Roderick's fatal fall that has already taken place, and a prefiguration of Hyacinth's death, which has not yet taken place but which is linked with Roderick's death as attributable to the Princess' influence" (*Book World,* 11).

Chapter 3: Expectations of Rastignac in *The Princess Casamassima*

1. Kermode, *Art of Telling,* 108.

2. John Carlos Rowe, the one critic to have recognized a significance in the tendency of *The Princess Casamassima* to undermine "the customary expectations of realistic narration," emphasizes that "[a]gainst the characteristic organicism and development of realistic narration, James repeatedly manipulates strategic discontinuities, shifts in action and perspective. . . . Everywhere one looks in *The Princess Casamassima,* the dramatic action turns on discontinuities . . ." (*Theoretical Dimensions of Henry James,* 181, 182); Rowe closely examines the break between the end of chapter 21 and the beginning of chapter 22 and other such discontinuities (181–86).

3. *Meaning in Henry James,* 180. "In a sense," Bell continues, "that *is* what happens, but in a way which substitutes for [Hyacinth's] recovered paternal relation a discovery of the culture which is the fruit of his father's class advantages"; Hyacinth regains his privileges, but "His privileges, so gained, are only the privileges of culture" (181).

4. The first chapter of James's *The Europeans* introduces the siblings Felix and Eugenia in the same way. Until they reveal their relationship in their conversation, the narrator refers to them as "the young man" and "the young woman"; then they are called "the brother" and "the sister"; only when they happen to

address each other by name during the course of the dialogue does the narrator begin to identify them by name.

5. In *The Theoretical Dimensions of Henry James,* Rowe views this gap as a sign that the revolutionary world and the world of high society are, metaphorically speaking, one and the same. He thus concludes that "*The Princess Casamassima* deconstructs the opposition between anarchists and aristocrats" (186). Millicent Bell argues in *Meaning in Henry James* that the gap is an "elision" that "serves to reinforce the idea that reality is full of lapses which balk our effort at story-making" (162).

6. A case could be made that abrupt transitions from the end of one chapter to the beginning of the next are results of the way the novel was divided into installments for its original serialization. James speaks in his preface to *The Ambassadors* of experimenting with the serial form: "I had been open from far back to any pleasant provocation for ingenuity that might reside in one's actively adopting . . . recurrent breaks and resumptions" (*LC2* 1313). Indeed, it seems that *The Princess Casamassima* is a case in point, for the surprising leaps made at the beginnings of chapters 4 and 22 begin new installments. Chapters 12, 14, 29, 33, 39, 41, and 45 (the novel's last three chapters, numbers 45 through 47, were incorrectly numbered 44 through 46 in the final installment of the novel in *Atlantic Monthly*) also begin installments, and each presents material very different from the preceding chapter. Yet this is hardly the case of chapters 17, 25, and 37 (nor, arguably, of 8), which also start installments. The surprising chapter 24 comes at the end, not the beginning, of an installment, and the abrupt transition from chapter 26 to 27 falls in the middle of the next installment. One would be mistaken to see the serial form as the only explanation for the transitions, although they surely are evidence of James's making the most of the serial form. Nor should one see an explanation for the transitions in James's 10 Aug. 1885 notebook entry on how vague the details of the novel's "future evolution" were to him (*CN* 31), for the abrupt transitions continue to occur until the novel's end, at which point James presumably had worked out the novel's evolution.

7. Chapter 24, which gives the expected but delayed complete account of Hyacinth's "vow" to Hoffendahl, also begins in the abrupt manner typical of *The Princess Casamassima*. After two chapters given entirely to Hyacinth's sensations and impressions of Medley, chapter 24 opens with the surprising " 'I can give you your friend's name—in a single guess. He is Diedrich Hoffendahl,' " followed by the context: "They had been strolling more and more slowly, the next morning, and as she made this announcement the Princess stopped altogether, standing there under a great beech with her eyes upon Hyacinth and her hands full of primroses," followed by the conversation as it led up to the announcement (*PC* 284–90). It is typical of *The Princess Casamassima* that the surprising fact of the Princess's relations with Hoffendahl and the startling manner in which the reader learns of them come in the same chapter where the reader's expectation of learning about Hyacinth's visit with Hoffendahl is at last satisfied. Since the passing of one surprise or frustrated expectation is often counterbalanced with the presentation of another, the reader is never left at ease for too long in this novel.

8. Pinnie is most responsible for Hyacinth's own expectations related to his parentage, as Margaret Scanlon points out: "Brushing off his questions, yet hinting importantly at Hyacinth's blue blood, she makes his parentage the focus for a strategy of fantasy and repression" ("Terrorism and the Realistic Novel: Henry James and *The Princess Casamassima*," *Texas Studies in Literature and Language* 34 [1992]: 388).

9. Miss Pynsent's worship of aristocracy (which is blind to the point that she can see no fault in the members of that class) and her cherished hopes over her foster child's connection to it are apparent from the novel's first pages, when they come into conflict with the pragmatic Mrs. Bowerbank's view of the boy's parents:

> [W]hat endeared [Hyacinth] to [Miss Pynsent] most was her conviction that he belonged, "by the left hand," as she had read in a novel, to an ancient and exalted race. . . . To believe in Hyacinth, for Miss Pynsent, was to believe that he *was* the son of the extremely immoral Lord Frederick. She had, from his earliest age, made him feel that there was a grandeur in his past. (*PC* 8)

10. At his first encounter with Rosy Muniment, the only character in the novel who worships the aristocracy as much as Miss Pynsent, Hyacinth "was thrilled by the familiarity and frequency of her allusions to a kind of life he had often wondered about." This inspires his imagination to "the hope of being carried to some brighter, happier vision—the vision of societies in which, in splendid rooms, with smiles and soft voices, distinguished men, with women who were both proud and gentle, talked about art, literature and history" (*PC* 98). In spite of his annoyance with Pinnie for cultivating unrealistic aspirations that he will one day be elevated to his "rightful" rank, Hyacinth "none the less continued to cherish the belief that he was a gentleman born" (124).

11. Larousse, *Grand dictionnaire* 7:1108.

12. *Coleridge to "Catch-22": Images of Society*, 97. Colmer quotes the Hyde Park passage in full (96–97), adding that this "centrally important passage . . . clearly establishes Hyacinth's role as a young man from the provinces" (96).

13. As Hyacinth grows older, the projection of his fantasy becomes more sophisticated; in the sweetshop window, the *Family Herald* and the *London Journal* represent the aristocratic world, whereas later in his life, Hyacinth associates his idea of nobility life with the more fashionable *Revue des Deux Mondes*, "un recueil influent qui représente en France la civilisation extérieure et la France à l'étranger" [an influential journal that represents foreign civilization in France and France to the world] (Larousse, *Grand dictionnaire* 13: 1130).

14. *"The Princess Casamassima,"* 168.

15. Ibid., 69. It would consume considerable space to credit correctly all the critics who concur or disagree with Trilling's position on the "Young Man from the Provinces." Since my point is that the novel leads readers to perceive Hyacinth against the backdrop of this "Young Man from the Provinces" tradition, I mention only critics who appear to do so as a result of their own reading rather than as a result of Trilling's influential remarks. Clinton Oliver, writing before Trilling's essay

appeared, sees the parallels to some of the same texts Trilling cites: "Hyacinth Robinson, in the Princess's salon . . . is not unlike Eugene Rastignac, in the salon of the Viscountess de Beauséant . . . or that of the Baroness de Nucingen." Oliver also is aware of how Hyacinth differs from the types of characters Trilling refers to:

> In his original impulse to kill, to destroy, in order to achieve status and to break through a society that is personally stultifying, he is not unlike Dostoevsky's Rodion Raskalnikov, or Richard Wright's Bigger Thomas. . . . He does not, like Eugene Rastignac, pledge eternal war against the inequities of his society, but from the first moment of his introduction to the great world of the Princess, he is plagued with doubts. ("Henry James as Social Critic," 252–53)

D. G. Halliburton says much the same sort of thing as Trilling about Hyacinth:

> In a narrow sense *The Princess Casamassima* is a study in frustrated male hypergamy: a socially disinherited young man attempts to escalate upwards in his society by aligning himself with a woman of superior station. Hyacinth is never conscious of this aspiration. But in reading James it is easy to forget the substratum of action on which the dialogues are erected; it is easy to overlook, to put it crudely, what is really going on.

Halliburton stresses the point that Trilling leaves out, the alignment "with a woman of superior station" as a means of escalation:

> For that remarkable woman becomes in James's hands a kind of mock deity, a female savior who is unable to save, not because she had been dispossessed of her powers, but because they had only existed in the imagination of another, merely human being. ("Self and Secularization in *The Princess Casamassima*," 123, 124)

John Roland Dove compares Hyacinth with Stendhal's "Young Man from the Provinces," Julien Sorel, in his article ("Alienated Hero"), and Ivo Vidan claims "it is appropriate to draw a parallel between the *Princess* and Balzac's *Les Illusions perdues*" ("*The Princess Casamassima* Between Balzac and Conrad," *Studia Romanica et Anglica Zagrebiensia* 21–22 [1966]: 262), which represents a failure of the type.

16. Trilling, *"Princess Casamassima,"* 67–68.
17. Ibid., 68–69.
18. Ibid., 68.
19. Ibid., 69–75.
20. Ibid., 69.
21. Ibid., 70.
22. Ibid., 68.
23. Flaubert, *Oeuvres* 2: 48–49.
24. Richard Brodhead calls Hyacinth the *"arriviste* straight out of Balzac"

(*School of Hawthorne*, 144). Millicent Bell is the only commentator on *The Princess Casamassima*, as far as I can tell, who acknowledges the extent to which James's novel is a play on the "Young Man from the Provinces" type (*Meaning in Henry James*, 162–63).

25. Trilling, *"Princess Casamassima,"* 68.

26. Ibid., 69. *Daniel Deronda* and *Bleak House* cannot be included in Trilling's category, but their plots also have at their cores a mysterious, and perhaps illegitimate, birth, and in each of these texts the interceding "hand" of a lost parent brings on the eventual revelation.

27. Serialization of *Little Lord Fauntleroy* "began in the children's magazine, *St. Nicholas,* in November 1885," two months after *The Princess Casamassima* began to appear in *Atlantic Monthly.* James's friend James Russell Lowell was an admirer of Burnett's book (Ann Thwaite, *Waiting for the Party: The Life of Frances Hodgson Burnett, 1849–1924* [New York: Scribners, 1974], 93, 94).

28. Hyacinth makes a conscious effort to not believe in the possibility of an intercession by his father's family on his behalf, but the frequency and passion with which he alleges his indifference to them betrays his unconscious desire for their attention:

> He sometimes saw the name of his father's relations in the newspaper, but he always turned away his eyes from it. He had nothing to ask of them, and he wished to prove to himself that he could ignore them (who had been willing to let him die like a rat) as completely as they ignored him. Decidedly, he cried to himself at times, he was with the people, and every possible vengeance of the people, as against such shameless egoism as that; but all the same he was happy to feel that he had blood in his veins which would account for the finest sensibilities. (*PC* 124)

Because of his happiness about the "blood in his veins," one suspects the lengths to which he must go "to prove to himself that he could ignore" the Purvises. His attempt to return apparent indifference for real indifference is actually a sign that the Purvises are not unimportant to him, that, despite himself, he does want them to recognize him. Even though Hyacinth recognizes his foster mother's romantic illusions for what they are and appears to ignore his paternal relatives' existence, Miss Pynsent has succeeded in filling him with expectations, or at least pretensions, to a great future.

29. The Princess remarks this directly to Hyacinth: " '[Y]ou have nothing of the people about you—to-day not even the dress' " (*PC* 205).

> "You haven't a vulgar intonation, you haven't a common gesture, you never make a mistake, you do and say everything exactly in the right way. You come out of the hole you have described to me, and yet you might have stayed in country-houses all your life." (295)

Sholto tells Muniment that Hyacinth is " 'simply astonishing' " for someone of his " 'low extraction' " (180). Madame Grandoni says to the Prince, " 'If you mean the little bookbinder, he isn't dirty, especially what we should call' " (215), and she and Sholto agree, " 'who is to know he's her bookbinder? It's the last thing you'd take him for' " (308).

30. David Seed, while trying to argue that "Lionel Trilling notwithstanding, Hyacinth is not in any sense a young man from the provinces or representative of *any* social class," is one critic who stresses how *The Princess Casamassima* differs from the tradition: "the proposition that it springs out of the 'young man from the provinces' line of nineteenth-century fiction overshadows the more prosaic, though more important question of how it diverges from this tradition." Despite his effort to refute Trilling, Seed concedes that romance with a lady of a higher rank is an integral part of the tradition:

> Apart from these local influences the "young man from the provinces" tradi-
> tion is present by implication in so far as the plot outline seems pre-deter-
> mined. The sequence of events more or less follows a contour of entry into
> urban life, romance with aristocratic lady, union with revolutionaries fol-
> lowed by betrayal and death; in other words a composite of this tradition.
> ("Hyacinth Robinson and the Politics of *The Princess Casamassima*," *Etudes
> Anglaises* 30 [1977]: 31, 30, 38)

31. *Grand dictionnaire* 13: 717.

32. The "crisis" is a particularly melodramatic moment in the play's action. James frequently mixed the action on the stage with the action in the auditorium in his theater scenes, as Adeline Tintner points out in *The Book World of Henry James* (10–12), and this is no less the case here. Sholto appears in the narrative at the most melodramatic moment of the play as a correlative for the expectation that Hya-cinth's own melodramatic crisis will now be reached. Although the notes to the Library of America volume of James novels that includes *The Princess Casamassima* mention that "A number of *Pearl of* . . . dramas were popular in the late 19th century, such as the French opera *La Perle du Brésil [The Pearl of Brazil]* that first played in 1851, and was revived in 1858 and again in 1883" (1282, n.), neither Tintner nor I have found an actual, historical text corresponding to the play Hya-cinth takes Millicent to see (*La Perle du Brésil* contains no scene like the one James describes his characters viewing). Whereas James's fictions are full of literary refer-ences to actual other texts, this is one instance where James appears to have invented a reference and a melodramatic situation, the particular "crisis" of the "dishevelled and distracted" title character "implor[ing] the stern hidalgo her father, to believe in her innocence in spite of the circumstances which seemed to condemn her—a midnight meeting with the wicked hero in the grove of cocoanuts" (*PC* 132). If indeed James did invent this scene, it indicates something of his view of the kinds of elements included in stereotypical melodrama.

33. Scanlon supports my point, arguing that this passage shows that the Princess "awakens . . . primitive longings" in Hyacinth ("Terrorism and the Realis-tic Novel," 388).

34. *"Princess Casamassima,"* 69–74.

35. In this sense, William Stowe's argument that *The Princess Casamassima* is about different ways of representing reality is particularly appropriate (*Balzac, James, and the Realistic Novel,* 77–99).

36. The novel contains several instances of ring composition: for example, most of the minor characters, like the Poupins, Milicent, Mr. Vetch, and Prince Casamassima, appear in the early books, virtually disappear during the middle books, and reappear in the last two books.

37. It is appropriate in the context of the allusion to Feuillet and the connections it points to between *Roderick Hudson* and *The Princess Casamassima* that in her last appearance in *Roderick Hudson,* Christina launches her Rastignac-like challenge—"her mysterious menace"—against the world (*RH* 488), thus placing herself also in the context of Rastignacian expectations; and it is fitting to my thesis that *The Princess Casamassima* is a record of the frustration of Rastignacian expectations to see that in the later novel Christina is not very effective at "getting back at" the " 'world' " (*RH* 488) for having forced her to marry the Prince (although she certainly is effective at making her husband suffer for it).

38. John Roland Dove and Jane Marie Luecke have stressed the role of illusion in Hyacinth's relationships with his friends. Dove traces the development of Hyacinth's idealized attachment to Paul, Millicent, and the Princess until they all opt for an alternative, physical love.

> At the end of *The Princess Casamassima* . . . the three individuals [the Princess, Paul, and Millicent] whom Hyacinth loved and idealized turn out to be as self-centered, as disloyal, and as coarse spiritually as the people to whom Stendhal introduces us in *Le Rouge et le Noir,* and Hyacinth finds himself forced to adopt a view of humanity as disillusioned as that of Julien Sorel. ("Alienated Hero in *Le Rouge et le noir* and *The Princess Casamassima,*" 153)

Luecke shows how "Hyacinth Robinson's selective consciousness" is responsible for his making Paul and the Princess "fit ideals he had long cherished." In Paul's case, "Hyacinth imagined him to fit his ideal of that 'grand friendship' he had 'dreamed' about all his life[;] . . . the Princess on the other hand pre-eminently embodies his preconceived general ideal . . ." ("*The Princess Casamassima:* Hyacinth's Fallible Consciousness," in *Henry James: Modern Judgements,* ed. Tony Tanner [London: Macmillan, 1968], 187, 188–89). William Stowe's idea of *The Princess Casamassima* as generally about representation implies Hyacinth's tendency to create illusions for himself: "In *The Princess Casamassima* . . . the central character represents himself to himself and to others in various guises, and perceives things and systems of things in the world as representations of his own fate (*Balzac, James, and the Realistic Novel,* 57, see also 90–99).

39. See, for example, Roger Lewis's "Money, Love, and Aspiration in *The Great Gatsby,*" in *New Essays on "The Great Gatsby,"* ed. Matthew J. Broccoli (Cambridge: Cambridge University Press, 1985), 41–57.

Chapter 4: Salvation, the Scaffold, and Origen in *The Ambassadors*

1. As James calls Paris (*Amb.* 64) and as Thackeray calls London (*The History of Pendennis: His Fortunes and Misfortunes, His Friends and His Greatest Enemy* [1850; reprint, Harmondsworth: Penguin, 1972], 304, chap. 28).

2. Because James alludes specifically to Thackeray's two novels, it is surprising that Tintner, who is usually so exhaustive in her tracing of literary allusions in James, speculates on the "specific indebtedness" of *The Ambassadors* to Balzac's "Madame Firmiani" (*Book World*, 301–6) while not writing about *Pendennis* and *The Newcomes*, which *The Ambassadors* specifically alludes to, even though she does mention the reference to *The Vicar of Wakefield* (*Book World*, 320). Oscar Cargill, on the other hand, noticing the proximity of Thackeray's Newcomes to James's Newsomes, suggested that "The mother-daughter relationship to Chad was possibly suggested by *Henry Esmond*," and that Colonel Newcome's "relation to [his son] Clive and his final humility [have] a faint bearing on the history of Chad and Strether. Maria Gostrey one morning reminds Strether 'of Major Pendennis breakfasting at his club' " (*Novels of Henry James*, 332, n. 30).

3. *Pendennis*, 37–39, chap. 1.

4. Ibid., 39, chap. 1.

5. Ibid., 596, chap. 57.

6. Mamie is only one letter—indeed, one stroke of the pen—removed from being Marie, suggesting either that there are more than two Marys in the text, which is borne out by her willingness to save, or that she is a failed Mary, a Marie manquée, which is borne out, too, by her ineffectiveness at saving anyone.

7. Tintner denies that the frequency with which "the metaphor of salvation" appears in *The Ambassadors* implies any connection to religious metaphors; because of James's Protestant background, she argues, the Virgin Mary—the female symbol of salvation in Western culture—has nothing to do with the continual recurrence of the idea of salvation or with the name Mary (*Book World*, 306). According to Tintner, all this saving and the double use of the name Mary are derived from Balzac's *Une Fille d'Eve*, which also has two Marys who, like James's characters, both save and need saving (*Book World*, 307–8). Since they "do not fit in with James's decidedly secular bias and with his concern for the human rather than the divine comedy," Tintner rejects the "number of religious interpretations" of *The Ambassadors* by Oscar Cargill (in *Novels of Henry James*), Richard Chase (in "James's *Ambassadors*," in *Twelve Original Essays on Great American Novels*, ed. Charles Shapiro [Detroit: Wayne State University Press, 1958]), William Troy (in "The Altar of Henry James," in *The Question of Henry James*, ed. F. W. Dupee [New York: Holt, 1945]), and William Gibson ("Metaphor in the Plot of *The Ambassadors*," *New England Quarterly* 24 [1951]: 291–305) that might "explain this phenomenon" of the two Marys (*Book World*, 306). Therefore, for Tintner, while Balzac's novella plays out the symbolic drama of "the dual nature of woman as Eve and as Mary" (*Book World*, 308), this is not the case in *The Ambassadors*, where the double use of the name Mary has nothing to do with the Virgin Mary as a symbol of salvation.

8. The Notre Dame scene and the subsequent lunch at the Tour d'Argent

are not only thematically but also physically at the center of the novel. The first chapter of the seventh of twelve books (also the first chapter of the second volume of the New York Edition of the novel) is devoted to this episode, and the metaphorical repetition of the earlier dinner in London with Miss Gostrey suggests a new, or second, beginning. This placement of the episode at the center of the novel suggests its significance, as does James's choice of photograph for the frontispiece to the first volume of the revised edition of 1909: while the frontispiece of volume 2 has a view of the Luxembourg Gardens (showing the scene where Strether reads his mail in the second book [*Amb.* 59–64]), that of the first volume "was a picture of the Pont Neuf connecting the left bank with the Ile de la Cité. James entitled it simply 'By Notre Dame' " (S. P. Rosenbaum, "Editions and Revisions," in Henry James's *The Ambassadors: An Authoritative Text, the Author on the Novel, Criticism* [New York: Norton, 1964], 366). The choice of view which is almost the same view Strether and Mme. de Vionnet would have had during their lunch—for the first volume's frontispiece emphasizes the significance of Notre Dame, and therefore of the scenes that occur in it and facing it, to the entire novel.

9. In 1866, James reviewed *Chastelard,* the first of Swinburne's three tragedies on Mary Stuart, for the *Nation.* He also owned the complete works of Swinburne and individual copies of *Chastelard* and *Bothwell* (cf. Leon Edel and Adeline Tintner, "The Library of Henry James, from Inventory, Catalogues, and Library Lists," *Henry James Review* 4 [1982]: 185). The subject of *Chastelard,* says James, "is one of the numerous flirtations of Queen Mary of Scotland" (*LC1* 1274), and Swinburne presents Mary "as a coquette on the heroic scale" (*LC1* 1276). The following passage from the review indicates what James held to be the typical view of Mary:

> Her figure has been repeatedly used, and it is likely it will continue to be used for a long time to come; for it adapts itself to the most diverse modes of treatment. In poetry, after all, the great point is that the objects of our interest should be romantic, and from every possible point of view Queen Mary answers this requisite, whether we accept her as a very conscientious or as a very profligate woman; as a martyr or simply as a criminal. For the fact remains that she was supremely unhappy; and when to this fact we add the consideration that she was in person supremely lovely, that she embodied, if not all the virtues, at least all the charms, of her sex, we shall not be at a loss to understand the ready application of her history to purposes of sentiment. (*LC1* 1274)

Possibly on the strength of his three tragedies, Swinburne was asked to contribute the article on Mary Stuart for the ninth edition of the *Encyclopaedia Britannica.* Because of the place of the *Britannica* in English-speaking culture, and also as James appears to have admired Swinburne (Edel, *The Life of Henry James,* vol. 1, *The Untried Years: 1843–1870* [Philadelphia: Lippincott, 1953], 289), the article can be seen as representative of the figure Mary presented in late Victorian culture. Before her incarceration in England (mostly in Fotheringay Castle, from which the actress with whom Thackeray's hero Arthur Pendennis falls in love takes her stage name), Mary had "very sufficient experience" of "[t]he passion of love," says Swinburne. Few, it seems, were "impervious" to Mary's "lifelong power of seduction and subjugation . . . George Douglas fell inevitably under the charm"; and her physical beauty was such that "no man could look upon her and refuse" her appeals for mercy after Bothwell's defeat at Carberry Hill. According to Swinburne, Mary's current husband, Darnley, certainly did not think he was the father of the future James I of England ("Mary Queen of Scots," in *Encyclopaedia Britannica* [9th ed., 1875–1889; reprint, 11th ed., 1910–1911], 17:823, 820, 818).

10. James alludes to Esmeralda, the heroine of *Notre-Dame de Paris,* in other novels: in *The Awkward Age* (see chap. 5, this volume) and in *The Bostonians,* where her innocence is an emblem of Verena Tarrant's (see note 1 of chap. 1, this volume).

11. *Victor Hugo: Oeuvres complètes,* vol. 1, *Roman I: Notre-Dame de Paris,* ed. Jacques Seebacher (Paris: Laffont, 1985), 677. All subsequent references are to this edition and will be cited parenthetically as *Notre-Dame* in the text.

12. Swinburne's *Encyclopaedia Britannica* article on Mary Stuart concludes with a comparison of Queen Elizabeth and Mary:

> Elizabeth, so shamefully [Mary's] inferior in personal loyalty, fidelity and gratitude, was as clearly her superior on the one all-important point of patriotism. The saving salt of Elizabeth's character, with all its wellnigh incredible mixture of heroism and egotism, meanness and magnificence, was simply this, that, overmuch as she loved herself, she did yet love England better. Her best though not her only fine qualities were national and political, the high public virtues of a good public servant; in the private and personal qualities which attract and attach a friend to his friend and a follower to his leader, no man or woman was ever more constant and more eminent than Mary Queen of Scots. ("Mary Queen of Scots," 17: 823–24)

With devotion to the Woollett mentality and the family business in place of Elizabeth's patriotism and love of public service, the passage would be a perfectly appropriate contrast of Mrs. Newsome and Mme. de Vionnet in *The Ambassadors.* Swinburne dedicated *Chastelard,* incidentally, to Victor Hugo.

13. Maria's red velvet band is an excellent example of Strether's own metaphorical "reading" differing from the reader's. At the moment of the comparison, Strether sees Maria's bare shoulders in contrast to Mrs. Newsome's modesty. The red and the velvet of the band are for Strether at the moment only signs of the sensuality of Mary Stuart. The reader, however, can read into the neck band the additional sense of the gruesome image of the band of blood that the executioner would make appear on Mary Stuart's neck.

14. I am following Sallie Sears's explanation of the relationship between Strether's "double consciousness," "the paradox of his character," and "the European-American antithesis," which is its "symbolic projection" (*The Negative Imagination: Form and Perspective in the Novels of Henry James* [Ithaca, N.Y.: Cornell University Press, 1968], 105ff.).

15. Ibid., 109–10.

16. Ibid., 109.

17. Ibid.

18. Ibid., 109–10.

19. Ibid., 110.

20. Ibid.

21. In *The Europeans,* a novel with many parallels to *The Ambassadors*—Americans and Europeans coming into contact, a charming and complex heroine, characters whose views change and who learn to enjoy life—the Unitarian minister, Mr. Brand, uses much the same words as Strether to Chad when he tries to convince Gertrude Wentworth not to abandon him for Felix Young: "You have new interests, new occupations . . . I don't know that I can say that you have new duties" (*Eur.* 939).

22. *Negative Imagination,* 109.

23. Millicent Bell's chapter on *The Ambassadors* in *Meaning in Henry James* very persuasively reads James's novel as "a contest enacted from page to page among different possibilities of story" (324); not unlike William Stowe, who sees Hyacinth in *The Princess Casamassima* as trying out different forms of representation, Bell sees Strether in *The Ambassadors* as trying out the situations and people he encounters in different fictional genres (*Meaning in Henry James,* 324–53).

24. Richard A. Hocks, *Henry James and Pragmatic Thought: A Study in the Relationship Between the Philosophy of William James and the Literary Art of Henry James* (Chapel Hill: University of North Carolina Press, 1974), 169.

25. William M. Thackeray, *The Newcomes* (1853; reprint, New York: Crowell, n.d.), 335–37, 343, chap. 33; 349, chap. 34; 383, chap. 37.

26. Ibid., 336, chap. 33. James's affection for *The Newcomes* is apparent from his critical writings; much as one might speak, for example, of Tolstoy as "the author of *War and Peace,*" James often alludes to "the author of *The Newcomes*" (*LC1* 26, 1344; *LC2* 698)—indeed more frequently than, as would seem more common today, to "the author of *Vanity Fair*" (*LC1* 1397).

27. Critics since Troy ("Altar of Henry James") and Gibson ("Metaphor in the Plot of *The Ambassadors*")—and despite Tintner (*Book World,* 306)—with their emphasis on the motif of the garden in *The Ambassadors* have agreed.

28. I am following Richard Hocks's definition of polarity and his reading of its role in *The Ambassadors.* "Polarity," he says, "differs from dichotomy by virtue of involving interpenetration rather than juxtaposition. It is a life-endowing relationship through opposition and, according to Coleridge anyway, the fundamental source and principle of life itself" (*Henry James and Pragmatic Thought,* 174ff).

29. Of course, the conventional form of the story is interested in the father figure's effort to understand, but this is not represented as a process as drawnout and involving as many reversals as in *The Ambassadors;* rather, it usually consists of a single revelation scene.

30. *Negative Imagination,* 109–10.

31. Parisian post offices are still linked by pneumatic tubes, and Parisians can

still mail *pneus,* though at a price. Before the telephone—and now the fax machine—became ubiquitous, they were used more often, and around the turn of the century, there was the same sort of romance about using the new technology that was associated later, for example, with early jet travel. Numerous examples of the romance of correspondence appeared over a decade after *The Ambassadors* in *A la recherche du temps perdu,* where, according to Alain Buisine, there is a significant connection between desire and letters and, most important, *pneumatiques:*

> Quel raffinement supplémentaire que le pneumatique dont le mode de transport doit combler tous les désirs proustiens! Merveilleuse invention du XIXe siècle en effet que cette façon de souffler les lettres, de créer une circulation presque éolienne de l'écriture!
>
> [The *pneumatique* offers a further refinement, for this means of transport fully satisfies all the Proustian desires! It is in fact one of the nineteenth century's more wonderful inventions, this method of blowing letters, of creating a virtually aeolian means of circulating writing!] (*Proust et ses lettres* [Lille: Presses Universitaires de Lille, 1983], 62)

32. William Shakespeare, *Macbeth,* in *The Riverside Shakespeare,* ed. G. Blakemore Evans (Boston: Houghton Mifflin, 1974), 5.5.24–26.

33. This phrase also evokes Shakespeare—the title *Love's Labour's Lost*—and indeed, from Maria's and Marie's viewpoints, *The Ambassadors* is unquestionably about love's labors lost.

34. *Macbeth,* 5.5.27.

35. In his preface to the New York Edition of the novel, James wrote:

> The whole case, in fine, is in Lambert Strether's irrepressible outbreak to little Bilham on the Sunday afternoon in Gloriani's garden, the candour with which he yields, for his young friend's enlightenment, to the charming admonition of that crisis. The idea of the tale resides indeed in the very fact that an hour of such unprecedented ease should have been felt by him *as* a crisis, and he is at pains to express it for us as neatly as we could desire. The remarks to which he thus gives utterance contain the essence of "The Ambassadors," his fingers close, before he has done, round the stem of the full-blown flower; which, after that fashion, he continues officiously to present us. (*LC2* 1304)

This "germ" was inspired by a story Jonathan Sturges told about William Dean Howells, and the history of the anecdote's effect on James can be followed in the author's notebooks (the 31 Oct. 1895 entry) and in the proposal, "Project of Novel," James sent Harper and Brothers in the fall of 1900 (*CN* 140–42, 541–76, esp. 541–43).

36. The passage is problematic in at least one other aspect: it is ironic that two Americans, natives of the self-styled land of freedom, meet in the Old World—where they speak of "the clock of . . . freedom ticking as loud as it seems to do

here"—the world Americans have been taught was that of tyranny, and learn there to recognize and appreciate the nature and value of freedom.

37. *The American Henry James* (New Brunswick, N.J.: Rutgers University Press, 1957), 213.

38. Tintner's article, "Henry James' Balzac Connection," (*AB Bookman's Weekly* 67 [1981]: 3219–28); James W. Gargano's "*The Ambassadors* and *Louis Lambert*" (*Modern Language Notes* 75 [1960]: 211–13); and a paragraph of Quentin Anderson's *The American Henry James* (213–14) are the only commentaries on the subject. Anderson offers little more than a brief summary of the points of comparison between *Louis Lambert* and *The Ambassadors:*

> But Lambert has qualities and experiences in common with James's character: the violent revolution in feeling and conviction undergone by Lambert; his propensity to systematic inquiry; his obsession with the faculty of will, which had for the two Henry Jameses such an unpleasantly righteous connotation; and, finally, his loss of his position in the world through devotion to a woman of another faith. (214)

39. In a passage from a letter that James quotes in his review (*LC2* 75–76), Balzac boasts:

> *Louis Lambert* m'a coûté tant de travaux! que d'ouvrages il m'a fallu pour écrire ce livre! Il jettera peut-être, un jour ou l'autre, la science dans des voies nouvelles. Si j'en avais fait une oeuvre purement savante, il eût attiré l'attention des penseurs, qui n'y jetteront pas les yeux. Mais, si le hasard le met entre leurs mains, ils en parleront peut-être! (*Correspondance,* vol. 2 [Paris: Garnier, 1962], 89)

> ["Louis Lambert" has cost me so much work! To write this book I have had to read so many books! Some day or other, perhaps, it will throw science into new paths. If I had made it a purely learned work, it would have attracted the attention of thinkers, who now will not drop their eyes upon it. But if chance puts it into their hands, perhaps they will speak of it!] (trans. by James, *LC2* 76)

40. "*The Ambassadors* and *Louis Lambert,*" 211.

41. Ibid., 212.

42. Ibid.

43. Ibid., 213.

44. "Balzac Connection," 3228; emphasis added.

45. Larousse, *Grand dictionnaire* 11: 1468.

46. "Balzac Connection," 3228.

47. The end of *The Ambassadors* is the source of the most disagreement among commentators on this text. Is the end positive or negative? Does Strether return to the United States the better for his stay in Paris, or does his refusal of

Maria indicate that he has failed to assimilate the lessons he appeared to have learned in France? These are the questions that the debate centers on, and virtually every critical piece on *The Ambassadors* offers some kind of resolution to them. Julie Rivkin's "The Logic of Delegation in *The Ambassadors*" provides a useful summary of the various readings of the novel's final scene (*PMLA* 101 [1986]: 830, n. 2).

48. *"The Ambassadors and Louis Lambert,"* 212–13.

49. Ibid., 213.

50. Ibid.

51. Ibid. 212.

52. Millicent Bell cites this scene as an example of the problem of "which story, farcical or tragical," Strether "should assign" Marie; Strether's reactions to the scene show that Marie "is both type and unfathomable individuality, unexpressed in either conventional story" (*Meaning in Henry James,* 351).

53. Paul Rosenzweig, "James's 'Special-Green Vision': *The Ambassadors* as Pastoral," *Studies in the Novel* 13 (1981): 385.

54. This is yet another motif the novel develops: young Chad will turn out to look "awfully old" and to have "grey hair" (*Amb.* 93), while the middle-aged Strether will learn to "toddle alone" (190) and will strike Miss Gostrey as youth itself—"you *are,* at this time of day, youth" (197). This reversal of apparent ages is reinforced in the way scenes at the end of the novel reverse a scene at the beginning: the early scene in which Strether performs his duty to Mrs. Newsome and tries to persuade Chad to think of his family, his future, and his career and to return to America (94–102) is mirrored not only by a scene where Strether reverses his position and asks Chad to stay in Paris (183–89) but also by a scene, almost identical in its details to the first, in which Chad urges Strether to consider his financial future and the security of his position in the Newsome family (332–40). The significance of these reversals is related to the central theme of polarities: if everything contains to some degree both its essence and its opposite, then youth contains age and old age contains youth; that is why Strether and Chad are both young and old.

Chapter 5: French Books in *The Awkward Age*

1. The function of *Paule Méré* in *Daisy Miller* is, as Adeline Tintner puts it in respect to literary references in general in James's fiction, "part of a pattern which in James more often than not is his way of suggesting to the reader that he should keep in mind a story parallel to the one James is telling" ("Review-Essay: Eight Ways of Looking at James," *Studies in the Novel* 9 [1977]: 86). Jean Blackall arrives at much the same conclusion about literary allusions in James in "Literary Allusion as Imaginative Event in *The Awkward Age*," *Modern Fiction Studies* 26 (1980): 195.

2. Paula V. Smith, "A Wilde Subtext for *The Awkward Age*," *Henry James Review* 9 (1988): 202. This essay presents a persuasive case for the parallel structures of *The Awkward Age* and Wilde's *The Importance of Being Earnest*.

3. Walter Isle, *Experiments in Form: Henry James's Novels, 1896–1901* (Cambridge: Harvard University Press, 1968), 180.

4. Daniel J. Schneider, in "James's *The Awkward Age:* A Reading and an Evaluation" (*Henry James Review* 1 [1980]: 219–20), gives a summary of the sides taken on this issue.

5. Isle writes that "Nanda, Mitchett, and Mr. Longdon are the generally praiseworthy characters in the novel, the ones who gain the greatest share of our sympathy. The 'evil' ones, or those who obstruct the good characters, are Mrs. Brookenham, Vanderbank, and the Duchess" (*Experiments in Form,* 170). Sklepowich levels some of the strongest diatribes against Mrs. Brookenham: "Mrs. Brook eventually brings about such chaos by doing to Nanda what she most probably knew Longdon would never do to *her*—'hitting below the belt' " ("Gilded Bondage: Games and Gamesplaying in *The Awkward Age*," *Essays in Literature* 5 [1978]: 190); Oscar Cargill says in *The Novels of Henry James* (267) that "she certainly outranks all his bad heroines, save the tragic Kate Croy"; while in *Henry James,* F. W. Dupee adopts a more moderate position, comparing Mrs. Brook to Falstaff: "She belongs with the charming rogues of literature, those characters whose energy redeems their badness and who, consequently, have no place in [James's] regular scheme" (172).

6. As Hall says:

> [T]he critical image of Mrs. Brookenham as a calculating creature, controlled and controlling, is altogether wide of the mark in its oversimplification. The sophistication, the interest, and the value of Mrs. Brook (and of the society of which she is the center) lie in her awareness, not in any manipulative consciousness. . . . ("James's Conception of Society in *The Awkward Age*," *Nineteenth-Century Fiction* 23 [1968]: 40)

Blackall, in "The Case for Mrs. Brookenham" (*Henry James Review* 2 [1981]: 159–60), praises Mrs. Brook's "protean social character"—her ability to

> assume . . . the right line for dealing with the matter in hand. . . . While Mrs. Brookenham is at fault if *The Awkward Age* is read as a study of the decadence of English manners, she is simultaneously the heroine of *The Awkward Age* regarded as an entertainment, a circus, a game of wits. Lacking any other capital, she matches her nuance against Longdon's money and wins.

Jones argues that "Mrs. Brook sacrifices herself and Van for Nanda," and as a result, "Nanda is free . . . to discover what she is. . . . Mrs. Brook, indeed, is responsible for it all: she has seen Nanda into being a young woman" (*Henry James's Psychology of Experience: Innocence, Responsibility, and Renunciation in the Fiction of Henry James* [The Hague: Mouton, 1975], 32–33). Schneider claims that in the society represented in *The Awkward Age,* "Mrs. Brook is fundamentally too decent, too sweet—she cares too much about people—to be entirely effective. . . . [S]he will not impose her will upon Nanda and Harold; she does not try to manipulate them or force them into arrangements against their will. . . . She is really very considerate of Nanda, whose life is so much easier than her own" ("James's *The Awkward Age*," 222).

7. Isle, *Experiments in Form*, 192.

8. For Krook, *The Awkward Age* "is essentially not a comedy at all, but a tragedy—the tragedy of Nanda Brookenham, the girl who is exposed to the full impact of the London *beau monde* figured in Buckingham Crescent" (*The Ordeal of Consciousness in Henry James* [Cambridge: Cambridge University Press, 1962], 138). Jacobson calls Nanda "a passive victim of society and specifically of her mother" (*Henry James and the Mass Market*, 136).

9. In *The Crystal Cage: Adventures of the Imagination in the Fiction of Henry James* ([Lawrence: Regents Press of Kansas, 1978], 57), Schneider writes that if Nanda "is surprisingly an example of 'the moral sense,' she also remains what she has been made: a creature who, like her mother, can plot and scheme with furious industry to achieve her ends." Hartsock criticizes the "tragic victim" interpretation of Nanda: "The suffering of Nanda Brookenham does not mean that a corrupt society destroys her nor that she is a tragic figure" ("The Exposed Mind: A View of *The Awkward Age*," *Critical Quarterly* 9 [1967]: 58). McCormack seconds the argument that Nanda shows herself to have become a younger, perhaps gentler, version of her mother at the end of the novel when she "replaces her mother as a verbal power broker" (*The Rule of Money: Gender, Class, and Exchange Economics in the Fiction of Henry James* [Ann Arbor, Mich.: UMI Research Press, 1990], 60). Greg W. Zacharias concurs when he writes that "Nanda . . . is the novel's 'experienced mariner.' She exerts influence . . . to reorganize the circumstances of her little society. Nanda improves her own life by improving the lives of those around her. Civic renewal spreads outward from her steady wake" ("The Marine Metaphor, Henry James, and the Moral Center of *The Awkward Age*," *Philological Quarterly* 69 [1990]: 102).

10. For Isle, for example, "Nanda is sacrificed figuratively in the continual talk of what to do about her, and literally in the climactic scene at Tishy Grendon's" (*Experiments in Form*, 198). Jacobson writes in *Henry James and the Mass Market* that Mrs. Brook is "childish toward the end of the novel when her entire circle of friends gathers at Tishy Grendon's house. She is rude to everyone and at the end of the evening succeeds in forcing her daughter to admit publicly to having read a scandalous French novel" (130). Sklepowich says, in "Gilded Bondage": "Egotism perverts the better social virtues as, in order to win the competition for Van's interest, she indiscriminately inflicts pain, embarrassing her vulnerable daughter and outraging Longdon and the more sensitive souls" (191).

11. Hall, "James's Conception," 42–45.

12. "Literary Allusion," 181.

13. Blackall thinks the heroine with the poodle is also Christina Light from *Roderick Hudson* ("Literary Allusion," 181). Christina certainly does have a poodle (and Roderick and Rowland do compare the poodle and its owner to Mephistopheles [*RH* 229]), but she cannot be seen as personifying any larger, cultural stereotype in the way Esmeralda and Gretchen stand for the type of the innocent victim,

so one can only speculate as to the role an allusion to her would have in *The Awkward Age*. Christina and her pet poodle can hardly be considered eminently recognizable to the novel reader of 1899, as Faust's poodle or Gretchen would have been, so if James was having a private joke with himself, it was one that only his most faithful readers could have perceived. Of course, the private joke is perfectly appropriate, because it compares Nanda with Christina, who is certainly forced by her mother into an unhappy future—and by implication, so is Nanda. The case is very different in *The Princess Casamassima*, where that novel's title and the recurrence of Christina in a major part make it far more clear that the reader should perceive a reference to *Roderick Hudson*.

14. Blackall, "Literary Allusion," 186.

15. Ibid., 184.

16. Ibid., 185–87.

17. Ibid., 188.

18. Ibid.

19. Ibid.

20. The suspicions, incidentally, do not come only from characters in the novel; at least one of James's readers, Schneider, who insinuates that Nanda has an affair with Cashmore, shares these suspicions ("James's *The Awkward Age*: A Reading and an Evaluation," *Henry James Review* 1 [1980]: 220–21).

21. Cartoons and caricatures of Zola used the character of Nana as an identifying trait for the figure of Zola, showing that Zola was most easily recognizable as the author of *Nana;* an example is the Russian cartoon (reproduced in Emile Zola, *Oeuvres complètes,* vol. 7, ed. Henri Mitterand [Paris: Cercle du Livre Précieux, 1966], 1135) occasioned by the publication of *Rome,* which depicts Zola in a pilgrim's robe, leading a little girl named Nana by the hand, knocking on the door of the Vatican.

22. Blackall claims that Van's allusion to Zola is to Camille Duvillard of *Paris,* the last of the trilogy entitled *Les Trois Villes* ("Literary Allusion," 188–90). Zola's *Paris* is pertinent to *The Awkward Age,* says Blackall, because Camille Duvillard and her mother compete for the affection of the same man. There is no question that there is a parallel between the mother-daughter-lover triangles in James's and Zola's novels, and there is evidence, which Blackall does not offer, to support a claim that a reader of *The Awkward Age* would associate *Paris* with an allusion to Zola. Both Zola and *Paris* were in the news in 1899: the serialization of *Paris* ended in early 1898, at the same time *L'Aurore* published Zola's famous indictment of the Dreyfus affair, "J'Accuse"; and the book publication in March 1898 came immediately after Zola's trial and flight to England. As a protester and victim of the Dreyfus scandal, Zola received extensive press coverage in both his own country and abroad, and publicity for his new novel benefited from this exposure. One English review states that the story line of *Paris* "has been done to death in the daily and weekly press" (J. E. H. W., "Paris—Metz—Chartres: A Trilogy of Translations," *The Bookman* 79, no. 14 [Apr. 1898]: 19). As a result, James had sufficient opportunity for exposure to *Paris* before he wrote *The Awkward Age* in the fall of 1898 (Edel, *The Life of Henry James,* vol. 4, *The Treacherous Years, 1895–1901* [Philadelphia:

Lippincott, 1969], 251). However, there is no concrete evidence that James read *Paris* before he finished *The Awkward Age:* he owned and signed a copy of the first edition (Edel and Tintner, "Library of Henry James," 190), but he dated it "1900" (see Tintner, *Cosmopolitan World*, 89–90), which makes it seem unlikely that James read it before the end of the century (of course, that does not rule out that James knew enough of the plot of *Paris* from other sources, such as the press and friends' conversation). Furthermore, James speaks specifically of *Lourdes* and *Rome*—but not of *Paris*—and the *Trois Villes* sequence in general in the 1903 article on Zola in such a way that only a reading of the first two volumes of the trilogy is certain (*LC2* 883–88, esp. 887–88, 897). Considering the sentimentality in the rendering of the Froment family life and the shallow and facile panegyric on the work ethic in *Paris,* it is hard to understand how James could have read *Paris* and not criticized in the 1903 article on Zola what must have seemed to him the novel's egregious failings. We also know from James's 4 March 1895 notebook entry that James had come to at least a general conception of the Brookenham-Vanderbank love triangle before Zola began *Paris* (with the similar Duvillard-Quinsac love triangle) in late 1896 (see *CN* 118).

What is curious about *Paris* in relation to James is that, as Tintner says, "one wonders if Zola knew *The Princess Casamassima*" (*Cosmopolitan World*, 90), for in the characters of Camille's brother, Hyacinthe, and his admirer, the princesse de Harth, who decidedly is capricious and who develops an interest in anarchists, Zola would seem to have created a parody of Hyacinth Robinson (and perhaps also of Oscar Wilde) and the Princess Casamassima, were it not for the fact that Zola's English was not good enough for him to have read *The Princess Casamassima*.

23. The corruption of the Second Empire is, of course, a constant theme throughout the *Rougon-Macquart* novels, and the process of corruption is paralleled by the decay of a human body not only in Nana's illness but also in the Emperor's illness during the Franco-Prussian War, which is so often mentioned in *La Débâcle,* where this bodily corruption is also contrasted with the equally frequently mentioned illusions/delusions of the cheering Paris crowds at the outbreak of the war. *La Débâcle* was published in 1892 and sold well, and we know that James read it at the time of its appearance (*LC2* 898) and liked it (*LC2* 892, 898).

24. The "awkward age" of the title could also seem to refer to Mrs. Brook's awkward age, for she has reached the age where a youthful appearance ceases to be among her principal attractions, and she is also at the age that is always difficult for parents, when the children start to "leave the roost." There is no question that Mrs. Brook is also at a difficult moment in life, but my point is that the "awkward ages" that most concern James's readers are Nanda's and the period's, and that this is most apparent once we consider, as I do below, the relation of James's novel to Gyp's novels on similar topics.

25. The association of Esmeralda and Gretchen is further reinforced by a perceived similarity in the nineteenth century between Hugo's heroine and another of Goethe's suffering innocents, Mignon: Larousse points out that Gautier called Esmeralda, "cette charmante soeur de la Mignon de Goethe" [that charming sister of Goethe's Mignon] (7: 877).

26. See notes 6 and 11 above.

27. Molière derived the name from the Greek ἀγνόδ , which means "pure" and "chaste."

28. James explored the Agnès situation in his first novel, *Watch and Ward*.

29. Perhaps it is a reference to King Gustav III of Sweden, who was noted for his progressiveness, for his homosexual predilections, and for being assassinated in 1792 by a reactionary conspiracy; he was the subject of Verdi's *Un ballo in maschera*.

30. Alexandre Dumas *fils*, *La Dame aux camélias* (1848; reprint with introduction by André Maurois; Paris: Gallimard, Folio, 1975), 37.

31. Alexandre Dumas, *Fernande*, 3 vols. (Paris: Dumont, 1844). Auger's authorship of this novel is claimed in Hector Talvart and Joseph Place's *Bibliographie des auteurs modernes de langue française, 1801–1934*, vol. 5 (Paris: Editions de la Chronique des Lettres Françaises, 1935), which refers to Joseph-Marie Quérard's *Les Sepercheries littéraires dévoilées*, vol. 1 (Paris: Quérard, 1847) as its source, and in the *Bibliographie de la France ou Journal général de l'Imprimerie et de la Librairie et des cartes géographiques, gravures, lithographies, oeuvres de musique*, 5 Apr. 1856, 365, n. 2833. The reference to *Fernande* in *La Dame aux camélias* does not appear to question the elder Dumas's authorship; but Dumas was known to use ghost writers, *Fernande* went out of print after Auger's authorship was revealed, and when one reads *Fernande*, it is hard to believe that one is reading the same writer whose *Le Comte de Monte-Cristo* and *Les Trois Mousquetaires* appeared in the same year as *Fernande*.

32. Dumas, *Fernande* 1: 186.

33. See Edel and Tintner, "The Library of Henry James," 169.

34. The name still bears such associations in French culture, as Georges Brassens's song "Fernande" attests.

35. In "De 'Madame de La Pommeraye' à 'Ruy Blas' " (*Revue d'histoire littéraire de la France* 66 [1966]: 238, 241–42, 243–46, 249), English Showalter, Jr., cites Hugo's *Ruy Blas*, Lytton's *The Lady of Lyons*, Léon de Wailly's *Angelica Kauffmann*, three purely fictitious French biographical dictionary articles on Angelica Kauffmann, Helen Maria Williams's *The History of Perourou, or the Bellows-Mender*, Croly's *Pride Shall Have a Fall*, Browning's *Pippa Passes*, Moncrieff's *The Beauty of Lyons*, H. J. Byron's *The Lady of Lyons*, Merivale's *The Lady of Lyons Married and Settled*, and Reece's *The Lady of Lyons Married and Claude Unsettled*. Wade Jennings makes a case in "Diderot: A Suggested Source of the Jules-Phene Episode in *Pippa Passes*" (*English Language Notes* 2 [1964]: 32–36) for the connections between Diderot's story and *The Lady of Lyons* and *Pippa Passes*. Finally, Henri Coulet argues in "Le Thème de la 'Madeleine repentie' chez Robert Challe, Prévost et Diderot" (*Saggi e ricerche di letteratura francese* 14 [1975]: 289–90) that the final scene of the story of Mme. de La Pommeraye is a conventional one that also appeared in *Manon Lescaut* and Challe's *Illustres françoises*, and that all three are derived from the figure of Mary Magdalene washing Jesus' feet. James certainly knew the manifestation of the type in *The Lady of Lyons;* he was generally familiar with the plays of both Bulwer-Lytton and H. J. Byron, and had seen Lytton's *The*

Lady of Lyons (see *SA* 122, 137, 146, 148, 158–59, 212; and *LC*1 1151). Byron's *The Lady of Lyons* was a satire of Lytton's work, a further indication of how pervasive representations of the basic type were.

36. English and American readers of *The Awkward Age* would be aware of Gretchen's two names in *Faust* and would naturally think of both names when the allusion is made; since Gretchen is not an obvious diminutive for Margaret to English-language readers, the free substitution of the one name for the other in Goethe's poem is invariably noticed because of the confusion it gives rise to, and footnotes are often required in modern American editions of *Faust*—see, e.g., the English translations of *Faust* by Peter Salm ([Toronto: Bantam, 1985], 323 n. 31) and Cyrus Hamlin ([New York: Norton, 1976], 318). Also, as Gounod's *Faust,* one of the best-known and most often performed operas of the late nineteenth century, uses the name Marguerite exclusively, James's readers would all the more naturally make the connection between Van's mention of Gretchen and the name Marguerite.

37. Sardou is best remembered today for creating the play upon which Puccini's *Tosca* is based.

38. James spoke favorably of Sardou's work in the several articles he wrote over the years on the Parisian stage and on its contrast with the London theaters (*SA* 8, 40–41, 48, 56, 101, 107–8, 165–66) and in his notebooks (*CN* 18, 53, 227).

39. See, for example, James's 28 Nov. 1889 letter to his brother William (*HJL* 3: 264–65).

40. If James saw *Fernande,* it would most likely have been while the play was being revived, either just before he left France for England in December 1876 or when he visited Paris in September 1877.

41. See Sarcey's in *Le Temps* (14 Mar. 1870, 1) and C. Buloz's "*Fernande* par M. Victorien Sardou" (*Revue des Deux Mondes,* 15 Mar. 1870, 509–10).

42. *Ferblande, ou l'abonné de Montmartre: Parodie en un acte, trois tableaux et deux intermèdes* (Paris: Dentu, 1870). The intermezzi are especially devoted to making fun of the plot's unoriginality. James would have been familiar with Busnach and Gastineau, for they dramatized his favorite Zola novel, *L'Assomoir.* Busnach also dramatized *Nana,* and James owned a copy of his *Trois Pièces* (see Edel and Tintner, "The Library of Henry James," 166).

43. Séamus Cooney, "Awkward Ages in *The Awkward Age,*" *Modern Language Notes* 75 (1960): 210.

44. This is clear, for example, in a conversation that Nanda and Mr. Longdon have during the visit to Mertle, the country house Mitchy rents for the weekend:

> "I dare say," [Nanda] said at last, "that I make allusions you don't like. But I keep forgetting."
> . . . "Keep forgetting what? . . . I hope you don't think I want you to be with me as you wouldn't be—as it were—with yourself. I hope you don't

think I don't want you to be frank. If you were to try to *appear* to me anything—!" [Mr. Longdon] ended in simple sadness; that, for instance, would
be so little what he should like.

"Anything different, you mean, from what I am?" (*AA* 140–41, chap.
17)

45. Nanda's relation to her mother is also clearly defined by her playing the
role of Fernande/Marguerite. In Diderot's version of the story, the daughter is the
instrument of Mme. de La Pommeraye's and the mother's intriguing; in Sardou's
play, the mother's role is minor, but Fernande is still the instrument of intrigue; in
Ancelot's *Léontine*, however, the girl, Léontine, is an orphan, and Mme. de Ceroni,
the Pommeraye figure, takes the place of the mother. In *The Awkward Age* the real
mother plays the role of Mme. de La Pommeraye; she manipulates the situation,
and she exposes Nanda's nature to the man she fears losing to her daughter.

46. Diderot, *Oeuvres romanesques*, ed. Henri Bénac (Paris: Garnier, 1962),
648; Victorien Sardou, *Fernande: Pièce en quatre actes en prose* (Paris: Calmann
Lévy, 1895), 210, act 4, scene 9.

47. Diderot, *Oeuvres romanesques*, 648.

48. *Fernande*, 210, act 4, scene 9, original ellipses. This view of the story is
complicated in *Jacques le fataliste;* the story proper ends with the impression that
the Marquis des Arcis has made a very happy marriage and that, by implication, one
of the best ways for a man to assure such happiness is to choose a fallen woman and
offer her a better existence. This is followed, however, by a long passage in the
narrator's own voice that suggests the reader might view the Marquis's treatment
of Mme. de La Pommeraye in a harsher light and consider her revenge most justified
(Diderot, *Oeuvres romanesques*, 651–52).

49. Mitchy, who is entirely aware of the extent of Nanda's knowledge and
would gladly have married her, does not qualify for the Marquis's role; he cannot
pardon Nanda because she was never at fault in his eyes.

50. As Jacobson writes, "The dialogue novel in English probably owes its
initial impetus to 'Gyp,' although her novels were not available in translation until
the mid-nineties and the form had appeared earlier in England" (*Henry James and
the Mass Market*, 122).

51. Gyp was proud of her publicly acknowledged anti-Semitism and was involved in a libel suit over her staunch anti-Dreyfusard views.

52. One of the ironies of the history of *The Awkward Age* is that contemporary critics did not notice the similarity of form of James's novel to Gyp's, as the
author pointed out in his preface:

What I now see to have happened is that I organised and arranged but too
well—too well, I mean, for any betrayal of the Gyp taint, however faded and
feeble. The trouble appears to have been that while I on the one hand exor-
cised the baleful association, I succeeded in rousing on nobody's part a sense
of any other association whatever, or of my having cast myself into any conceivable or calculable form. My private inspiration had been in the Gyp plan

(artfully dissimulated, for dear life, and applied with the very subtlest consistency, but none the less kept in secret view); yet I was to fail to make out in the event that the book succeeded in producing the impression of *any* plan on any person. (*LC 2* 1128–29)

This suggests that the critics were not by any means the sort of tricultural (Franco-Anglo-American) readers that James's texts so often require. *The Awkward Age* was one of the least successful—both critically and commercially—of James's novels, and it is my hypothesis that the failure of the critics to be stirred up in any way by it is not coincidental to their limited acquaintance (in contrast to James's own, for example) with Gyp and contemporary French fiction. The absence of any comparison of *The Awkward Age* with the French author's work suggests that the reviewers had little knowledge of French fiction, and I believe that this lacuna contributed to their inability to appreciate this James novel.

53. Perosa, *Henry James and the Experimental Novel*, 69; Cargill, *Novels of Henry James*, 263–65; Isle, *Experiments in Form*, 167.

54. "Literary Convention," 633.

55. In 1884, its second year of publication, *Autour du mariage* was already in its fifty-second printing.

56. The whereabouts of this copy, an 1895 reprint, and the 1897 reprint of its sequel, *Autour du divorce*, which James also owned, are no longer known (see Edel and Tintner, "Library of Henry James," 173).

57. Tintner has examined the importance of a number of Gyp's novels to James's *The Awkward Age* in a short section of *Cosmopolitan Age;* she argues that Arletty in Gyp's *Monsieur le duc* "can serve as a model for . . . Aggie in *The Awkward Age*" (144), that "Gyp's *Le Mariage de Chiffon* . . . has a young girl so close to Nanda in certain respects that the feeling is inescapable that James was influenced by the content, as well as the technique, of Gyp's novels" (145). "Gyp's novels," maintains Tintner, "not only offered James a technique for handling his ironic view of English society, . . . but evidently also provided him with the very subject matter of *The Awkward Age*. . . . His novel . . . owes much of its theme to Gyp," and "his plan . . . was to use a different occasion or scene to create different divisions," just as Gyp had in her *Le Petit Bob* (145–46). Tintner also sees Marcel Prévost's *Les Demi-Vierges* (149–53) and Jules Lemaître's *L'Age difficile* (155) as contexts for *The Awkward Age*. That Tintner saw such connections, especially without knowing that I had already asserted there was a relationship between *The Awkward Age* and *Autour du mariage* ("Reading the French Intertexts in Novels of Henry James" [Ph.D. diss., Columbia University, 1989], 311–28), demonstrates, among other things, that there is more than one reader of James who finds it natural to read him in the context of contemporary popular French literature and specifically to read *The Awkward Age* in the context of Gyp's many novels on adolescents and marriage politics.

58. *Autour du mariage* (Paris: Calmann Lévy, 1884), 10, chap. 1. All subsequent references to this novel will be cited parenthetically as *AM*, with page and chapter numbers in the text. All ellipses in the citations from this text are from the original.

59. And once again, the heroine makes the same request to be accepted as she is, as do the maligned wives in the Madame de La Pommeraye story and Sardou's *Fernande*.

60. *Monsieur, Madame et Bébé* is a novel by Gustave Droz, published in Paris by Hetzel (Jules Verne's publisher) in 1868. While its first part has some suggestive passages, it is really a paean of the happy domestic life. As a result, d'Alaly should be more upset that his wife does not like the book than that she had read it before their marriage. *Ma Tante en Vénus* is actually the title of the book's raciest chapter.

61. There is a wonderful irony in the mention of *La Vie parisienne* in the "Mauvaises lectures" chapter. The journal is mentioned because it is a clear sign of Paulette's taste for off-color reading, a sign of her bad upbringing and all that the text presents as wrong with "modern girls." The irony is that Paulette and the novel she appears in subsequently became as much a stock type for exactly the same thing as the journal in which they appeared.

62. Gyp, quoted in Michel Missoffe, *Gyp et ses amis* (Paris: Flammarion, 1932), 62–63.

63. "Revue du théâtre: Drame et comédie," *La Nouvelle revue* 25 (1883): 196.

64. "Romans, contes et nouvelles," *Polybiblion: Revue bibliographique universelle* 40 (1884): 15–16.

65. Indeed, one could consider the similarities between Paulette and an equally willful young female fictional character whom James created six years previously, Daisy Miller.

66. *Impressions de théâtre: Neuvième série* (Paris: Lecène, 1896), 316.

67. Anatole France, *La Vie littéraire*, vol. 2 (Paris: Calmann Lévy, 1890), 245.

68. Pierre Moreau, "Gyp," *Le Dix-neuvième siècle*, vol. 1, ed. Pierre Moreau and Louis Pichard, vol. 6 of *Dictionnaire des lettres françaises* (Paris: Fayard, 1964–1972), 469.

69. *Cosmopolitan World*, 144–46.

70. *Henry James and the Structure of the Romantic Imagination* (Baton Rouge: Louisiana State University Press, 1981), 15.

71. Isle, *Experiments in Form*, 177.

72. This is a fundamental premise of Rowe's *Theoretical Dimensions of Henry James*, especially of the first chapters. One of the central arguments of Anesko's *"Friction with the Market"* is that while James willingly cultivated the image of himself as an avant-garde writer who cared only for art for art's sake, he in fact cared very much about making a living from his literary labor and about writing work that would make money.

Chapter 6: The Experimental and Sentimental Novels in *Washington Square*

1. William Veeder has shown how the rigidity of this tragic bind is reflected throughout the novel, even in its rhetoric, in *Henry James—the Lessons of the Master*, 197–200.

2. Much of James's fiction is ultimately about the problem of representation; this can take the form, as I argue in the chapter on *The Ambassadors*, of Lambert Strether's attempts to come to terms more thoroughly with the dynamics of the social world around him or of James's fictional inquiry into the nature of art, artistic representation, and the artistic life in *The Tragic Muse*. Or it can take the form William Stowe claims it does in *The Princess Casamassima*, where "representation . . . is the central process" (*Balzac, James, and the Realistic Novel*, 57).

3. *Henry James and the Naturalist Movement*, 2.

4. "Style as Subject: *Washington Square*," *Sewanee Review* 83 (1975): 19.

5. Bell also notes James's attitude toward Balzac and Hawthorne and the relevance of the publication of *Hawthorne* a year earlier to *Washington Square* ("Style as Subject," 21–24). She states that the years immediately previous to the writing of *Washington Square* and *The Portrait of a Lady* were "pivotal in James's career, a time when Balzac's and all other models both teased and repelled" (23), and she suggests that *Washington Square* "dramatize[d this] moment of awkward choice-making" (19). While this thesis may have much in common with my own, it is limited to the relationship between *Washington Square* and James's precursors; there is no mention of how *Washington Square* dramatizes James's criticism (indeed, there is no consideration of James's criticism) of Zola or of any contemporary practitioners of the novel. In her chapter on *Daisy Miller* and *Washington Square* in her later *Meaning in Henry James*, Bell's view of *Washington Square* has clearly evolved from her earlier article and remains similar in several respects to my own thesis. *Washington Square*, she states,

> is the testing ground of its affinities, which offer other modes of interpretation besides the realistic, as well as challenging the conditions of objective social reality and its confining categories. In this skeptical fiction James examines by means of his story and its presentational devices literary modes and their analogous life attitudes, such as those of the ironist, the melodramatist, and the romantic fabulist. . . . Releasing himself from the grip of one system of forms, he found that he wanted to try to escape from others, from all. (52–53)

Bell is like me in seeing the principal characters of *Washington Square* as corresponding to modes (she prefers the term "styles") of fictional representation— "sentimental melodrama to Mrs. Penniman, satiric comedy to Dr. Sloper, and to Townsend something of each genre by turns" (*Meaning in Henry James*, 73). She also sees, as I do, that James's novel "exposes the fallacy of romance by means of Mrs. Penniman's grotesque parody. But it also exposes the limitations of Sloper's science" (170). Darshan Singh Maini's argument that " *Washington Square* is a dramatic study in the limits of irony" (" *Washington Square*: A Centennial Essay," *Henry James Review* 1 [1979]: 91) is indebted to the thesis of Bell's earlier article (and related to her later book) and also slightly related to my own.

6. As James told William Dean Howells in 1884, "Daudet, Goncourt, and

Zola . . . do the only kind of work, today, that I respect" (*HJL* 3: 28). This statement is far from ambivalent, and my argument is that such unequivocality about the French naturalists is not at all typical of James.

7. Between the beginning of 1880 and the end of 1884, James published nine critical articles besides "The Art of Fiction": a review of Sainte-Beuve's letters in *The North American Review* (even it contains a mention of Zola [*LC2* 692]) and the *Nana* review in the *Parisian* in 1880; his review of Daudet's brother's *Mon Frère et moi* in the *Atlantic Monthly* in 1882; articles on Daudet (both Daudet articles contain significant passages on naturalism and Zola) and on Trollope in the *Century Magazine,* and reviews of Renan's *Souvenirs* and the *Correspondence of Carlyle and Emerson* in 1883; and articles on Turgenev, in the *Fortnightly Review,* and on Arnold, in the *English Illustrated Magazine,* in 1884.

8. Bell cites many of these same passages in support of a similar view of Mrs. Penniman (*Meaning in Henry James,* 74–75, 77).

9. William Veeder has written an excellent analysis, in *Henry James—the Lessons of the Master,* of how the doctor's actions in this scene fail to fulfill the conventions expected of a loving father in popular romance and drama and, rather, take on the characteristics of a conventional villain (270 n. 9).

10. *The Comic Sense of Henry James: A Study of the Early Novels* (1960; reprint, New York: Oxford University Press, Galaxy, 1967), 148.

11. Poirier is the only critic of *Washington Square,* as far as I can tell, to notice the relationship between Zola's "Le Roman experimental" and Dr. Sloper (*Comic Sense of Henry James,* 147–48, 172, 177–78); however, he does not relate James's composition of *Washington Square* to his stance as a critic in relationship to naturalism. Bell, who in "Style as Subject" does place *Washington Square* in the context of James's working out of his position on realism and romance in the criticism up to 1880, makes no mention of Zola or any other contemporary novelists, a lacuna she rectifies in *Meaning in Henry James,* where she points out that "Scientific or naturalistic observation and analysis were the intellectual methods of Dr. Sloper" (170).

12. Two of the best pieces of commentary on *Washington Square,* Poirier's chapter on the novel in *The Comic Sense of Henry James* (165–82) and Veeder's in *Henry James—the Lessons of the Master* (184–205), exemplify the variety of difference in critical opinion of the character of the doctor. This difference both testifies to and is a natural result of the ambivalent response to the doctor that readers of *Washington Square* cannot help but have.

13. Over twenty years after *Washington Square,* after he had moderated his criticism of Zola, James still complained about the extent to which the experimental method dominated Zola's art: "Method and system, in the chronicle of the tribe of the Rougon-Macquart, . . . have spread so from centre to circumference that they have ended by being almost the only thing we feel" (*LC2* 106), James wrote in 1902, a year before the appearance in the *Atlantic Monthly* of his least qualified praise of his French colleague. James still complained in "The Lesson of Balzac" (1905) of the obtrusiveness of the mechanics of the experimental method in Zola's fiction: "It is exactly here that we get the difference between such a solid, square,

symmetrical structure as 'Les Rougon-Macquart,' vitiated, in a high degree, by its mechanical side, and the monument left by Balzac" (*LC2* 130).

14. Bell argues in her book that in Catherine "James presents a heroine whose style is so mute and motionless as to be almost a surrender of style" (*Meaning in Henry James,* 53), and in her article that to be silent is the only way for Catherine to triumph over "the imposition of others' styles" upon her ("Style as Subject," 38). This may be Catherine's triumph, but it cannot be seen as James's, for silence is not a viable solution to an author in search of his own unique form of representation.

15. Powers, *Henry James and the Naturalist Movement,* 1–2.

16. "Style as Subject," 38. Bell has a more positive conclusion about Catherine in *Meaning in Henry James;* Catherine resists her aunt's and her father's attempts to force their styles of representation on her by adopting "the antirhetoric of . . . silence" (77), and in the end, she gives "form to her life, imposed style upon it in making her own ending" (78). This form of Catherine's own, Bell sees as represented in the "morsel of fancy-work" Catherine picks up as she seats herself in the final paragraph of the novel—"for life, as it were" (*WS* 189). The fancywork or embroidery, argues Bell, is Catherine's own style or artistic genre; it is the tapestry *she* chooses to weave, and it "has a greater dignity, after all, than Mrs. Penniman's preposterous embroidery of plot" (*Meaning in Henry James,* 78–79). This argument is convincing in several respects, but what it means is that if the Mrs. Penniman model of sentimental melodrama (as both Bell and I would argue) the Dr. Sloper model of a Balzacian "categorizing instinct" (as Bell argues in her *Meaning in Henry James,* 73), and the model of Dr. Sloper as experimental novelist (that I see) are all inadequate, what is adequate is "Catherine's plain art" (*Meaning in Henry James,* 79), the small piece of embroidery—something that sounds very much like the stories of Sarah Orne Jewett or Mary Wilkins Freeman, writers for whom James certainly expressed his admiration later in his life (*LC1* 174–75, 700–702), but who can hardly stand for the direction the ambitious and aspiring novelist sought in the early 1880s.

17. Interestingly, Andrew J. Scheiber has argued in "Eros, Art, and Ideology in *The Bostonians*" (*Henry James Review* 13 [1992]) that "*The Bostonians* is a war of signification in which Verena is treated as a blank page on which Ransom and Olive attempt to inscribe their competing desires" (235). This view of the triangular relationship of the novel's central characters strikes me as bearing comparison to my view of Catherine, Lavinia, and Dr. Sloper in *Washington Square:* as I view Catherine as voiceless, Scheiber sees Verena as "a blank page"; and as I see Catherine's aunt and father competing to speak for or represent the situation in which Catherine finds herself, Scheiber sees Basil and Olive competing to write on Verena's blank page.

18. The composition of *The Princess Casamassima* results, if we are to believe the account James gave twenty years later in the New York Edition preface to that novel, from Christina's insistence on speaking (*LC2* 1098).

Chapter 7: Mountebanks, Artist, Representation, and *The Tragic Muse*

1. The representation can never be the same as the represented; representation is always at the same time inherently *mis*-representation, thus the term "(mis)-representation."

2. Ovid, *The Art of Love and Other Poems,* trans. J. H. Mozley, vol. 2 of The Loeb Classical Library Ovid (Cambridge: Harvard University Press, 1979), 313.

3. *The Gentle Art of Making Enemies: As Pleasingly Exemplified in Many Instances, Wherein the Serious Ones of This Earth, Carefully Exasperated, Have Been Prettily Spurred on to Unseemliness and Indiscretion, While Overcome by an Undue Sense of Right* (London: Heinemann, 1890), 115. It seems ironic to compare Whistler's maxim with *The Tragic Muse,* for in this novel, more so than in any of James's fictions after *The Portrait of a Lady,* the narrative voice is "omniscient and often intrusive," as Judith Funston points out in " 'All Art Is One': Narrative Technique in Henry James's *The Tragic Muse*" (*Studies in the Novel* 15 [1983]: 345), making this novel seem as a result full of the kind of "blemish" of which Whistler writes. These authorial intrusions call the reader's attention to the fact that the novel is an artifice; "by calling attention to the mechanics of narration, [James's narrator] destroys any illusion of life and again emphasizes the 'art' of fiction," says Funston (" 'All Art Is One,' " 348). Because the theme of *The Tragic Muse* is based on the paradox that all realistic representation is fiction masquerading as truth—in other words, that it is artifice—it is particularly appropriate that this novel should call attention to its own artificiality to the extent it does.

4. Johann Wolfgang von Goethe, *Wilhelm Meister's Apprenticeship [and Wilhelm Meister's Travels],* trans. Thomas Carlyle (New York: Lovell, 1839), 188, bk. 4, chap. 15; emphasis added.

5. Typical examples of the standard approach to *The Tragic Muse* appear in Alan Bellringer's " *The Tragic Muse:* The Objective Centre," *Journal of American Studies* 4 (1970): 73–89; John Kimmey's " *The Tragic Muse* and Its Forerunners," *American Literature* 41 (1970): 518–31; Wagenknecht's *Eve and Henry James* (73); Donald Stone's *Novelists in a Changing World: Meredith, James, and the Transformation of English Fiction in the 1880's* (Cambridge: Harvard University Press, 1972), 309; and Krook's *The Ordeal of Consciousness in Henry James,* 63. Schneider, in one of the best close readings of *The Tragic Muse,* provides an excellent summary of previous discussion of the novel and its treatment of "art and 'the world' " ("The Theme of Freedom in James's *The Tragic Muse,*" *Connecticut Review* 7, no. 4 [1974]: 5). Anesko is one of the few to argue against the standard view of *The Tragic Muse:* "Many readers have accepted rather uncritically . . . the simple dichotomy between art and the world that James addressed in his 1908 preface. . . . The dualistic logic behind such interpretations . . . falsely converts a richly ironic novel into simple melodrama" (*"Friction with the Market,"* 138). Joseph Litvak (like Anesko and myself) sees the conflict between "art" and "the world" as more complex and paradoxical than has generally been understood. In *Caught in*

the Act: Theatricality in the Nineteenth-Century English Novel, he writes that "Nick and Miriam . . . threaten to abbreviate, rather than expand, the distance between James and a 'world' from which he would 'contract' " ([Berkeley: University of California Press, 1992], 250–51) and concludes that

> the parallel trajectories of Nick's and Miriam's stories seem to promise a way out of this double bind by having the protagonists transcend or repudiate the patriarchal imperative to sell oneself to the public. Yet neither evasion quite succeeds: Miriam ends up marrying her manager, consolidating her status as a commodity even in her apotheosis as the "divinest" Juliet, and Nick ends up giving in to the "bribery" of the politically ambitious Julia Dallow, who seems to lure him away from an aesthetic priesthood he has by now reconceptualized . . . by remaking him as a fashionable amateur painter and setting him up as a "great social institution"—exactly what he thought he was renouncing. (268)

6. Edel, *Middle Years,* 256–63; Krook, *Ordeal of Consciousness in Henry James,* 64; Lyall H. Powers, "James's *The Tragic Muse*—Ave Atque Vale," in *Henry James: Modern Judgements,* ed. Tony Tanner (London: Macmillan, 1968), 202–3.

7. As Robert Falk points out, *The Tragic Muse* "has been often dealt with in biographical terms related to James's ebbing popularity and his discouragement in the late Eighties over his diminished reputation" ("*The Tragic Muse:* Henry James's Loosest, Baggiest Novel?" in *Themes and Directions in American Literature: Essays in Honor of Leon Howard,* ed. Ray B. Browne and Donald Pizer [Lafayette, Ind.: Purdue University Studies, 1969], 148). Typical readings of *The Tragic Muse* of this type are provided by Edel in *The Middle Years* (256–63), where he maintains that the novel shows the truly dedicated artist putting a commitment to creating "enduring masterpieces" (259) before more worldly and commercial considerations, and by Krook, who speaks of James's "unconcealed partisanship—for there is never a doubt, of course, that he himself stands firmly on the side of the angels, that of the artist and his world" (*Ordeal of Consciousness,* 64). Powers understands the novel in a similar way: "the theme of the conflict between art and the world seems to be worked out to its logical conclusion—the persistent triumph of art" ("James's *The Tragic Muse*—Ave Atque Vale," 202–3). Jacobson's *Henry James and the Mass Market* and Anesko's *"Friction with the Market"* question the position that James subscribed to a view of the artist as transcending the material, and Schneider argues against the expression of this view in *The Tragic Muse:* "can James be saying, as so many critics argue, that the artist must cleave to his line in the face of the philistine world? That version of his 'meaning' would scarcely seem adequate in view of the fact that . . . the diplomat must also cleave to *his* line if he is to 'succeed' " ("Theme of Freedom in James's *The Tragic Muse,*" 7).

8. As Kenneth Graham says at the beginning of his chapter on *The Tragic Muse:* "Any account of *The Tragic Muse* still seems to require an opening note of apology and defence" (*Henry James: The Drama of Fulfilment: An Approach to the Novels* [Oxford: Clarendon Press, 1975], 79). Despite defenses of *The Tragic Muse*

such as Krook's (*Ordeal of Consciousness,* 103, 62) and Robert Falk's ("*The Tragic Muse:* James's Loosest, Baggiest Novel?"), critics still feel they must defend this longest of James's novels. See, e.g., William Macnaughton's "In Defense of James's *The Tragic Muse,*" *Henry James Review* 7 (1985): 5–12, and "The New York Edition of Henry James's *The Tragic Muse,*" *Henry James Review* 13 (1992): 19, 24.

9. "The Allegory of Representation in *The Tragic Muse,*" *The Journal of Narrative Technique* 8 (1978): 152. Goetz is the one critic who understands the degree to which *The Tragic Muse* is about representation, and part of the brilliance of his article lies in its perception of the pun on representation in both the political and the artistic senses as central to the novel's significance. Goetz argues that "the three principal kinds of activity between which the characters must choose—politics, painting and drama—each involve a distinct type of representation" (153). Mark Seltzer, though only in a parenthetical remark, makes a point similar to Goetz's when he calls *The Tragic Muse* "virtually an inventory of aesthetic and political modes of representation, and their entanglement" (*Henry James and the Art of Power* [Ithaca, N.Y.: Cornell University Press, 1984], 155). Donald Stone, though also only in an aside, hints at the same point when he mentions that "Nick prefers the satisfaction of representing his constituents upon canvas to representing them in Parliament" (*Novelists in a Changing World,* 317).

10. "Mountebank" and "humbug" are the two synonyms for "charlatan" or "fake" that appear most frequently in *The Tragic Muse.* The chart shows the appearances of the two words in *The Tragic Muse:*

Word	Page	Speaker
humbugging	772	Nick
humbug	773	Julia, quoting Nick
humbug	786	Mme. Carré
mountebank	805	narrator, indirect discourse for Nash
humbug and charlatan	818	Nick
mountebank	832	narrator, indirect discourse for Peter
mountebank	882	narrator, indirect discourse for Nick
humbug	915	Nick
mountebanks	941	Mme. Carré
mountebank	949	Peter
humbug	963	Nick
humbuggery	978	Nick
mountebanks	980	Nick
humbug	1041	narrator, indirect discourse for Peter
humbug humbuggery and humbug	1092	Peter; Nash
mountebanks	1104	Miriam
humbug	1191	Miriam

humbugging 1207 narrator, indirect discourse for Nick
humbug 1226 Miriam

It is interesting that Miriam never uses the words "humbug" and "mounte-bank" in the first half of the novel (although Peter accuses the general actress, apparently including Miriam, of being a "mountebank" [*TM* 832]), but she utters the two words more often than anyone else in the novel's second half, the last time flat out calling herself a "humbug" (1226). When Nick uses "mountebank" or "humbug," it is usually to describe himself and his involvement in politics (772, 882, 915, 963), which seems appropriate, considering how uncertain he is about engaging in politics. However, near the novel's end, Nick responds to Miriam's comment about how much of "a humbug" she has become by saying, "That's the way I used to be" (1226), apparently confirming the notion that by choosing to become a painter, he has followed his true self. But the paradox is that artistic representation by definition involves pretending, fakery, and counterfeiting. That is why the same Nick who wonders whether Nash is a "humbug" (818) and calls Peter's interest in the theater going "in for mountebanks and mimes" (980) can believe at the end of the novel that he *"used to be"* a humbug (1226) at the same time that he acknowledges his own "humbugging genius" (1207). At the same time Miriam, who is called a "mountebank" (832) before she treads the boards, can acknowledge, once she has tasted success, that she has become a humbug (1226).

11. After reciting the Musset poem, Miriam reverts to English and recites two poems by Tennyson, "Edward Gray" and "The Lotos-Eaters" (*TM* 790). On another occasion, Miriam performs Constance from Shakespeare's *King John* for Madame Carré (931) prompting Peter (938) to warn her not to "mix" Constance with Juliet, the role Miriam plays at the novel's end. There is also an allusion in the novel to Goethe's *Wilhelm Meister* when Peter mentally contrasts Mignon and Philina, comparing Miriam to the latter (1046). Peter's comparison of Miriam to Philina is certainly appropriate, for Philina is a consummate social performer, particularly adept at using her theatrical skills to win people's favor: she "soon wormed herself into favor . . . being always cheerful, having the knack of giving little presents, and of talking to each in his own vein; at the same time always contriving to do exactly what she pleased" (*Wilhelm Meister,* 177, bk. 4, chap. 9). Donald Stone argues that "In *The Tragic Muse* James wrote a *Bildungsroman* in reverse. If Goethe treats Wilhelm Meister's apprenticeship in art as a necessary step to prepare him for life, James characteristically puts his characters through a training in life . . . so that they can become artists like himself" (*Novelists in a Changing World,* 329). James's text also alludes to *Faust,* a dramatic poem, when, after Nick calls him "Mephistopheles," Nash asks whom, then, "do you call Margaret?" (*TM* 1088).

12. The only literary allusions in the novel that do not involve a pairing come when Miriam is seen as "representing Mary Stuart in Schiller's play" (*TM* 1102–3), when Biddy is alluded to as "a devoted Electra, laying a cool, healing hand on a distracted Orestes [i.e., Nick]" (1147), and almost at the end of the novel, when Nick's unfinished portrait of Nash fades away "as in some delicate Hawthorne tale" (1236). That the vast majority of the novel's literary allusions

come in opposed pairs cannot be pure coincidence. It should be noted that the reference to Schiller's *Mary Stuart* fits in perfectly with the motif of charlatanism, since Mary in this version of her story is condemned for her pretensions to the English throne, for being a pretender.

13. These dramatic references each serve a formal function in *The Tragic Muse*, even when they are not particularly about deceit and representation, as with the Constance/Juliet opposition. This pair is an example of James's playful, humorous touch with the literary allusion, and it is a sign that Miriam has, by the novel's end, gained autonomy from her mother. When Miriam first appears, she resembles other young heroines of James's—such as Christina Light in *Roderick Hudson*— who are dragged around by ambitious mothers. In performing Constance from *King John* for Mme. Carré, Miriam not only recites speeches that were popular with actresses in the past for their language, but also plays Shakespeare's pushy mother par excellence—an ironic comment on her relation with her mother; by concluding with her performance of Juliet, the novel marks Miriam's attainment of independence by casting her in the role of Shakespeare's best-known rebellious daughter. Graham suggests a connection between Miriam's recital of Constance's speech and Lady Agnes's appeal to Nick, after the results of the Harsh polls, "to save his family" (*Drama of Fulfilment*, 90).

14. In *The Antitheatrical Prejudice*, Jonas Barish points to this conversation as an example of James's doing "battle with the philistines," saying that in *The Tragic Muse*, "[m]ost of the familiar antitheatrical positions are thus rehearsed, sifted, and weighed in the course of the story, usually in the end being somehow mysteriously assimilated and purified, converted from minuses to pluses" ([Berkeley: University of California Press, 1981], 388). Mme. Carré's speech would normally be seen as a typical example of one of the novel's characters mouthing an artistic view dear to James; my point is not to deny this but to show what else the scene accomplishes.

15. James used this quintessentially naturalist image of the insensitive night sky in his previous long novel: when Hyacinth waits in the street for Schinkel to deliver the letter from Hoffendahl, he looks at "the terrible, mysterious, far-off stars, which appeared to him more than ever to see everything and tell nothing" (*PC* 513). In *The Princess Casamassima*, the image apparently reflects the awareness of meaninglessness and hopelessness to which Hyacinth has come by the end of that novel, but we must recall that if Hyacinth finds that the London sky does not tell him anything, the beauty of Paris and Venice did: that the great monuments of art and architecture were worth the human suffering upon which they were built; thus art has a redemptive or consoling power. In *The Tragic Muse*, there is a slightly different emphasis, for if art could be a consolation in *The Princess Casamassima*, it is the only alternative in *The Tragic Muse*.

16. "The Lotos-Eaters," in *Poems of Tennyson*, ed. Jerome Hamilton Buckley (Boston: Houghton Mifflin, Riverside, 1958), 50–55, 84–85.

17. Ibid., 54–57.

18. *Drama of Fulfilment*, 90. Graham's point here is not too different from my own argument about the effect upon Strether and Bilham of their ability to

"see"; to see things from various points of view—which is precisely what the imagination makes possible—renders the viewer impotent.

19. Alfred de Musset, *Poésies complètes,* ed. Maurice Allem (Paris: Gallimard, Pléiade, 1957), 309.

20. Sandeau resolves the situation in the novel on which he based the play by having Bernard die after falling from a horse.

21. That James's characters emphasize the "painterly" quality of Balzac's and Augier's works, calling them both portraits, coincides with Funston's reading of the narrative technique in *The Tragic Muse* as primarily and fundamentally informed by the metaphor of the portrait painter: "James's narrator . . . functions in a distinctly 'painterly' manner. He paints the characters by concentrating on their pictorial qualities" (" 'All Art Is One,' " 345). But the other art represented in the novel—the drama, as Funston points out (354)—is also central to *The Tragic Muse* in a number of ways. My emphasis on the literary texts *The Tragic Muse* alludes to attempts to demonstrate that the paradox at the heart of the dramatic art (and indeed at the heart of all art)—that art's power derives from its being fiction masquerading as truth—is at stake, is in fact *mise en abîme,* by these allusions.

22. We recall James's play on Taine's comment, "Balzac aime sa Valérie," in his contrast between Madame Marneffe and Thackeray's Becky Sharp in "The Lesson of Balzac" (*LC2* 131–33).

23. In fact—and this is an example of how difficult it is to distinguish a voice in *The Tragic Muse* that corresponds to James's own critical and artistic views—as a critic, James was highly complimentary of Augier; see the essay on the French playwright that James published in the *Nation* in 1878 (*SA* 116–17).

24. Miriam Rooth is the stage performer who is not a *cocotte,* while Valérie and Séraphine are the cocottes who are not—at least literally speaking—stage performers. By alluding to the two texts in which these cocottes who are not (but in fact are) actresses appear, *The Tragic Muse* yet again manages to remind that acting pervades realms of society other than the theater.

25. Paul Morillot, *Emile Augier, 1820–1889: Etude biographique et critique* (Grenoble: Gratier, 1901), 87.

26. Ibid., 87–88.

27. Stowe's count of theatrical allusions is slightly different (*Balzac, James, and the Realistic Novel,* 194 n. 38). For Stowe's account of drama as a function in *La Cousine Bette,* see the third part of his chapter on this novel (112–29).

28. Stowe mentions the two "Scenes from High Comedy" (*Balzac, James, and the Realistic Novel,* 114).

29. For Stowe, following the examples of P. Barrière and Peter Brooks, this passage is one of several that indicates the extent to which *La Cousine Bette* is structured as a neoclassical tragedy and a mid-nineteenth-century melodrama (*Balzac, James, and the Realistic Novel,* 116–18).

30. There are several other passages in the novel that describe Valérie in theatrical or artistic terms: the narrator states that if Valérie did not have the renown of a few dissipated fortunes to her credit, it would be like having "un Corrège dans un grenier" [a Correggio in an attic] (*Comédie* 7: 186); Valérie is compared to "les

ténors qui chantent un air mieux un jour que l'autre" [tenors who sing an aria better one day than another] (7: 236); the night Steinbock first comes to dinner, "Madame Marneffe . . . se comporta comme une actrice applaudie. Elle fut charmante et obtint un triomphe complet" [Madame Marneffe . . . behaved like an applauded actress. She was charming and obtained a total triumph] (7: 258); and finally Hulot and Valérie agree on a rendezvous "absolument comme autrefois la Comédie-Italienne annonçait à la fin de la représentation le spectacle du lendemain" [just as in the past when the Comédie-Italienne announced at the end of a performance the next day's show] (7: 302), and when they are surprised by Valérie's husband and the police, she "jeta le cri perçant que les actrices ont inventé pour annoncer la folie au théâtre" [she let out the piercing cry that actresses had invented for suggesting insanity in the theater] (7: 304).

31. This paradox is the central premise of Michael Riffaterre's *Fictional Truth;* in a related vein, Edward Jayne argues, in *Negative Poetics,* "that misrepresentation is fiction's sine qua non, its distinctive and most irreducible feature" ([Iowa City: University of Iowa Press, 1992], 1). Of course, the fictional novel insisting on its truth is a convention of the nineteenth century, from *Père Goriot,* which claims at the end of its first paragraph that it is "ni une fiction, ni un roman" [neither a fiction nor a novel] (adding in English, for extra emphasis, *"All is true"* [3: 50]), to the opening paragraph of *The Adventures of Huckleberry Finn.*

32. This is why Balzac's novel includes a digression on artistic appreciation (*Comédie* 7: 127), another on the deleterious effect of conjugal bliss on Wenceslas Steinbock's creative impulse (7: 245–47), another comparing the procrastinating Wenceslas's daydreams to the caprices of a courtesan (7: 241), and a lengthy exchange among Chanor, Rivet, and Stidmann on the opposing influences of artistic creation and material gain (7: 115). It is also, no doubt, why Balzac situates the building that Bette, Steinbock, and the Marneffes initially inhabit in the rue du Doyenné, apparently alluding to the "impasse du Doyenné group" of writers, which included Arsène Houssaye, Gérard de Nerval, Théophile Gautier, and Jules Sandeau.

33. Schneider is perhaps the only critic of *The Tragic Muse* to have noticed that the novel presents all the professions as fundamentally similar: "the two ways of life [art and politics] are identical in their being concerned exclusively with Appearances" ("Theme of Freedom in James's *The Tragic Muse,*" 8). Through his examination of the imagery in the novel, Schneider demonstrates that *The Tragic Muse* is "concerned . . . with the general problem of freedom," showing that this "novel examines two forms of 'limitation'—the artistic life and the political life—and it reveals . . . that neither the artist nor the politician is free of the narrow system in which he functions" ("Theme of Freedom in James's *The Tragic Muse,*" 6).

34. See note 10.

35. This in spite of the belief of at least one critic that Nick is "a true artist" (Bellringer, *"The Tragic Muse,"* 82).

36. Of course we know from James's story of that title the irony that reality is not a prerequisite of "the real thing." "The Real Thing" was published two years after *The Tragic Muse* and corresponds very strongly to the earlier and longer work

in its treatment of the paradoxical nature at the heart of realistic and evocative artistic representation, as Barish has recognized (*Antitheatrical Prejudice*, 381–90, esp. 382).

37. It does not matter if Miriam's remark is only false modesty (which it probably is); the point is still that this is another instance of the motif of charlatanism.

38. It is not my purpose to write a history of the evolution of literary movements from Romanticism to Modernism; suffice it to say that it seems to me that the crucible of Musset's poet is emblematic of much that is typically Romantic, just as Eliot's "objective correlative" is typically high Modernist; the vision of the artist *The Tragic Muse* provides is a way point between these two extremes and is yet another instance in which James can be seen as an important transitional figure between Romanticism and Modernism.

39. *Middle Years*, 261.

40. Graham, *Drama of Fulfilment*, 88. Graham also suggests that Nash's idealistic view of art is shared by Peter and that both men have a love/hate relationship with art. Nash hates the compromises the artist has no choice but to accept, and Peter's "view of art . . . is fatally idealistic: too idealistic, too tinged with aestheticism . . . for all that he belongs to the world of affairs, [Peter] is a little touched by Gabriel Nash's debility" (109–10).

41. Jonathan Freedman argues that one of Nash's roles in the novel is to express the professional artist's dependence on a market and its mechanisms: the artist cannot avoid the mass market, the theaters catering to suburban audiences, or the Salon and Royal Academy exhibits, for the only alternative is the older patronage system, which is what Nash predicts for Nick when he prophesies an eventual reconciliation with Julia (*TM* 1232–33). The artist is caught, says Freedman, and "Nash's ultimate role . . . is to suggest that the artist is caught between a rock and a hard place" (*Professions of Taste: Henry James, British Aestheticism, and Commodity Culture* [Stanford, Calif.: Stanford University Press, 1990], 190). The role of compromise is emphasized in *The Tragic Muse* by the fact that there is never any mention of alternative venues, such as the French impressionists' exhibitions (the first of which was held in 1874), which were organized out of frustration with such official venues as the Paris Salon and the Royal Academy, for in the world of the artist in *The Tragic Muse*, there are no alternatives to compromise.

42. For seeing the relevance of this passage to *The Tragic Muse*, I am indebted to Graham, who writes that this novel shows that "There is no excellence without action, in art or in life, and there is no action without shortcoming" (*Drama of Fulfilment*, 123). Anesko also cites the passage on compromise (*"Friction with the Market,"* 137).

43. See note 7.

44. *Drama of Fulfilment*, 123.

45. As William F. Hall suggests in "Gabriel Nash: 'Famous Centre' of *The Tragic Muse*," *Nineteenth-Century Fiction* 21 (1966): 183, n. 23.

46. Nash, who speaks for such an ideal, is (as Powers points out) the impetus

that gets Nick's and Miriam's careers going ("James's *The Tragic Muse*—Ave Atque Vale," 199). The ideal is a necessary starting point, but it is not everything.

47. *Drama of Fulfilment*, 110–11.

48. "In Defense of James's *The Tragic Muse*," 7–9.

Conclusion

1. *Book World*, xx, xxii. Tintner argues or implies the same point in virtually everything she has written: "James . . . does [not] simply use as models the works of fiction of the last years of the nineteenth century. He 'corrects' them . . . he alters the content" (*Cosmopolitan World*, 4); "James appropriated the literary classics and remade them into his own" (*Cosmopolitan World*, xiii); "James's intention was to use the material of popular art to make it into a permanent work of art, something that would make one think about life in its most serious form; the appeal was to consciousness rather than to sensation" (*Pop World*, xxiii).

2. *Book World*, xx–xxi.

3. Tintner is not very interested in the literary theory of the period since the mid-1950s (note her inappropriate use of the term "intertextual" in the subtitle of *The Cosmopolitan World of Henry James* and her dismissal of Harold Bloom [*Book World*, xxii], even though she could use Bloom's theory of the anxiety of influence in a number of ways to support her argument). Even though Steven Knapp and Walter Benn Michaels found considerable resistance to their article "Against Theory" (in *Against Theory: Literary Studies and the New Pragmatism*, ed. W. J. T. Mitchell [Chicago: University of Chicago Press, 1985], 11–30), Tintner might have found a way out of her circular reasoning through their central claim that intention and meaning amount to the same thing.

4. "Eight Ways of Looking at James," 86.

5. Similarly, the unspoken secret of Jake's wound in *The Sun Also Rises* is repeatedly made apparent through reference to and contrast with male figures who are not impotent: an imitation of the cab ride in *Madame Bovary* (Ernest Hemingway, *The Sun Also Rises* [New York: Collier-Macmillan, 1986], 25–27) and mention of statues of the lion of Belfort in the place Denfert-Rochereau (27), the statue in front of Jake's flat of Marshal Ney waving his sword (29), and "the statue of the inventor of the semaphore" (41).

Works Cited

Ancelot, Jacques. *Léontine*. In his *Oeuvres complètes*, 337–71. Paris: Delahays, 1855.

Anderson, Charles R. *Person, Place, and Thing in Henry James's Novels*. Durham, N.C.: Duke University Press, 1977.

Anderson, Quentin. *The American Henry James*. New Brunswick, N.J.: Rutgers University Press, 1957.

Anesko, Michael. *"Friction with the Market": Henry James and the Profession of Authorship*. New York: Oxford University Press, 1986.

Augier, Emile. *Théâtre complet*. 7 vols. Paris: Calmann-Lévy, 1897–1899.

Bader, Julia. "The Dissolving Vision: Realism in Jewett, Freeman, and Gilman." In *American Realism: New Essays*, edited by Eric J. Sundquist, 176–98. Baltimore: Johns Hopkins University Press, 1982.

Badger, Reid. "The Character and Myth of Hyacinth: A Key to *The Princess Casamassima*." *Arizona Quarterly* 32 (1976): 316–26.

Balzac, Honoré de. *La Comédie humaine*. Ed. Pierre-Georges Castex. 12 vols. Paris: Gallimard, Pléiade, 1976–1981.

———. *Correspondance*. 5 vols. Paris: Garnier, 1960–1969.

Barish, Jonas. *The Antitheatrical Prejudice*. Berkeley: University of California Press, 1981.

Barstow, Jane Missner. "Originality and Conventionality in *The Princess Casamassima*." *Genre* 11 (1978): 445–58.

Bell, Millicent. *Meaning in Henry James*. Cambridge: Harvard University Press, 1991.

———. "Style as Subject: *Washington Square*." *Sewanee Review* 83 (1975): 19–38.

Bellringer, Alan W. "*The Tragic Muse:* The Objective Centre." *Journal of American Studies* 4 (1970): 73–89.

Blackall, Jean Frantz. "The Case for Mrs. Brookenham." *Henry James Review* 2 (1981): 155–61.

———. "Literary Allusion as Imaginative Event in *The Awkward Age*." *Modern Fiction Studies* 26 (1980): 179–97.

Bogan, Louise. "James on a Revolutionary Theme." *Nation*, 23 Apr. 1938, 471–74.

Boissin, Firmin. "Romans, contes et nouvelles." *Polybiblion: Revue bibliographique universelle* 40 (1884): 5–33.

Bornier, Henri de. "Revue du théâtre: Drame et comédie." *La Nouvelle revue* 25 (1883): 192–201.

Bourgin, Georges. *La Commune*. Rev. ed. Ed. Paul Chauvet. Paris: Presses Universitaires de France, 1969.

Brodhead, Richard H. *The School of Hawthorne*. New York: Oxford University Press, 1986.

Brooks, Peter. *The Melodramatic Imagination: Balzac, Henry James, Melodrama, and the Mode of Excess*. 1976. Reprint, New York: Columbia University Press, 1984.

Buisine, Alain. *Proust et ses lettres*. Lille: Presses Universitaires de Lille, 1983.

Buloz, C. "*Fernande* par M. Victorien Sardou." *Revue des deux mondes*, 15 Mar. 1870, 509–11.

Busnach, William, Octave Gastineau, and Clairville. *Ferblande, ou l'abonné de Montmartre*. Paris: Dentu, 1870.

Cargill, Oscar. *The Novels of Henry James*. New York: Macmillan, 1961.

Chase, Richard. "James' *Ambassadors*." In *Twelve Original Essays on Great American Novels*. Ed. Charles Shapiro. Detroit: Wayne State University Press, 1958.

Cherbuliez, Victor. *Paule Méré*. 1866. Reprint, Paris: Hachette, 1906.

Colmer, John. *Coleridge to "Catch-22": Images of Society*. London: Macmillan, 1978.

Cooney, Séamus. "Awkward Ages in *The Awkward Age*." *Modern Language Notes* 75 (1960): 208–11.

Coulet, Henri. "Le Thème de la 'Madeleine repentie' chez Robert Challe, Prévost et Diderot." *Saggi e ricerche di letteratura francese* 14 (1975): 287–304.

Crick, Patricia. Notes to *The Princess Casamassima*, by Henry James. Harmondsworth: Penguin, 1987.

Culler, Jonathan. *The Pursuit of Signs: Semiotics, Literature, Deconstruction*. Ithaca, N.Y.: Cornell University Press, 1981.

Culver, Stuart. "Censorship and Intimacy: Awkwardness in *The Awkward Age*." *ELH* 48 (1981): 369–86.

Daugherty, Sarah. *The Literary Criticism of Henry James*. [Athens]: Ohio University Press, 1982.

Davidson, Cathy N. " 'Circumsexualocution' in Henry James's *Daisy Miller*." *Arizona Quarterly* 32 (1976): 353–66.

Deakin, Motley F. "Daisy Miller, Tradition, and the European Heroine." *Comparative Literature Studies* 6 (1969): 45–59.

Delbaere-Garant, Jeanne. "Henry James's Divergences from his Russian Model in *The Princess Casamassima*." *Revue des langues vivantes* 37 (1971): 535–44.

Diderot, Denis. *Oeuvres romanesques*. Ed. Henri Bénac. Paris: Garnier, 1962.

Dove, John Roland. "The Alienated Hero in *Le Rouge et le noir* and *The Princess Casamassima*." In *Studies in Comparative Literature*. Ed. Waldo F. McNeir.

Louisiana State University Studies, Humanities Series 11. Baton Rouge: Louisiana State University Press, 1962.

Droz, Gustave. *Monsieur, Madame et Bébé.* Paris: Hetzel, 1868.

Dunbar, Viola. "A Note on the Genesis of *Daisy Miller.*" *Philological Quarterly* 27 (1948): 184–86.

Dupee, F. W. *Henry James.* 1951. Reprint, New York: Delta, 1965.

Edel, Leon. *Henry James: A Life.* New York: Harper and Row, 1985.

———. *Henry James: The Middle Years: 1882–1895.* Vol. 3 of *The Life of Henry James.* Philadelphia: Lippincott, 1962.

———. *Henry James: The Treacherous Years: 1895–1901.* Vol. 4 of *The Life of Henry James.* Philadelphia: Lippincott, 1969.

———. *Henry James: The Untried Years: 1843–1870.* Vol. 1 of *The Life of Henry James.* Philadelphia: Lippincott, 1953.

Edel, Leon, and Dan H. Laurence. *A Bibliography of Henry James.* 3rd ed. Oxford: Clarendon Press, 1982. Edel, Leon, and Adeline Tintner. "The Library of Henry James, from Inventory, Catalogues, and Library Lists." *Henry James Review* 4 (1982): 158–90.

Falk, Robert. "*The Tragic Muse:* Henry James's Loosest, Baggiest Novel?" In *Themes and Directions in American Literature: Essays in Honor of Leon Howard.* Ed. Ray B. Browne and Donald Pizer, 148–62. Lafayette, Ind.: Purdue University Studies, 1969.

Feuillet, Octave. "Les Amours de Philippe." *Revue des Deux Mondes,* 1 July 1877, 5–32; 15 July 1877, 241–63; 1 Aug. 1877, 481–524.

———. "Histoire d'une parisienne." *Revue des Deux Mondes,* 1 Apr. 1881, 481–514; 15 Apr. 1881, 721–62.

———. "Le Journal d'une femme." *Revue des Deux Mondes,* 15 July 1878, 241–93; 1 Aug. 1878, 481–518.

———. "Julia de Trécoeur." *Revue des Deux Mondes,* 1 Mar. 1872, 5–56.

———. "Un Mariage dans le monde." *Revue des Deux Mondes,* 1 Sept. 1875, 5–28; 15 Sept. 1875, 241–62; 1 Oct. 1875, 481–521.

———. "La Morte." *Revue des Deux Mondes,* 15 Dec. 1885, 721–48; 1 Jan. 1886, 5–41; 15 Jan. 1886, 241–82.

———. "La Veuve." *Revue des Deux Mondes,* 1 Dec. 1883, 481–511; 15 Dec. 1883, 721–47.

———. "Le Voyageur; Scènes dialoguées." *Revue des Deux Mondes,* 1 Jan. 1884, 5–27.

Fiedler, Leslie. *Love and Death in the American Novel.* New York: Stein and Day, 1966.

Fish, Stanley. *Is There a Text in This Class? The Authority of Interpretive Communities.* Cambridge: Harvard University Press, 1980.

Flaubert, Gustave. *L'Education sentimentale: Histoire d'un jeune homme.* Vol. 2 of *Oeuvres.* Ed. André Thibaudet and René Dumesnil. Paris: Gallimard, Pléiade, 1952.

France, Anatole. *La Vie littéraire.* 4 vols. Paris: Calmann-Lévy, 1888–1897.

Freedman, Jonathan. *Professions of Taste: Henry James, British Aestheticism, and Commodity Culture.* Stanford, Calif.: Stanford University Press, 1990.

Fryer, Judith. *The Faces of Eve: Women in the Nineteenth Century American Novel.* New York: Oxford University Press, 1976.

Funston, Judith E. " 'All Art Is One': Narrative Technique in Henry James's *The Tragic Muse.*" *Studies in the Novel* 15 (1983): 344–55.

Fussell, Edwin Sill. *The French Side of Henry James.* New York: Columbia University Press, 1990.

Gargano, James W. "*The Ambassadors* and *Louis Lambert.*" *Modern Language Notes* 75 (1960): 211–13.

———. "Daisy Miller: An Abortive Quest for Innocence." *South Atlantic Quarterly* 59 (1960): 114–20.

Gibson, William M. "Metaphor in the Plot of *The Ambassadors.*" *New England Quarterly* 24 (1951): 291–305.

Goethe, Johann Wolfgang von. *Wilhelm Meister's Apprenticeship [and Wilhelm Meister's Travels].* Trans. Thomas Carlyle. New York: Lovell, 1839.

Goetz, William R. "The Allegory of Representation in *The Tragic Muse.*" *Journal of Narrative Technique* 8 (1978): 151–64.

Graham, [George] Kenneth. *Henry James: The Drama of Fulfilment: An Approach to the Novels.* Oxford: Clarendon Press, 1975.

Grenander, M. E. "Henry James's *Capricciosa:* Christina Light in *Roderick Hudson* and *The Princess Casamassima.*" *PMLA* 75 (1960): 309–19.

Grover, Philip. *Henry James and the French Novel: A Study in Inspiration.* New York: Barnes and Noble, 1973.

Gyp. *Autour du divorce.* Paris: Calmann-Lévy, 1886.

———. *Autour du mariage.* Paris: Calmann-Lévy, 1884.

———. *Les Gens chics.* Paris: Charpentier et Fasquelle, 1895.

———. *Mademoiselle Eve.* Paris: Calmann-Lévy, 1889.

———. *Mademoiselle Loulou.* Paris: Calmann-Lévy, 1888.

———. *Le Mariage de Chiffon.* Paris: Calmann-Lévy, 1895.

———. *Miquette.* Paris: Calmann-Lévy, 1898.

———. *Ohé! les psychologues.* Paris: Calmann-Lévy, 1889.

———. *Une Passionnette.* Paris: Calmann-Lévy, 1891.

———. *Petit Bob.* Paris: Calmann-Lévy, 1887.

Hall, William F. "Gabriel Nash: 'Famous Centre' of *The Tragic Muse.*" *Nineteenth-Century Fiction* 21 (1966): 167–84.

———. "James's Conception of Society in *The Awkward Age.*" *Nineteenth-Century Fiction* 23 (1968): 28–48.

Halliburton, D. G. "Self and Secularization in *The Princess Casamassima.*" *Modern Fiction Studies* 11 (1965): 116–28.

Hamilton, Eunice C. "Henry James's *The Princess Casamassima* and Ivan Turgenev's *Virgin Soil.*" *South Atlantic Quarterly* 61 (1962): 354–64.

Hamlin, Cyrus, ed. *Faust: A Tragedy,* by Johann Wolfgang von Goethe. New York: Norton, 1976.

Hartsock, Mildred. "The Exposed Mind: A View of *The Awkward Age*." *Critical Quarterly* 9 (1967): 49–59.

———. "*The Princess Casamassima:* The Politics of Power." *Studies in the Novel* 1 (1969): 297–309.

Harvey, Paul, and J. E. Heseltine, eds. *The Oxford Companion to French Literature.* Oxford: Oxford University Press, Clarendon, 1959.

Hasler, Jörg. *Switzerland in the Life and Work of Henry James.* The Cooper Monographs 10. Bern: Francke, 1966.

Hemingway, Ernest. *The Sun Also Rises.* New York: Macmillan, Collier, 1986.

Hocks, Richard A. *Henry James and Pragmatic Thought: A Study in the Relationship Between the Philosophy of William James and the Literary Art of Henry James.* Chapel Hill: University of North Carolina Press, 1974.

Hoffman, Frederick J. *The Mortal No: Death and the Modern Imagination.* Princeton: Princeton University Press, 1964.

Hugo, Victor. *Notre-Dame de Paris. Roman I.* Ed. Jacques Seebacher. Vol. 1 of *Victor Hugo: Oeuvres complètes.* Paris: Laffont, 1985.

Isle, Walter. *Experiments in Form: Henry James's Novels, 1896–1901.* Cambridge: Harvard University Press, 1968.

Jacobson, Marcia. *Henry James and the Mass Market.* University: University of Alabama Press, 1983.

———. "Literary Convention and Social Criticism in Henry James's *The Awkward Age. Philological Quarterly* 54 (1975): 633–46.

James, Henry. *The Ambassadors.* 1903, rev. 1908. Reprint, ed. S. P. Rosenbaum. New York: Norton, 1964.

———. *The Awkward Age.* 1899. Reprint, Harmondsworth: Penguin, 1966.

———. *The Complete Notebooks of Henry James.* Ed. Leon Edel and Lyall H. Powers. New York: Oxford University Press, 1987.

———. *Daisy Miller* [: *A Study*]. Ed. Geoffrey Moore. 1878. Reprint, Harmondsworth: Penguin, 1986.

———. *The Europeans.* In *Novels 1871–1880: "Watch and Ward," "Roderick Hudson," "The American," "The Europeans," "Confidence."* Ed. William T. Stafford. New York: Library of America, 1983.

———. *Letters.* Ed. Leon Edel. 4 vols. Cambridge: Harvard University Press-Belknap Press, 1974–1984.

———. *The Letters of Henry James.* Ed. Percy Lubbock. 2 vols. London: Macmillan, 1920.

———. *Literary Criticism: Essays on Literature, American Writers, English Writers.* Ed. Leon Edel and Mark Wilson. New York: Library of America, 1984.

———. *Literary Criticism: French Writers, Other European Writers, the Prefaces to the New York Edition.* Ed. Leon Edel and Mark Wilson. New York: Library of America, 1984.

———. *A Little Tour in France.* In *Collected Travel Writings: The Continent.* Ed. Richard Howard. New York: Library of America, 1993.

———. *The Princess Casamassima.* In *Novels 1886–1890: "The Princess Casamassima," "The Reverberator," "The Tragic Muse."* Ed. Daniel Mark Fogel. New York: Library of America, 1989.

———. *Roderick Hudson*. In *Novels 1871–1880: "Watch and Ward," "Roderick Hudson," "The American," "The Europeans," "Confidence."* Ed. William T. Stafford. New York: Library of America, 1983.

———. *The Scenic Art: Notes on Acting and the Drama, 1872–1901*. Ed. Allan Wade. New York: Hill and Wang, 1957.

———. "Swiss Notes." In *Collected Travel Writings*. Ed. Richard Howard. New York: Library of America, 1993.

———. *The Tragic Muse*. In *Novels 1886–1890: "The Princess Casamassima," "The Reverberator," "The Tragic Muse."* Ed. Daniel Mark Fogel. New York: Library of America, 1989.

———. *Washington Square*. In *Novels 1881–1886: Washington Square, The Portrait of a Lady, The Bostonians*. Ed. William T. Stafford. New York: Library of America, 1985.

Jayne, Edward. *Negative Poetics*. Iowa City: University of Iowa Press, 1992.

Jennings, C. Wade. "Diderot: A Suggested Source of the Jules-Phene Episode in *Pippa Passes*." *English Language Notes* 2 (1964): 32–36.

Jones, Granville H. *Henry James's Psychology of Experience: Innocence, Responsibility, and Renunciation in the Fiction of Henry James*. The Hague: Mouton, 1975.

Kaplan, Fred. *Henry James: The Imagination of Genius: A Biography*. New York: William Morrow, 1992.

Kermode, Frank. *The Art of Telling: Essays on Fiction*. Cambridge: Harvard University Press, 1983.

———. *The Genesis of Secrecy: On the Interpretation of Narrative*. Cambridge: Harvard University Press, 1979.

———. *The Sense of an Ending: Studies in the Theory of Fiction*. New York: Oxford University Press, 1967.

Kimmey, John L. "*The Princess Casamassima* and the Quality of Bewilderment." *Nineteenth-Century Fiction* 22 (1967): 47–62.

———. "*The Tragic Muse* and Its Forerunners." *American Literature* 41 (1970): 518–31.

Knapp, Steven, and Walter Benn Michaels. "Against Theory." In *Against Theory: Literary Studies and the New Pragmatism*. Ed. W. J. T. Mitchell, 11–30. Chicago: University of Chicago Press, 1985.

Koprince, Susan. "The Clue from *Manfred* in *Daisy Miller*." *Arizona Quarterly* 42 (1986): 293–304.

Kraft, James. *The Early Tales of Henry James*. Carbondale: Southern Illinois University Press, 1969.

Krook, Dorothea. *The Ordeal of Consciousness in Henry James*. Cambridge: Cambridge University Press, 1962.

Larousse, Pierre. *Grand dictionnaire universel du dix-neuvième siècle*. 15 vols. Paris: Administration du Grand Dictionnaire Universel, 1866–1876.

Leavis, F. R. *The Great Tradition: George Eliot, Henry James, Joseph Conrad*. New York: New York University Press/Gotham Library, 1967.

Lemaître, Jules. *Impressions de théâtre: Neuvième série*. Paris: Lecène, 1896.

Lerner, Daniel. "The Influence of Turgenev on Henry James." *Slavonic and East European Review* 20 (1941): 28–54.

Lewis, Roger. "Money, Love, and Aspiration in *The Great Gatsby*." In *New Essays on "The Great Gatsby."* Ed. Matthew J. Broccoli, 41–57. Cambridge: Cambridge University Press, 1985.

Lissagaray, [Prosper Olivier]. *Histoire de la Commune de 1871.* Rev. ed. Paris: Marcel Rivière, 1947.

Litvak, Joseph. *Caught in the Act: Theatricality in the Nineteenth-Century English Novel.* Berkeley: University of California Press, 1992.

Long, Robert Emmet. *The Great Succession: Henry James and the Legacy of Hawthorne.* Pittsburgh: University of Pittsburgh Press, 1979.

Luecke, Jane Marie. "*The Princess Casamassima:* Hyacinth's Fallible Consciousness." In *Henry James: Modern Judgements.* Ed. Tony Tanner. London: Macmillan, 1968.

Lukacs, Paul. "Unambiguous Ambiguity: The International Theme of *Daisy Miller*." *Studies in American Fiction* 16 (1988): 209–16.

Macnaughton, William R. "In Defense of James's *The Tragic Muse*." *Henry James Review* 7 (1985): 5–12.

———. "The New York Edition of Henry James's *The Tragic Muse*." *Henry James Review* 13 (1992): 19–26.

Maini, Darshan Singh. "*Washington Square:* A Centennial Essay." *Henry James Review* 1 (1979): 81–101.

Margolis, Anne T. *Henry James and the Problem of Audience: An International Act.* Ann Arbor, Mich.: UMI Research Press, 1985.

McCormack, Peggy. *The Rule of Money: Gender, Class, and Exchange Economics in the Fiction of Henry James.* Ann Arbor, Mich.: UMI Research Press, 1990.

Meyers, Jeffrey. "Velázquez and 'Daisy Miller.' " *Studies in Short Fiction* 16 (1979): 171–78.

Missoffe, Michel. *Gyp et ses amis.* Paris: Flammarion, 1932.

Moreau, Pierre. "Gyp." In *Le Dix-neuvième siècle,* Vol. 1. Ed. Pierre Moreau and Louis Pichard. Vol. 6 of *Dictionnaire des lettres françaises.* Paris: Fayard, 1972.

Morillot, Paul. *Emile Augier, 1820–1889: Etude biographique et critique.* Grenoble: Gratier, 1901.

Musset, Alfred de. *Il ne faut jurer de rien.* In his *Théâtre complet.* Ed. Simon Jeune. Paris: Gallimard, Pléiade, 1990.

———. *Poésies complètes.* Ed. Maurice Allem. Paris: Gallimard, Pléiade, 1957.

Ohmann, Carol. "*Daisy Miller:* A Study of Changing Intentions." *American Literature* 36 (1964): 1–11.

Oliver, Clinton. "Henry James as Social Critic." *Antioch Review* 7 (1947): 243–58.

Ovid. *The Art of Love and Other Poems.* Trans. J. H. Mozley. Vol. 2 of Loeb Classical Library Ovid. Cambridge: Harvard University Press, 1979.

Page, Philip. "*The Princess Casamassima:* Suicide and 'the Penetrating Imagination.' " *Tennessee Studies in Literature* 22 (1977): 162–69.

Perry, T. S. "Victor Cherbuliez." *Atlantic Monthly* 37 (1876): 279–87.

Perosa, Sergio. *Henry James and the Experimental Novel.* 1978. Reprint, New York: New York University Press, Gotham Library, 1983.

Poirier, Richard. *The Comic Sense of Henry James: A Study of the Early Novels.* 1960. Reprint, New York: Oxford University Press, Galaxy, 1967.

Powers, Lyall H. *Henry James and the Naturalist Movement.* [East Lansing]: Michigan State University Press, 1971.

———. "James's *The Tragic Muse*—Ave Atque Vale." In *Henry James: Modern Judgements.* Ed. Tony Tanner. London: Macmillan, 1968.

Randall, John H. "The Genteel Reader and *Daisy Miller.*" *American Quarterly* 17 (1965): 568–81.

Riffaterre, Michael. *Fictional Truth.* Baltimore: Johns Hopkins University Press, 1990.

———. "Interpretation and Undecidability." *New Literary History* 12 (1981): 227–42.

———. "Intertextual Representation: On Mimesis as Interpretive Discourse." *Critical Inquiry* 11 (1984): 141–62.

Rivkin, Julie. "The Logic of Delegation in *The Ambassadors.*" *PMLA* 101 (1986): 819–31.

Rosenbaum, S. P. "Editions and Revisions." In *The Ambassadors: An Authoritative Text, the Author on the Novel, Criticism,* by Henry James. New York: Norton, 1964.

Rosenzweig, Paul. "James's 'Special-Green Vision': *The Ambassadors* as Pastoral." *Studies in the Novel* 13 (1981): 367–87.

Rowe, John Carlos. *The Theoretical Dimensions of Henry James.* Madison: University of Wisconsin Press, 1984.

Salm, Peter, ed. *Faust: Part One,* by Johann Wolfgang von Goethe. Toronto: Bantam, 1985.

Sandeau, Jules. *Mademoiselle de la Seiglière.* Paris: Michel Lévy, 1847.

———. *Mademoiselle de la Seiglière: Comédie en quatre actes et en prose.* Paris: Michel Lévy, 1851.

Sarcey, Francisque. "Chronique théâtrale." *Le Temps,* 14 Mar. 1870, 1.

Sardou, Victorien. *Fernande: Pièce en quatre actes en prose.* Paris: Calmann-Lévy, 1895.

Scanlon, Margaret. "Terrorism and the Realistic Novel: Henry James and *The Princess Casamassima.*" *Texas Studies in Literature and Language* 34 (1992): 380–402.

Scheiber, Andrew J. "Eros, Art, and Ideology in *The Bostonians.*" *Henry James Review* 13 (1992): 235–52.

Schneider, Daniel J. *The Crystal Cage: Adventures of the Imagination in the Fiction of Henry James.* Lawrence: Regents Press of Kansas, 1978.

———. "James's *The Awkward Age*: A Reading and an Evaluation." *Henry James Review* 1 (1980): 219–27.

———. "The Theme of Freedom in James's *The Tragic Muse.*" *Connecticut Review* 7, no. 4 (1974): 5–15.

Sears, Sallie. *The Negative Imagination: Form and Perspective in the Novels of Henry James.* Ithaca, N.Y.: Cornell University Press, 1968.

Seed, David. "Hyacinth Robinson and the Politics of *The Princess Casamassima.*" *Etudes Anglaises* 30 (1977): 30–39.

Seltzer, Mark. *Henry James and the Art of Power.* Ithaca, N.Y.: Cornell University Press, 1984.

Shakespeare, William. *The Riverside Shakespeare.* Ed. G. Blakemore Evans. Boston: Houghton Mifflin, 1974.

Showalter, English, Jr. "De 'Madame de La Pommeraye' à 'Ruy Blas.' " *Revue d'Histoire Littéraire de la France* 66 (1966): 238–52.

Siebers, Tobin. *Cold War Criticism and the Politics of Skepticism.* New York: Oxford University Press, 1993

———. *Morals and Stories.* New York: Columbia University Press, 1992.

Sklepowich, E. A. "Gilded Bondage: Games and Gamesplaying in *The Awkward Age.*" *Essays in Literature* 5 (1978): 187–93.

Smith, Paula V. "A Wilde Subtext for *The Awkward Age.*" *Henry James Review* 9 (1988): 199–208.

Stone, Donald David. *Novelists in a Changing World: Meredith, James, and the Transformation of English Fiction in the 1880's.* Cambridge: Harvard University Press, 1972.

Stone, Edward. *The Battle and the Books: Some Aspects of Henry James.* Athens: Ohio University Press, 1964.

———. "A Further Note on *Daisy Miller* and Cherbuliez." *Philological Quarterly* 29 (1950): 213–16.

Stowe, William W. *Balzac, James, and the Realistic Novel.* Princeton: Princeton University Press, 1983.

Swinburne, A. C. "Mary Queen of Scots." In *Encyclopaedia Britannica.* 9th ed. 1875–1889. Reprint, 11th ed. 1910–1911.

Tennyson, Alfred. *Poems of Tennyson.* Ed. Jerome Hamilton Buckley. Boston: Houghton Mifflin, Riverside, 1958.

Thackeray, William M. *The History of Pendennis: His Fortunes and Misfortunes, His Friends and His Greatest Enemy.* 1850. Reprint, Harmondsworth: Penguin, 1972.

———. *The Newcomes.* 1853. Reprint, New York: Crowell, n.d.

Thwaite, Ann. *Waiting for the Party: The Life of Frances Hodgson Burnett, 1849–1924.* New York: Scribner, 1974.

Tilley, W. H. *The Background of "The Princess Casamassima."* University of Florida Monographs, Humanities 5. Gainesville: University of Florida Press, 1960.

Tintner, Adeline. "Arsène Houssaye's 'Capricieuse' and James's 'Capricciosa.' " *Revue de la littérature comparée* 50 (1976): 478–81.

———. *The Book World of Henry James: Appropriating the Classics.* Ann Arbor, Mich.: UMI Research Press, 1987.

———. *The Cosmopolitan World of Henry James: An Intertextual Study.* Baton Rouge: Louisiana State University Press, 1991.

———. "Henry James' Balzac Connection." *AB Bookman's Weekly* 67 (1981): 3219–28.

———. "Hyacinth at Play: The Play Within the Play as a Novelistic Device in James." *Journal of Narrative Technique* 2 (1972): 171–85.

———. "Keats and James and *The Princess Casamassima.*" *Nineteenth-Century Fiction* 28 (1973): 179–93.

———. "Octave Feuillet: *La Petite Comtesse* and Henry James." *Revue de la littérature comparée* 48 (1974): 218–32.

———. *The Pop World of Henry James: From Fairy Tales to Science Fiction.* Ann Arbor, Mich.: UMI Research Press, 1989.

———. "Review-Essay: Eight Ways of Looking at James." *Studies in the Novel* 9 (1977): 73–94.

———. "Two Innocents in Rome: Daisy Miller and Innocent the Tenth." *Essays in Literature* 6 (1979): 71–78.

———. "Vanda de Margi and Rose Muniment." *Revue de la littérature comparée* 55 (1981): 110–12.

Trilling, Lionel. "*The Princess Casamassima.*" In his *The Liberal Imagination: Essays on Literature and Society.* 1950. Reprint, New York: Doubleday/Anchor, 1954.

Troy, William. "The Altar of Henry James." In *The Question of Henry James.* Ed. F. W. Dupee. New York: Holt, 1945.

Veeder, William. *Henry James—the Lessons of the Master: Popular Fiction and Personal Style in the Nineteenth Century.* Chicago: University of Chicago Press, 1975.

Vidan, Ivo. "*The Princess Casamassima* Between Balzac and Conrad." *Studia Romanica et Anglica Zagrebiensia* 21–22 (1966): 259–76.

W., J. E. H. "Paris—Metz—Chartres: A Trilogy of Translations." *The Bookman* 79, no. 14 (Apr. 1898): 18–19.

Wagenknecht, Edward. *Eve and Henry James: Portraits of Women and Girls in His Fiction.* Norman: University of Oklahoma Press, 1978.

Whistler, James McNeill. *The Gentle Art of Making Enemies: As Pleasingly Exemplified in Many Instances, Wherein the Serious Ones of This Earth, Carefully Exasperated, Have Been Prettily Spurred on to Unseemliness and Indiscretion, While Overcome by an Undue Sense of Right.* London: Heinemann, 1890.

Wood, Carl. "Frederick Winterbourne, James's Prisoner of Chillon." *Studies in the Novel* 9 (1977): 33–45.

Zacharias, Greg W. "The Marine Metaphor, Henry James, and the Moral Center of *The Awkward Age.*" *Philological Quarterly* 69 (1990): 91–105.

Zola, Émile. *Oeuvres complètes.* Ed. Henri Mitterand. 15 vols. Paris: Cercle du Livre Précieux, 1966.

———. *Les Rougon-Macquart: Histoire naturelle et sociale d'une famille sous le second empire.* Ed. Armand Lanoux and Henri Mitterand. 5 vols. Paris: Gallimard, Pléiade, 1960–1967.

Index